THE LIVY SERIES

General Editor: T. A. Dorey, M.A., Ph.D.

T. LIVI
AB VRBE CONDITA
LIBER XXI

edited by

P. G. WALSH, M.A., PH.D.

Professor of Humanity in the University of Glasgow

UNIVERSITY TUTORIAL PRESS LTD

9-10 GREAT SUTTON STREET, LONDON, EC1V 0DA

This edition is set in 8 pt and 10 pt Baskerville

Published 1973

ISBN: 0 7231 0566 9

PRINTED IN GREAT BRITAIN BY UNIVERSITY TUTORIAL PRESS LTD
FOXTON, NEAR CAMBRIDGE

PREFACE

This book, like its companions in this series edited by Dr T. A. Dorey, has been designed with the needs of G.C.E. Advanced Level candidates specially in mind, but undergraduates will not find it useless. The Commentary seeks to explain points of historical and literary importance and to elucidate grammatical peculiarities and passages of unusual difficulty. There is a general introduction on Livy and the approach to historiography at Rome, and an introduction specifically to Book XXI. There are a full vocabulary, an index of names, and illustrative maps and plates.

I have indicated in the Notes the places where I think the reading is dubious, notably the following:

5.3: iungendoque	31.11: semper ⟨per⟩ vada
5.9: praeducto	33.4: perversis rupibus
5.16: in tanto pavore	34.4: † asperandos †
10.2: non cum adsensu	35.3: praecipites
10.13: ego ita censeo	35.10: ne . . . quidem
20.9: in exspectationem	36.7: [ut a lubrica]
21.9: prospera	37.5: apricos
22.2: firmatque eum	38.9: Sedunoveragri
22.3: ducenti equites	41.4: [neque] . . . [erat]
23.6: ipse	44.7: ⟨ademisti?⟩
24.3: et vel	44.9: ⟨incitamentum⟩
27.8: lintres, eques	46.7: ad pedes pugna abierat
28.5: variata	46.7: paulum
28.5: nantem	49.7: tueri
28.8: tres	52.2: uno . . . comminutus
29.3: sexaginta	55.2: ⟨ac⟩
30.7: pervias paucis esse	56.6-7: (transposition)
31.7: delata	

I should like to thank Mr J. R. G. Wright of the University of Edinburgh, and Mr J. D. Christie of the University of Glasgow, for their careful reading of the proofs which has resulted in the excision of sundry errors and inconsistencies.

PREFACE

The debt I owe to both is greater than a mere acknowledgement can convey.

The text is the Oxford Classical Text Volume III, edited by C. F. Walters and R. S. Conway (1929), by kind permission of The Clarendon Press, Oxford.

P.G.W.

University of Glasgow.

CONTENTS

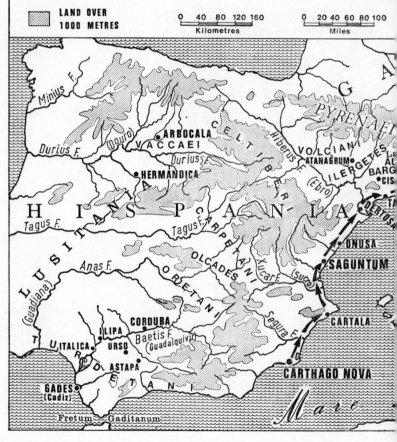

HANNIBAL'S OPERATIONS in Spain, France and Northern Italy.

LAND OVER
1000 METRES

0 40 80 120 160
Kilometres

0 20 40 60 80 100
Miles

Minius F.

PYRENAE

Durius F.

(Douro)

ARBOCALA
VACCAEI

CELTIB

Hiberus F. (Ebro)

VOLCIANI
ATANAGRUM

ILERGETES

BARG
CIS

Durius F.

HERMANDICA

H I S P A N I A

DEROSA

Tagus F.

Tagus F.

CARPETANI

ONUSA

L U S I T A N I

OLCADES

Xucar F. (Sucro)

SAGUNTUM

Anas F.

O R E T A N I

(Guadiana)

Segura F.

CARTALA

CORDUBA

ILIPA

Baetis F.
(Guadalquivir)

URSO

T U ITALICA
R D
E ASTAPA
T
A
N
I

CARTHAGO NOVA

GADES
(Cadiz)

Fretum Gaditanum

Mare

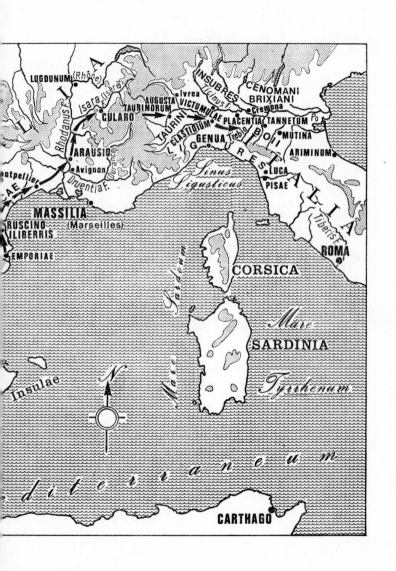

THE LIVY SERIES

Book I.   Ed. K. R. Prowse
Book IX.   Ed. R. M. Ogilvie
    (*In preparation*)
Book XXI.   Ed. P. G. Walsh
Book XXXIII.   Ed. T. A. Dorey and C. W. F.
                 Lydall
    (*Ready*)

THE PALATINE CLASSICS

CAESAR: GALLIC WAR
    Book II.   Ed. E. C. Kennedy
    Book V.   Ed. N. T. Newhouse and C. Greig
    Book VI.   Ed. E. C. Kennedy
A CHOICE OF OVID.   Ed. E. C. Kennedy
PLAUTUS: RUDENS.   Ed. H. C. Fay
SALLUST: BELLUM IUGURTHINUM.   Ed. L. Watkiss
VERGIL: AENEID
    Book IV.   Ed. B. Tilly
    Book V.   Ed. B. Tilly
    Book XII. Ed. B. Tilly

VARRO: THE FARMER (A Selection from the Res Rusticae).   Ed. B. Tilly

---

UNIVERSITY TUTORIAL PRESS

General Introduction

N.B. Notes on some of the persons referred to in the General Introduction and the Introduction to Book XXI are given on pp. 110-13

I

Historical composition at Rome sprang from two main sources: first, the *Tabulae Pontificum*, on which the Pontifex Maximus had recorded the names of magistrates and events of significance to the state religion, such as portents, dedications, triumphs, and festivals of thanksgiving or supplication on the occasion of victories or national disasters. Second, the private records kept in the archives of families whose members had held curule office, which would provide the material to be used from time to time in funeral orations, laudatory not only of the individual deceased but of his distinguished ancestors.

It was the Second Punic War that brought to birth the writing of history as a literary form in Rome. A great war acts as a stimulus to historians. Just as the Persian Wars produced Herodotus, the Peloponnesian War, Thucydides, and Alexander's conquests inspired a vast outburst of historical writing that flowed on until the Middle Ages, so at Rome the Hannibalic War acted as a catalyst to historical composition. The first Roman historian was Q. Fabius Pictor, a member of the Senate eminent enough to be sent officially to consult the Delphic Oracle on Rome's behalf after the disaster at Cannae in 216. His work covered the period from the foundation of Rome to the closing stages, probably, of the Second Punic War. It seems to have dealt with the early legends in some detail, given a rather meagre outline of the early Republic, and then a more comprehensive account of the events of Fabius's own lifetime. He was an important source for Polybius's account of the First Punic War, and he seems to have been an accurate and truthful historian, though with a considerable pro-Roman bias. His partisanship also shows in the prominence that he gives to the exploits of the Fabian *gens* in the early Republic, and in his invariably favourable portrayal of the actions and policies of his great kinsman, Q. Fabius Maximus Cunctator. His partisan approach to history was followed by most of his successors, for they, like him, were usually members of the Senate who regarded the composition of histories or historical monographs as an extension of the active political life in which they were engaged. Fabius Pictor wrote his histories in Greek, partly because he was writing for the Greek world with which Rome was now coming into contact and to which he was trying to justify Rome's policies, and partly because Latin was not as yet sufficiently developed to be a suitable vehicle for a large-scale piece of prose literature.

The three next historians also wrote in Greek: L. Cincius Alimentus, whose chief claim to fame was that for a time he had been a prisoner-of-war in Hannibal's camp, and two phil-Hellenic members of the Senate who wrote in the middle of the 2nd century B.C., C. Acilius and A. Postumius. It was at this period that there appeared the first history written in Latin, the *Origines* of Cato the Censor, which, starting with a description of the foundation of the more important Italian cities, proceeded with an account of Roman history down to Cato's own times, the latter section being interwoven with an admixture of political propaganda. In the next generation L. Calpurnius Piso, consul in 133, carried on still further the tradition of history-writing as a form of activity by which leading public men could at the same time justify their own and their party's political principles and convey moral instruction by means of suitable examples. Towards the end of the century L. Coelius Antipater, a jurist and teacher of rhetoric, introduced new elements into historical composition. First, he wrote an historical monograph rather than a full-scale history, an account of the Hannibalic War in seven books, for which he used, in addition to the normal Roman sources, a Carthaginian source, Silenus of Calatia, who had served in Hannibal's camp. Secondly, he was the first Roman historian to show any consciousness of the importance of style and to pay attention to literary presentation. He seems to have been a competent historian, and his most notable fault was an excessive love of the supernatural and the sensational.

In the first century B.C. Licinius Macer, an opponent of the Senate in politics, wrote a history of Rome from its foundation, in which political events of the early Republic were interpreted in contemporary terms and undue prominence given to members of the family of the Licinii. He was important in that he used an alternative tradition for the lists of magistrates, the *libri lintei* found in the temple of Juno Moneta on the Capitol at Rome, and not the lists based on the *Annales Maximi*, which apparently consisted of the Tabulae Pontificum with some additional matter derived from the state archives. In this he was followed by Aelius Tubero, a contemporary of Cicero. However, it was two historians from outside the ranks of the senatorial class, Q. Claudius Quadrigarius and Valerius Antias, who gave a new twist to the historiographical tradition. In their hands history became not an investigation of the truth, not even a means of conveying moral instruction, but merely a form of entertainment, in which carelessness about facts was combined with gross exaggeration as regards figures. They did, however, retail with reasonable accuracy the dry details of official appointments, religious phenomena, and the like that formed the greater part of the *Annales Maximi*. Claudius, who took as his starting point the capture of Rome by the Gauls, based the earlier part of his book on the history of C. Acilius. He had some merit as a stylist; Valerius, it seems, had none.

This is a brief summary of the work of some of the more important of Livy's predecessors. A more comprehensive account will be found in Professor E. Badian's chapter "The Early Historians" in *Latin Historians*.

Book XXI

II

Yet in the middle of the 1st century B.C. Rome still lacked an adequate history. In the *De Legibus*, written at the end of his life, Cicero emphasises this deficiency (I, ii). The earlier historians, he says, such as Fabius, Cato, and Piso, had been dry and lifeless. Coelius Antipater's style was more vigorous, but uncouth, while his successors did not reach even his standards. Licinius Macer (c. 115-66 B.C.) was verbose, and his work uneven, while his contemporary Sisenna (who wrote an account of the Social and Civil Wars), though the best historian yet, did not achieve any great merit. There was a great need for a history of Rome to be written by a consummate orator such as Cicero himself (as one of the characters in the dialogue suggests), since the composition of history is a task particularly suited to an orator—*opus unum hoc oratorium maxime*.

This point of view had already been set out at greater length in Cicero's *De Oratore* (II, 51-4). The great Greek historians had been outstanding orators, which was the reason why in this branch of literature the Romans fell so far short of the Greeks. At Rome, history had originally been nothing more than the compilation of a yearly record—*nihil aliud nisi annalium confectio*—following the methods and style of the *Annales* of the Pontifex Maximus. The earliest Roman historians, Fabius Pictor, Cato, and Calpurnius Piso, merely left records of dates, names, places, and events, set down without any literary embellishment—*sine ullis ornamentis monumenta solum temporum hominum locorum gestarumque rerum reliquerunt*. The only things they aimed at were clarity and brevity, and they merely recounted events without embellishing them—*non exornatores rerum, sed tantummodo narratores*. Coelius Antipater gave the voice of history a somewhat richer tone—*maiorem sonum vocis*—yet even he did not adorn his work with variations of light and shade, careful arrangement of words, or a smooth and flowing style.

In a subsequent passage (II, 62-4), Cicero gives his opinion

4

on the duties of an historian. The primary rule, he says, is never to say what is untrue; the next, never to suppress what is true; then, not to allow any trace of prejudice or partiality to affect one's writing. These are foundation-principles, Cicero asserts, that are familiar to everyone. Accordingly he dismisses them after only the most perfunctory consideration. Unfortunately, familiarity with these principles did not lead to their greater observance among Roman historians, who followed Cicero in giving more attention to presentation than investigation. For it is not with the foundations but with the "superstructure" of historical composition, comprising both subject-matter and language, that Cicero is chiefly concerned. In dealing with the subject-matter, the historian will have to handle both chronology and topography. He must describe and discuss the deliberations that preceded an action, tell how the action was carried out, assess the reasons for the ensuing result and allot praise or blame, and provide biographical sketches and character-studies of the most important people involved. As regards the language, it should be easy and flowing, moving forward smoothly and without jerkiness.

From this account of the functions of an historian it is not difficult to see why Cicero regarded the writing of history as a task for which an orator was specially fitted. For, in common with most Romans, he believed that the paramount duty of an historian, after the primary rules outlined above, was the presentation of his material in an attractive manner.

These were the ideas prevalent at the time when Livy starting writing his history, and the task which confronted him was very similar to what Cicero had outlined in the *De Legibus*, to write a history of Rome worthy of Rome's greatness, one that would stand comparison with the best histories of the Greeks, written in a style that embodied all the advances that had been made during the Ciceronian age in the development of Latin prose as a suitable vehicle for great literature. In spite of the activities of Pollio, Sallust, and Aelius Tubero, no adequate history of Rome had yet appeared, and Livy had full scope for his genius.

III

Livy's theme was the grandeur of Rome, and the men who made her great. His motive in writing was somewhat similar to that of Herodotus, a desire to perpetuate the great deeds of famous men: *iuvabit tamen rerum gestarum memoriae principis terrarum populi et ipsum consuluisse* (Preface, 3). Like Herodotus —and like most people who have derived keenest enjoyment from his work—he had a genuine love of the past. Unlike many of his immediate audience, who, guided by Sallust, were enthralled by the examination of contemporary society in the grip of corruption, he found his greatest pleasure in the opportunity that history gave him to escape, for however short a time, from the evils of the present (Pref., 5).

There was, too, a didactic element in Livy's purpose. He invites his readers not to make a critical assessment of the truth or falsehood of the early myths, but rather to consider the way of life and types of men that made possible the growth of Rome's power, and then to see how the national character disintegrated and progressively collapsed. From such a study as this, Livy says (Pref., 10), you may find clearly exposed to view examples of what to imitate and what to avoid. This strain of didacticism had been introduced into historiography in the 4th century B.C. by the Greek teacher Isocrates, and had played an important part in historical thought, both Greek and Roman, ever since. In Livy's case, it confirmed his natural Roman tendency to see his characters not as individuals but as examples of certain types of vices or virtues.

Livy was fully conscious of the importance of literary style. At the start of his Preface he admits that the only justification for embarking on a subject that had been often handled before was that the historian could either make some positive addition to the knowledge of the subject-matter or could in matters of style surpass the unsophisticated efforts of his predecessors—*scribendi arte rudem uetustatem superaturos*. Livy had no intention to add anything new: all his sources were the existing works of previous historians. It was in the field of style, in the presentation of his material, that he hoped to justify his efforts.

The writing of Latin Prose—and, later, of Latin Poetry— was greatly influenced by rhetoric. It was the purpose of rhetoric to enable a speaker to persuade his hearers either by presenting an argument in an attractive form or by moving the emotions of his audience. Livy himself may have been a teacher of rhetoric; in any case he made good use of the rhetorical technique. Speeches in his work followed the established pattern of rhetorical compositions, with an introduction designed to arouse interest, an exposition of arguments that would appeal to the rational faculties, and a peroration to stir the emotions. The narrative, too, was so constructed as to persuade the readers to adopt a certain point of view or to accept certain impressions without question; for example, that virtues such as fortitude, self-restraint, and patriotism are not only laudable in themselves but lead to satisfactory results, while vices like recklessness, indiscipline, or arrogance tend to bring disaster, both on the individual and the community. But Livy goes further than this. He persuades his readers to believe that the traditional virtues were generally displayed by Romans and the corresponding vices by non-Romans, or, where internal politics were concerned, virtues were to be found in the Senate and the supporters of Senatorial rule, whom Livy admired, and vices in the demagogues and the opponents of the Senate. By these methods Livy presents a picture of events that, without being false, is made to conform to the writer's preconceived ideas.

It was inevitable that this kind of approach to the writing of history led to bias and partisanship on the part of the historians. Livy and Tacitus represented the outlook of the Senatorial aristocracy, Caesar and Sallust that of the opponents of the Senate, Velleius Paterculus that of the Principate. As a result, even where accuracy was not seriously affected, impartiality suffered.

As an historian, Livy has been under-estimated in recent years. He suffers by comparison with Thucydides and Polybius, with Sallust and Tacitus. Yet Thucydides had the advantage of confining himself, for almost the whole of his work, to events of his own adult lifetime. Polybius, though unparalleled in the ancient world as a scientific historian, had little stylistic ability—it is said that he was readable in any language except his own—and indulged too frequently in long-winded digressions. Sallust, though his political judgement was shrewd, was far less conscientious than Livy, and less accurate, while Tacitus, though he surpassed Livy in intellectual calibre, also surpassed him in the violence of his prejudices. If we are to judge Livy by comparison with others, we should compare him not merely with those few historians of the front rank whose work has survived, but with the many whose work has largely been lost, with Coelius Antipater, whom we know to be excessively prone to the sensational, or with Valerius Antias and Claudius Quadrigarius, who were frequently guilty of gross exaggeration. We should also compare him with the later historians whose work has survived, Cassius Dio, for example, or Appian. Finally, we should view the monumental size of the task that he undertook, a work of 142 Books covering three quarters of a millennium, and presenting a record of events that, where it can be tested, has generally been found reliable on most matters of import-ance. It is true that, from time to time, Livy misunderstands or misinterprets the source that he is following, especially in the case of technical military details; sometimes he distorts or suppresses facts when they are inconsistent with the character that he is trying to portray; at times he falls into confusion from trying to conflate or reconcile two inconsistent sources. But viewed in the context of the work as a whole, these errors can be seen in a fairer perspective; they detract only slightly from the mass of valuable information that Livy provides. We must remember, too, that he carried out his work suffering from certain handicaps. The size of his history inevitably prevented his doing much first-hand research into public or private records or documentary material. All his sources were the works of earlier historians, and he had to use what material he found in them. It is to his great credit that he came more and more to rely on better sources such as Polybius and to distrust manifestly worse ones such as Valerius Antias. It is probable that his knowledge of Greek was deficient, while he had not the benefit of first-hand acquaintance with military or political affairs. When we take all these points into consideration, we can form a surer judgement on his merits. No one can doubt that Thucydides and Polybius were greater historians than Livy, but the very magnitude of his work, the unequalled length of time that it covered, and the sustained quality of his achievement place Livy above other Romans.

In constructing his narrative, Livy tended to follow one source at a time, expanding the material where necessary and recasting it in a more suitable literary form. Then, with a change of scene or of subject, he would often change to another source. Sometimes the transition was not accomplished with complete success, and this method resulted in a number of errors of chronology, with events being set out in the wrong order when the earlier parts of the new source overlap the later parts of the old one. Livy tended to follow later rather than earlier historians, mainly because they provided a fuller narrative. His main sources were: for Books I-X, Licinius Macer, Aelius Tubero, Valerius Antias, and, for the latter half of the decade, Claudius Quadrigarius; for XXI-XXX, Coelius Antipater, Polybius, Valerius, and Claudius; and for XXXI-XLV, Polybius for affairs in Greece and the East, and Claudius and Valerius for events in Italy and Spain. But Livy would also refer to the older historians such as Fabius, Cincius Alimentus, and Piso for corroborative evidence on disputed points, especially with reference to troop numbers and battle casualties. Fabius, as the oldest authority and a witness of the Second Punic War, was considered to have special weight.

Livy pays great attention to the human element. His narrative is usually cast in the form of a drama, with frequent reversals of fortune. In his descriptions of battles, emphasis is placed not on the technical details but on the emotions of the combatants, and the effects of surprise, terror, and fortitude are skilfully portrayed.

In his character-sketches Livy depicts types rather than individuals, and he ignores or suppresses details that conflict with the pattern that he has in mind. His characters tend to represent certain stock qualities, such as dignity (*grauitas*), recklessness (*temeritas*), arrogance (*superbia*), or self-restraint (*modestia*). But this is in accordance with the Roman literary tradition, both in drama and in history. The depicting of certain types of character, good and bad, was one of the most acceptable methods of conveying moral instruction. It is significant that the use of set character-types is common in Sallust and Tacitus also.

Livy followed the custom, firmly established among ancient historians, of including formal speeches in his work. They were normally inserted at certain conventional points, the speeches of the opposing generals before a battle, for example, or those made during a debate on some important political matter, such as the proposal to migrate to Veii in Book V, the ransoming of prisoners in Book XXII, or the question of invading Africa in Book XXVIII. Some of the speeches had an historical basis; Polybius records the exhortations of Scipio and Hannibal before the battle of Ticinus and the conversation between Hannibal and Scipio before that of Zama. But in cases such as these Livy has expanded his original and embellished it with all the ornaments of contemporary rhetoric. On other occasions the speeches are Livy's own composition, modelled on the rules of formal rhetoric and intended not to represent the actual words of a real speaker but to depict the attitudes and points of view of the various groups of people involved.

In style Livy followed Cicero, using the periodic structure for his sentences, in which the main idea or main action was stated in the main clause, with the various attending circumstances, causes, or results expressed in subordinate clauses that are attached to it. In this type of sentence the attending circumstances are expressed in such a way that they lead up logically to the main idea. The language that Livy used was smooth and flowing; he avoided both the archaisms of Pollio—except where archaic forms are used deliberately to give special solemnity to a particular passage—and Sallust's terseness and deliberate variation of constructions. The result is a style of considerable dignity and grandeur.

IV

Little is known of Livy's life. Even the usually accepted dates for his birth and death, 59 B.C.-A.D. 17, have been challenged, and a life-span of 64 B.C.-A.D. 12 suggested. He was born at Patavium (Padua) in Cisalpine Gaul, and was probably a teacher of rhetoric by profession. At any rate he was later made tutor to the future emperor, Claudius. He does not seem to have been connected with either of the main literary circles of Rome, that of Maecenas, to which Horace and Virgil belonged, or that of Messalla. Augustus, towards whom he seems to have been friendly but not subservient, once called him a "Pompeian", a mark of his republican sympathies; he did, in fact, long for the great days of Senatorial rule, and had a boundless admiration for Cicero. He probably started his history just after 30 B.C., and worked at it till shortly before his death. His 142 Books covered the period from the foundation of Rome to the death of Drusus in 9 B.C. The last nine books, covering the period from 28-9 B.C., may have been published posthumously.

Of the thirty-five extant books, I-V cover the period down

Book XXI

to the capture of Rome by the Gauls, a period for which Livy himself laments the shortage of written records (VI, 1), VI-X go down to the Third Samnite War, XXI-XXX cover the War with Hannibal, while XXXI-XLV deal with the era of Rome's eastern conquests to the end of the Third Macedonian War in 167 B.C.

For a more detailed discussion of Livy's life, see R. M. Ogilvie, *A Commentary on Livy I-V* (Oxford University Press), Introduction, and Dorey and Lydall, *Livy XXIX* (K. Mason), Introduction.

V

Livy's success was immediate and, in spite of periods of reaction, lasting. It is significant that no Latin historian ever attempted to re-write the history of the Republic. Tacitus, his great successor, started his "Annals" approximately where Livy ended his "Ab Urbe Condita"; similarly, two hundred years later, Ammianus Marcellinus wrote his Histories as a continuation of Tacitus. Other historians either appended a brief summary of Republican history to a work on contemporary affairs, as did Velleius Paterculus, or were Epitomators, like Florus, Eutropius, and Orosius. The only full length histories that dealt with the period that Livy had covered were written in Greek, by men such as Appian or Cassius Dio.

Livy presented the aristocratic view of history. The theme recurs throughout his work that a country only prospers, whether in peace or war, under the type of stable government that was best provided by a self-perpetuating aristocracy. Livy admires the aristocratic virtues of moderation and self-control (*temperantia, modestia, uerecundia*) and contrasts with them both the irresponsibility of the masses (*furor, insania*) and the arrogance and self-seeking of those individuals who from time to time try to rise above their fellows (*superbia, ambitio*). His condemnation of men like Flaminius and Varro (the Roman commanders at Trasimene and Cannae respectively) is not so much for bad generalship as for their political rabble-rousing. One of the most moving scenes in Livy's portrayal of Scipio Africanus is the one where he tells the Spanish tribes that it is more noble to act like a king than be called a king. It is interesting to note, too, how Livy applies the concepts of Stoicism, the prevalent school of thought in Rome at that time, to the political system by implicitly identifying the philosophical "good men" (*boni*), who alone deserved to wield power, with the political *boni*, the aristocrats, who alone, under the Republic, did wield power.

Livy's interpretation of history on these lines made his work acceptable to subsequent aristocratic societies, both in the city-states of the Renaissance and in 19th century England. It was through Livy that European writers derived their knowledge of the Roman institutions which had such a great influence on political thought during and after the Renaissance. Machiavelli, in particular, was a life-long student of Livy, and often uses or adapts his phraseology. His *Discorsi sopra Tito Livio*, a sustained work of political philosophy, is expressly based on Livy; his more famous *The Prince*, too, draws heavily on Livy (Books I-X), although this short book is not true history or philosophy, but an *ad hoc* tract for the use of Cesare Borgia—with the inevitable over-emphasis such a purpose entails. Machiavelli did not admire Livy blindly, but re-interpreted him in the light of current political conditions. For example, he contrasts Livy's picture of the Roman people as a whole, representing a nation bound together by civic virtues, with Livy's view of the undisciplined multitude, and, drawing on his own experience, regards the arrogance of the nobles as a greater threat to political cohesion than the unruliness of the populace. Machiavelli, like Livy, writes as a moralist, and sees in the history of Rome a rich store of those lessons in behaviour, good and bad, that are so dear to moralists.

Like Machiavelli, Montesquieu in 18th century France was influenced by Livy's moral attitudes, and takes his idealised picture of Roman history as portraying the sober truth. He did not approach Livy critically as an historian, but used the contents of Livy's work as raw material for his own great critical studies on social and political development.

In England, too, Livy had great influence, in two different ways. First, the Whig historians of the 18th and 19th centuries were particularly interested in the supremacy of Parliament. They tended to equate the Senate with Parliament, regarding the struggles of the early Republic against oppression as reflecting the struggles of Parliament against despotism, and seeing Livy's condemnation of the masses in terms of their own opposition to the current cult of equality that had been fostered by the French Revolution. Macaulay, in particular, followed Livy, not only as regards his uncritical attitude, but also his partisan approach and his belief in the importance of high ethical standards.

In the second place, as a result of this emphasis on morality, and above all the principle by which Livy makes success or failure depend on the exercise of good or bad qualities, his works helped to transmit the Roman-Stoic virtues of courage, patriotism, and self-control to Victorian England, where these virtues came to be regarded as indispensable to the acquisition and maintenance of imperial power.

Livy has been little appreciated in recent years, but at the present time, when so many societies are moving either towards despotism or towards mob-rule, the lessons that he can provide are very relevant.

T. A. D.

Chronological Table

264-41	First Punic War.
256-5	Regulus' defeat in Africa.
241	Naval victory off Aegates Islands ends war. Peace of Lutatius Catulus.
241-38	Mercenary War in Africa. Carthage finally puts down the revolt.
238	Rome claims Sardinia.
237-1	Rome's conquest of Corsica.
229-8	First Illyrian War.
227	Sardinia and Corsica constituted a Roman province.
226-5	Ebro treaty between Rome and Hasdrubal.
225	Celtic invasion of Etruria; Roman defeat near Montepulciano followed by crushing victory at Telamon.
224-2	Campaigns against Boii and Insubres. Roman capture of Milan.
220	Flaminius builds Via Flaminia from Rome to Ariminum.
219	Second Illyrian War; defeat of Demetrius.
(219-18	For a table of Spanish and Italian events, see p. 33.)
218-201	Second Punic War.
218	Roman reverse at the Ticinus; heavy defeat at the Trebia.
217	Roman defeat at Lake Trasimene. Fabius Maximus Cunctator becomes dictator.
216	Roman disaster at Cannae. Revolt of Capua.
216-03	Hannibal in Italy. Roman resistance effectively led by Fabius Maximus Cunctator and Claudius Marcellus.
215	Syracuse and Philip of Macedon allied with Carthage.
214-05	First Macedonian War.

Book XXI

Introduction to Book XXI

A. ROME AND CARTHAGE

With the defeat of Pyrrhus and the humbling of the sea power Tarentum, Rome had by 270 B.C. emerged as mistress of Italy and a major Mediterranean power. The clash which now took place with Carthage, the leading economic power in the west, seems retrospectively to have been almost inevitable. Yet to a Roman statesman of the early third century such a development would have seemed most unlikely; previous relations between the two cities had been so sensibly and realistically based on mutual self-interest that the prospect of two major and exhausting wars, spanning the years 264-241 and 218-201 B.C., would have appeared incredible.

Carthage had been founded, according to the traditional date, in 814 by a group of Phoenicians from Tyre led by Elissa, whom Virgil calls Dido. The date is approximately acceptable, though some archaeologists, troubled by the absence of eighth-century remains, prefer a date of a century later. In Phoenician, Carthage is "Qart Hadasht", "new city" or "new capital", and its foundation was an attempt to establish a large-scale Phoenician base on the route to Spain and Britain. The mines of Spain, with their silver, iron, tin, and lead, were the chief magnet for commercial exploitation, in which there was fierce competition with Greek traders; Carthage was only one of a series of inter-mediate stations established about this date—there were others in Africa, Sicily, Sardinia—to welcome and defend the merchant-ships plying their trade between the eastern and the western Mediterranean.

By 700 it was a rich and powerful city, a dominant commercial centre which was to last for the next five hundred years. Its history between 700 and 300 is the story of an economic struggle with the western Greeks; and in this struggle she sought alliance successively with the Etruscans and then with Rome. In this protracted rivalry her fortunes were on occasion at a low ebb. At the end of the fourth century, however, came a decisive turn bringing fresh prosperity. After Alexander the Great died in 323, the ensuing change in the balance of power in the eastern Mediterranean saw King Ptolemy joining Syria and Palestine to Egypt as a sort of common market, in which the measures and the currency of the Phoenicians were adopted as the standard. This was a great opportunity for Carthage to renew her traditional role as economic entrepreneur between east and west, and there is good evidence to show how she intensifies her trade after this date with Phoenicia, with Italy, and with the Greek cities.

Carthage now becomes virtually a Hellenistic city, acquiring Greek tastes in her building and ornamentation. Her craftsmen were undistinguished imitators; the abundant archaeological remains present a damningly clear picture. Carthage was in standards of manufacture the ancient Hong Kong. Any aesthetically impressive objects found at the site are imported; the good pottery is Greek, the good glassware from Egypt. Not merely were the Carthaginians imitators; unlike the Etruscans they were shoddy imitators.

This was the city confronting Rome, newly reaching the status of a Mediterranean Power—a civilisation of great commercial energy and resource, but a city virtually without literature or art, a nation wholly dominated by trade. Its politics had always been formulated with an eye to economic growth. There had been treaties of mutual help with Rome in 509, 348, 306, and as recently as 279, when Pyrrhus had been the common enemy. There was no pressing circumstance impelling the two sides to war, though the decline in the fortunes of the western Greeks was encouraging Carthage to exploit her presence in Sicily, where Greeks held the eastern seaboard.

INTRODUCTION TO BOOK XXI

In a situation in which there is no logical reason for war, war often breaks out because a chance happening triggers off a chain of reactions on each side, arousing mutual fears of external domination. It is a far cry from the crisis of Messene in 264 to the crisis confronting President Kennedy in Cuba a few years ago, but the parallel is striking. Messene, on the north-east tip of Sicily, had been previously seized by a group of Campanian mercenaries who called themselves Mamertines ("sons of Mamers", the Sabellian Mars), and who had been fighting for Agathocles of Syracuse against the Carthaginians. After holding the city for about twenty years (288-68) they were defeated by Hiero of Syracuse and sought external support. Some were for inviting the Carthaginians to take over the city, others the Romans. The Carthaginians got there first, but were ousted by trickery and the Romans seized the citadel. Immediately King Hiero, enraged by this dubious Roman action, allied himself with the Carthaginians. The Romans under Appius Claudius successively defeated Greeks and Carthaginians, and the war was under way.

The First Punic War was primarily a sea-war, with Sicily the prize. The Romans' greatest liability was naval in-experience. Yet in spite of losses in storms, they gained the upper hand at sea, initially with the crude device of the grapnel (*corvus*) at Mylae and Ecnomus (260, 256), but finally by more orthodox methods at the Aegates Islands (241); only one naval battle was lost, at Drepana (249). But on land, the operations in Africa (where Regulus was humiliated by the Spartan mercenary Xanthippus) and in Sicily (where Hamilcar easily repelled the Romans near Mt Eryx) showed that the Carthaginian forces were a match for Roman citizen-troops. The vital difference between the two sides lay in the superior organisation and steady resolution in the Roman political centre, the Senate.

The peace-terms imposed by the treaty of Catulus (241) were harsh. The Carthaginians agreed to pay a heavy twenty-year indemnity and to quit Sicily, which thus became the first overseas possession of Rome. A further serious reverse for Carthage followed. A mercenary war, precipitated by the failure of Carthage to pay her foreign troops, afflicted the city for over three years, and Rome exploited her difficulties to claim Sardinia as well. Within twenty-five years the Carthaginians had lost their foothold in the profitable grain-areas of Sicily and Sardinia.

But as always Carthage showed great powers of recovery and resilience. One area remained open for her to exploit, apart from the agricultural development possible in North Africa itself. That area was Spain, where Phoenicians had been commercially active since the ninth century, when Gades (Cadiz) was established. In order to increase her revenues, Carthage decided to dominate the country as far as the Ebro. This was what Hamilcar, Hasdrubal, and Hannibal achieved, largely by following the military strategy and battle-tactics of Alexander the Great.

Meanwhile Rome was preoccupied with the menace of the Gauls. In the Po valley the tribes were in revolt, and were being assisted by kinsmen from across the Alps. Because of this distraction on their northern border the Romans allowed the Carthaginians in Spain to proceed unhindered. In 226 a treaty was made with Hasdrubal making the Ebro the limit of the Carthaginian advance, and thereby tacitly admitting (or so the Carthaginians must have assumed) that the area further south was under Carthaginian control. But about the same time, or a little earlier, Rome had made an alliance with Saguntum, a city south of the Ebro and therefore now within the Carthaginian sphere. Once the Gallic danger receded, the Romans decided to put a brake on Carthaginian aspirations in Spain, and her ally Saguntum offered one obvious avenue of interference. So about 221 some Roman arbitrators put to death the pro-Carthaginian partisans in Saguntum. Hannibal, the new Carthaginian general, had hoped that he would win over Saguntum by persuading the inhabitants to renounce the Roman alliance; but once his supporters there were executed, the alternatives for him were either to accept a hostile Saguntum within the Carthaginian sphere, or to capture it by force. In 219 he decided on the second course. Rome hesitated for so long before deciding to go to war that her Saguntine allies were finally overwhelmed (219), but she eventually declared war and the Second Punic War (218-201) began.

The fundamental causes of this war are much clearer than those of the First Punic War; Polybius (III.8) and Livy (XXI. 1) present similar analyses. Fundamentally there is the deep resentment on the Carthaginian side at the loss of Sicily and Sardinia, areas exploited for their agriculture and mineral wealth for half a millennium; the opportunist Roman seizure of Sardinia especially rankled. Livy presents this resentment as the peculiar dynamic of the Barcines Hamilcar and Hannibal, but they undoubtedly had the mass support of the Carthaginians. On the Roman side there is the apprehensive suspicion that Spain was being developed as a Carthaginian colony to challenge the Roman supremacy, and certainly the three leaders had converted their armies into a more efficient war-machine than Carthage had previously possessed. More immediately, the Roman failure to observe the spirit of the Ebro treaty, reflected in their execution of the pro-Carthaginian faction at Saguntum, presented Hannibal with a challenge which he could ignore only with loss of face. It may well be that Hannibal formally contravened the treaty of Catulus by attacking a Roman ally (even though Saguntum was not an ally in 241), but the Romans had manoeuvred him into a corner. Even so, the lack of Roman preparation suggests miscalculation rather than a meditated challenge. Rome assumed that Carthage would withdraw from Saguntum, or make restitution after it had fallen. Hannibal likewise hoped that Rome would not go to war over a Spanish town—and indeed it took the Romans a year to decide to do so.

Book XXI

So began a global struggle, for in this war of 218-201 there was fighting in Italy, in Spain, in Sicily, in Greece, in Africa. It began with the epic and foolhardy crossing of the Alps by Hannibal. If Carthage had had long-laid plans for invading Italy, she ought logically to have built up a naval force and mounted the invasion by sea. The overland march was a gesture in the tradition of Alexander the Great; Hannibal staked all on a rapid conquest of Italy, and if this failed he was cut off from effective reinforcements.

The strategy almost succeeded. Great victories at the Trebia (218), Trasimene (217), and Cannae (216) achieved the massacre of three Roman armies. But his prospects of seizing Rome without siege-equipment were slight, and his hopes rested on the possible collapse of Roman morale which might induce the city to make terms. Hence his decision not to make for the capital, but to try to win over the Italian communities. He obtained Gallic support in the north, and backing from Greeks and Italians in the south; but the tribes of central Italy and many southern towns remained loyal.

After the disaster of Cannae, Rome avoided full-scale engagements and concentrated on detaching Hannibal from Italian sources of supplies. Gradually she recovered towns lost until the Carthaginians were penned in the south. Hannibal's only hope was for reinforcements from Carthage or Spain; but when his brother Hasdrubal, succeeding in bringing an army over the Alps, was defeated and killed at the Metaurus in 207, his prospects were bleak. Rome could go over to the offensive in Italy as she had already done in Spain and Sicily. In Sicily, Marcellus had captured Syracuse in 212; the young Scipio, appointed commander in 210, by a series of brilliant victories expelled the Carthaginians from the whole of Spain by 206. The way was open for the invasion of Africa, led by Scipio himself in 204. Hannibal was recalled to defend his homeland, but the Romans with the invaluable aid of the Numidian Massinissa and his cavalry won a series of victories which culminated at Zama in 202.

The peace-terms now imposed on Carthage ended her career as a Mediterranean power. An enormous annual indemnity was imposed, and her fleet destroyed. Henceforward she was confined to her own territory in what is now eastern Tunisia. Massinissa was made king of Numidia to circumscribe her on the west, and she was specifically forbidden to make war on him without Roman consent. Astonishingly she made yet another economic recovery, intensifying her agricultural efficiency, and her commercial activities in the areas to the south. But as Rome after the battle of Pydna (168) became increasingly suspicious of independent allies and increasingly impatient of diplomatic processes, Massinissa was able to awaken deep-seated fears of the resurgence of Carthage. By his skilful policy of piecemeal seizure of Carthaginian territories, he finally induced Carthage to retaliate and so to break the treaty of 201. So the obsessively anti-Carthaginian Cato and his supporters were able to persuade the Roman Senate to decide on war. Carthage finally fell and was destroyed in 146.

Suggestions for further reading

Dorey, T. A., and Dudley, D. R., *Rome against Carthage* (London 1971).

McDonald, A. H. *Republican Rome* (London, 1966).

Harden, Donald, *The Phoenicians* (London, 1962).

Picard, G., *Carthage* (English edition, London, 1964).

Scullard, H. H., *History of the Roman World 753-146 B.C.* (London, 1961).

Warmington, B. H., *Carthage* (London, 1969).

Book XXI

B. Livy as Historian

The theme of Rome's struggle with Carthage, by which she became mistress of the Mediterranean, serves as a useful focus for measuring Livy's virtues and limitations as historian. Unfortunately his account of the First and Third Wars is lost;[1] but the ten books allotted to the Second Punic War have survived, and here the historian has everything in his favour. The theme was a challenging one, appealing deeply to his engaged patriotism; and he has by this stage the experience of twenty books behind him, and more important, access to reasonably adequate historical authorities.

There are two possible ways of measuring the adequacy of Livy's account of 219-201 B.C. The first is to assume the mantle of the modern historian, and to subject Books XXI-XXX to sharp scientific scrutiny. The second, more rewarding approach is to visualise Livy's achievement within a framework of history-writing quite alien from ours—in other words, to ask what Livy's contemporaries expected of him, and how good is his history by the standards of Augustan Rome.

The modern historian finds much to censure. First, Livy reports virtually the whole war from an engaged Roman standpoint. Before the African operations of Book XXX, there are only four brief sections allotted to Carthaginian affairs,[2] and these are imaginative rather than real reports of Carthaginian debates, shedding oblique glory on Rome and blaming Carthage for the war. The extent of our ignorance of the Carthaginian administration (always less centralised than the Roman, with more discretion left to army-commanders) becomes more glaring as we note the laudable cumulation of detail about Roman central planning.

Secondly, as military historian Livy has grave faults. It would be possible to review the main campaigns in Italy,

---

[1] Of the 142 books composed by Livy, covering the years 753-9 B.C., only 35 have survived, I-X (753-293 B.C.) and XXI-XLV (219-167 B.C.).

[2] XXI.10 f.; XXIII.11 ff.; XXIII.32; XXIX.3 f.

Spain, Sicily, Greece, and Africa as he describes them, and to demonstrate the recurrent failures. There is his failure to recount vital detail of topography, of dispositions, of tactics in the major battles at Lake Trasimene, Cannae, and the Metaurus: his defective chronology, especially in the Spanish campaigns: his uncritical acceptance of biassed sources, which makes his account of military reverses an indictment of a Flaminius, a Minucius, a Terentius Varro: his idealising of individual figures like Marcellus, Fabius Cunctator, and above all Scipio Africanus.

In non-military contexts the modern historian will be prepared to make certain concessions in Livy's favour. He would acknowledge above all the value of his documentation of the Roman central administration. For Livy provides for every year of the war a list of commanders and their various spheres of duty. These lists of operational commands may make dreary reading for young students but are of great value in depicting the efficiency of senatorial planning. From these catalogues too can be assembled an almost complete chart of legionary dispositions in the various theatres of war: such information on strategic planning is often more valuable for an assessment of the causes of victory than are the descriptions of actual fighting.

Similarly our modern historian would willingly admit the extent of social and economic information provided by Livy. There is no systematic analysis of this evidence, but scattered items of information, when gathered together as in Tenney Frank's *Economic Survey of Ancient Rome*, offer a striking amount of information on state-income during the Hannibalic War. There are figures of direct taxation, of purchase-tax on salt and slaves, of income from booty, of moneys raised from the sale of public land. There are details of liturgies imposed on the rich, of loans made by widows and minors from trust funds, of collections of gold, silver, and jewelry from patriotic citizens, of the refusal of some knights and centurions to accept their army pay. There is an important account of contributions in kind made by individual cities towards the invasion of Africa; the list of commodities offered provides precious information about local industries, as well as insights into the sustained patriotic sacrifices which helped Rome's recovery from earlier disasters.

Detail of Roman diplomacy is also copious, for Livy systematically records the dispatch of Roman legations and the reception of foreign embassies. Treaties are set down in detail. But at this point our modern historian registers further protest, for many of these accounts of diplomatic activities have been patriotically falsified by Livy's sources, and he has failed to eliminate the distortions. We shall see, for example, how in Book XXI the treaties of Catulus and of the Ebro are misrepresented, and the same is true of his version of the peace-terms imposed after Zama.

This reliance on biassed sources is a fault which extends beyond diplomatic history, but it is here at its most blatant. It leads the modern historian into the central criticism that Livy is content to record rather than to interpret, to set down the received version rather than to organise the evidence into a significant pattern. The reader will not find any explicit explanation in Livy of why the Romans won the war. He provides the basic facts to establish the reasons—the efficacy and determination of the senatorial direction of the war, the fidelity of colonies and allied cities in Italy, the remoteness of the Carthaginian government from military planning and operations—but he does not try to pose such general questions, much less to set the factors into a synthesis. This is why it is tempting to call him a scholarly compiler rather than a historian. A Polybius or a Tacitus selects from the material to mould events into a meaningful pattern: Livy is content to dramatise individual events in a memorable way, without relating them to each other.

Clearly these are important criticisms, but we must now try to view them in the light of the conditions and the formative traditions within which Livy wrote. So against the indictment of patriotic bias, the reporting of the war from the Roman side only, we must set the fact that in the 20s B.C., when there was so much talk of founding a new Rome, the temptation to idealise the achievements of the old and middle Republics against the degeneracy of recent times was overwhelming. Even more important, the whole tradition of Roman historiography was that of propaganda history, beginning with Fabius Pictor who wrote his history of Rome in Greek for the benefit of the Greek world. Apart from Coelius Antipater, whose monograph on the Second Punic War exploited the work of at least one historian writing from the Hannibalic viewpoint, Livy's Roman sources automatically write pro-Roman apologetics. One of our historian's great merits is that he recoils from the tendentious misrepresentations of a Valerius Antias: he is a patriot, but tries to be an honest patriot. Finally, we must acknowledge that a historian who takes as his theme the whole history of a nation has not the time and leisure to search out such evidence of the Carthaginian viewpoint as may have existed in African or Greek libraries.

This argument, that histories on the scale of Livy's must forgo much primary research and depend on easily accessible sources, is important also in rebutting the charge of consultation of biassed authorities. It is salutary to visualise the physical conditions under which the historian worked, probably in the new library of Apollo, laboriously unwinding and rewinding each roll which he consulted. This must have been a basic factor dictating his technique of composition, which is to build up his account of an incident on the basis of a single source and to append differing versions at the end of each section in what are virtually footnotes. While we must remain critical of Livy's handling of his sources, we must acknowledge that he was circumscribed in his choice if he was to work quickly in obtaining full information from the Roman viewpoint.

Thirdly we must put the military weaknesses, the frequent misunderstanding of tactics and topography, into context.

Book XXI

Roman historians are distressingly cavalier in this respect. Sallust's *Jugurtha* is full of such geographical and military failings. Tacitus was called "the most unmilitary of historians" by Mommsen in connection with his account of military operations in Britain, and his accounts of other campaigns (*e.g.*, the eastern operations of Corbulo) raise similarly vexing difficulties. The truth is that Roman historians did not write for military specialists, and their contemporaries did not demand much technical virtuosity in such matters.

This brings us to the central consideration of the Roman conception of *historia*. The ancient historian is not concerned primarily with abstractions such as the evolution of political institutions, the impersonal laws of economics, or the science of warfare. For the Romans, history is the *magistra vitae*, the guide to the good life; it is a description of how earlier individuals and communities confronted historical situations, presented in such a way that we may apply the moral lessons to our own lives. For Livy, history is essentially not about political institutions, but about political virtues and vices of politicians: not about warfare, but about the behaviour of leaders and armies in war: not about social structures or economic laws, but about the personal qualities of individuals. It is his aim to demonstrate how such mental and moral attributes have a decisive impact on events.

But the term *historia* embraces more than categories of content. It also recommends the ways in which the material is to be presented, and the rules which Livy follows are laid down in Cicero's *De Oratore*.[1] Within the annalistic framework of events recounted year by year, the causes of those events should be explained, and their outcome outlined, so that the description of particular happenings should incorporate a trinity of *consilia, acta, eventus*—the motives and plans of

[1] 2.62 ff.

the people involved, the operations themselves, and their subsequent impact.

In this sense one may say that Livy's chief aim is to write psychological history, to delineate the attitudes of mind with which individuals and communities confronted particular situations—a theory of historiography remarkably parallel to that recommended by Collingwood in *The Idea of History*. But the ancients go beyond this aim of analysing particular attitudes of mind at particular moments. They seek to build up these psychological insights into a coherent pattern of characterisation. So characterisation, visualised as the expression of mental and moral qualities, is the method by which Livy achieves his didactic purpose.

So in his narrative of the Second Punic War, the historian presents full portraits of the main Roman leaders—Fabius Cunctator, *cautior quam promptior*, Marcellus, the hard man of the war, but whose ruthlessness is compensated by courage and magnanimity, and above all Scipio Africanus, Livy's ideal Roman. The character of Hannibal is likewise explored in depth. There are brief sketches of all these four, but Livy develops these pen-portraits by his presentation of their deeds and their words. Those who wish to get to grips with these techniques of characterisation must study above all the Livian speech. In recounting what actually happened, the historian was circumscribed by the requirement of truth and honesty ("nihil falsi dicere audeat, nihil veri non dicere")[1], but the ancient convention permitted him to proceed more imaginatively with the words. He was permitted to insert speeches at apposite points in the narrative, and Livy's speeches are "adapted to the characters and the occasions".[2] In such speeches as those of Books XXI and XXX, before the Italian operations commence and before the fateful battle of Zama, Hannibal is characterised as the leader who relies on fortune, *Scipio pater* and *Scipio filius* as exemplars

[1] Cic. *De Or.* 2.62.
[2] Quint. 10.1.101.

of Roman *pietas*. In other speeches are stressed Scipio Africanus' courage, foresight, diligence, clemency, and powers of self-control: the tendency towards idealised portrayal is a constant danger for a patriot, and Scipio is drawn too much the saint, Hannibal too much the devil.

As we survey Livy as purveyor of the ancient theories of historiography, we become increasingly critical of their defects but increasingly indulgent to Livy as their prisoner. The inability to see causes for events other than the virtues or follies of men (and chance or divine agency) leads to an excessive preoccupation with psychological analysis which tempts the historian to manufacture mental states to account for events. So too there is an excess of moralising didacticism, which leads to distortion of what really happened, and manipulation of what really was said. But if we make allowances for these weaknesses of the tradition, Livy emerges with some honour as a man who advanced that tradition to a more honest and respectable level.

In summary, the modern historian regards Livy as guilty of two main failures. First, he gets the facts wrong too often through being insufficiently critical of his sources. Secondly, he fails to assemble the facts into a historical pattern; a French scholar has recently called this "the lack of historical reflection on the evolution of major phenomena", instancing this from the first decade with Livy's discussion of the constitutional changes at Rome, and again of Rome's strategic advance to the middle of the peninsula.[1] The pattern of development is never made clear. Instead Livy depicts a series of separate and independent incidents, each brilliantly and memorably described but not coherently connected with the next.

I have tried to account for this failure by suggesting that Livy is not interested primarily in this type of interpretation. His chief conviction is that history is about the impact of human manners, a process of intellectual understanding not

[1] J. Bayet, in the Budé edition of Livy VII, Appendix.

of impersonal laws or forces but of human character. By study of the Hannibals and Scipios, the Marcelluses and the Fabiuses, and by a study of the behaviour of the Roman people in adversity and in victory, every age may obtain exemplars for political and private life. As Livy says in his Preface, "hoc illud est praecipue in cognitione rerum salubre ac frugiferum, omnis te exempli documenta in inlustri posita monumento intueri; inde tibi tuaeque rei publicae quod imitere capias, inde foedum inceptu foedum exitu quod vites."

SUGGESTIONS FOR FURTHER READING

Dorey, T. A. (ed.), *Latin Historians* (London, 1966).

Laistner, M. L. W., *The Greater Roman Historians* (Berkeley, 1947).

McDonald, A. H., "The Roman Historians" in *Fifty Years of Classical Scholarship* (Oxford, 1954).

Ogilvie, R. M., *A Commentary on Livy Books 1-5* (Oxford, 1965), Introduction.

Walsh, P. G., *Livy* (Cambridge, 4th Imp., 1970).

Book XXI

C. Book XXI

We must now scrutinise Book XXI in greater detail, with the double purpose of trying to establish what really happened and of seeking to elucidate Livy's main purposes and emphases. With characteristic neatness he divides the book into three equal sections. The first discusses Carthaginian consolidation in Spain up to the outbreak of war. The second describes Hannibal's remarkable expedition against Italy. The third describes the first operations in Italy in the autumn of 218 and the winter of 218-17.

Livy's account of the Carthaginian development of her Spanish interests under Hamilcar (237-229), Hasdrubal (229-221), and Hannibal (221-219) is an acceptable summary, though it should be noted that his version of the Ebro treaty with Rome (?226-5) is tendentious (2.7 n.). There is also too much emphasis on the Spanish operations as a Barcine rather than a national enterprise. A further criticism refers specifically to Hannibal's operations, curiously visualised as a strategic chain ultimately aimed at destroying Saguntum (5.3 n.). The account of the battle of the Tagus is confused (5.9 n.). In general, however, the narrative is clear and orderly.

Once Livy embarks on the Saguntum episode, however, his whole account becomes chronologically confused and factually dubious. He accepts into his account a deliberate distortion by which the siege of Saguntum was dated to 218 instead of 219. It was not a mistake he need have made, because he shows that he has read and approves the correct chronology (15.3 n.). But he is unwilling to go back and revise his version, although the entire presentation of the diplomatic exchanges between Carthage and Rome, and Saguntum and Rome, is vitiated by this falsification (10.1 n., 10.6 n.). It will therefore be useful to tabulate the approximate chronology of these events of 219-18.[1]

[1] See the useful articles by G. V. Sumner listed at the end of this section.

INTRODUCTION TO BOOK XXI

219 April/May	Hannibal's departure from New Carthage, and the siege of Saguntum begins.
219/18 Dec./Jan.	Saguntum captured.
218 Jan./Feb.	P. Cornelius Scipio, Ti. Sempronius Longus elected consuls.
Mar./April	Roman embassy goes to Carthage.
April	Comitia Centuriata votes war.
April/May	Hannibal leaves New Carthage.
May	Hannibal crosses Ebro.
May/June	Boii revolt.
June	News of Hannibal's crossing of the Ebro reaches Rome.
July/Aug.	Hannibal crosses Pyrenees.
Aug.	Scipio sails to Pisa, then to Massilia. Hannibal crosses the Rhône.
Late Sept.	Hannibal completes crossing of the Alps.

Livy is not primarily concerned with disentangling the precise sequence of events from the contradictory versions he found in the sources. His first aim is to depict the Barcine trio as a family dedicated to the development of Carthaginian imperialism and the destruction of Rome. This series of characterisations finds its climax in Hannibal, who is first described in a Sallustian portrait (4.2), and later in the speeches of Hanno, who depicts him as the *furia faxque huius belli* (10.11). The portrayal reaches its climax in the description of the famous dream, in which Hannibal is represented as a monstrous dragon menacing Rome (22.6 n.).

Secondly, the siege of Saguntum takes pride of place as the central event of this Spanish section. Described in three acts, it develops as a psychological account of the besieged, who pass from confidence to desperation and finally to madness. This account is followed by an analysis of the Roman reaction to this tragedy of their allies, and here too Livy concentrates on the psychological climate at Rome, harnessing the device of *oratio obliqua* to describe the causes of their apprehension

(16.3-6); this is a particularly clear example of the dangers of such imaginative analysis, for all the evidence suggests that the Romans were planning for campaigns overseas, and not in Italy itself (17.1 n.).

II

The problems raised by Livy's account of Hannibal's Alpine crossing are notorious.[1] Speculation has proceeded since the sixteenth century; literally hundreds of itineraries have been suggested, for controversy begins with the crossing of the Rhône, and the permutations are almost infinite. The difficulties cannot be solved by practical experimentation; only careful analysis of the sources can help.

Livy's account squares with that of Polybius[2] as far as the notorious "Island" on the Rhône; indeed, it supplies extra topographical detail (24.1f., 26.6). We may therefore assume that the crossing of the river was in the vicinity of Tarascon/Arles (27.1 n.), and that the army marched northward along the east bank to "The Island". If this name, used by both Polybius and Livy, could be indisputably identified, controversy on the initial stages of the route would disappear.

"The Island" is described as a triangular area, bounded on two sides by the Rhône and the Skaras (Polybius) or Arar (Livy)—these being almost certainly corrupt forms of the same river, not readily identifiable. From Polybius we infer that it was 600 stades (just under 70 miles) from the point of the Rhône crossing, and took four days. It is 40 miles to the Aygues and 100 to the Isère. The "Island" must be one of these junctions. From there Hannibal continued "along the river", i.e. either from the Aygues up the Rhône to the Isère and along that river, or from Pont de l'Isère directly along the Isère to Grenoble. From this point Polybius' account is naked of recognisable names, but he states that on his descent

[1] See Walbank's *JRS* article, listed at the end of this section.
[2] On Polybius, see below, p. 40.

Hannibal arrived in the territory of the Insubres, which suggests that he thought the pass used was the Little Saint Bernard.[1] The evidence of Polybius, therefore, consistently suggests that Hannibal took the northerly route; if this were the sole available version, the only controversy would relate to the identity of the final pass.

Livy's version, however, partly contradicts Polybius. He suggests that after leaving "The Island", Hannibal heads *northward*, but a little later he claims that he reached the Durance via the Tricastini, Vocontii, and Tricorii. It seems clear that he has followed the same tradition as Polybius up to 31.8, but has then turned to a different source, presumably Valerius Antias, which contained the theory of a more southerly route (31.9 nn. and the map on p. 73). The likely reason for his changing sources in midstream was that the northerly route as described by Polybius and Coelius would have brought Hannibal down to Aosta and then to Vercelli instead of to Turin (38.7 nn.). Though Livy does not name the pass, he implies that it was the Mt Genèvre or one of the Mt Cenis passes, and here his account must be preferred to that of Polybius. But because he has begun with the northern route as described by Coelius/Polybius, and then introduced dissonant material from Valerius, his version is self-contradictory.

The likelihood is that Polybius, who follows the account of Silenus, Hannibal's companion on the march, has described the route correctly up to the final stage. Hannibal will have taken the northerly route along the Isère, but the final pass will have been not the Little St Bernard but one of the Mt Cenis passes or the Mt Genèvre.

But Livy is not primarily concerned with a meticulous reproduction of the route followed. He wishes rather to implant in the reader's mind a psychological picture of the progress of the Carthaginians on this epic journey. Their hazards and privations are vividly recounted as they meet the

[1] Pol. III.49.5 ff. with Walbank's notes.

Book XXI

hostile Volcae at the Rhône, as they ship the elephants across the river, as they confront the snow-topped Alps merging with the sky, as they plod wearily and fearfully through the unfamiliar snow, and as they make the descent which takes toll of animals and men.

III

Hannibal's arrival in Italy marks the commencement of the struggle, and this is fittingly prefaced in Livy by the contrasting orations of Scipio the elder and the Carthaginian leader before the engagement at the Ticinus. Balanced in length and content, the speeches seek to bring out the fundamentally different religious attitudes of the Roman and the Carthaginian, who in Book XXX before Zama is to admit that he relied overmuch on fortune.

As military narrative, this final section leaves much to be desired. After the skirmish at the Ticinus, Livy confuses the rivers Ticinus and Po in describing the Roman retreat (47.2 n.). The battle of the Trebia becomes confused in his version because he sites the first Roman camp east instead of west of the Trebia (47.8 n.), makes them cross the river east to west instead of west to east (48.6 n.), and stages the battle on the east bank instead of the west (56.8 n.). Sempronius' alleged march to Lucca, following upon highly dubious accounts of Carthaginian bestiality at Victumulae and an attempt to cross the Apennines (57.13, 58.1 nn.) is rejected by almost all scholars since it contradicts 63.1 (59.10 n.). Likewise the version of Spanish operations contains its problems (61.4-8 nn.). On the credit side must be set the usefulness of his fuller account of Sicilian operations (49-51).

Livy's eyes are trained in this section on the events of 218 as a prelude to the great disasters to follow, which he seeks both to presage with the appropriate atmosphere of cosmic gloom and to explain by moralising. The importance of the lists of prodigies (46.1, 62.1ff.) in creating the feeling of disaster should be noted. In accounting for the disaster of the

Trebia, the *temeritas* and *ferocitas* of Sempronius are contrasted with the *prudentia* of Hannibal. The unpreparedness of the Roman troops, wet, hungry, and cold, is set against the astute preparations of the Carthaginians, who are warm, dry, and well-fed. And the final chapters set the scene for the disaster of Trasimene by dilating on the *impietas* and *discordia* associated with Flaminius. Note also the psychological description of the Roman reaction to the disaster of Trebia, as earlier after Saguntum reinforced with the imaginative use of *oratio obliqua* (57.1 n.).

The contrasts in each of the three sections of the book between the priorities of the modern historian and the primary aims of Livy provide a striking lesson about the limitations of ancient historiographical theory.

SUGGESTIONS FOR FURTHER READING

Spain before the Second Punic War:—

E. Badian, *Foreign Clientelae* (Oxford, 1958), 47ff.

G. V. Sumner, "Roman Policy in Spain before the Hannibalic War", in *Harvard Studies in Classical Philology* (1968), 205-46.

G. V. Sumner, "The Chronology of the Outbreak of the Second Punic War", in *Proc. Afr. Class. Ass.* (1966), 5-30.

Alpine Crossing:—

Dennis Proctor, *Hannibal's March in History* (Oxford, 1971).

F. W. Walbank, "Some Reflections on Hannibal's Pass", in *Journal of Roman Studies* (1956), 37-45.

Italian section and Book XXI generally:—

P. G. Walsh, "Livy", in *Latin Historians*, ed. Dorey, ch. 5.

Book XXI

D. The Sources

Livy's massive theme of the entire history of Rome, written in 142 books, allowed him little time for research into original documents. He was content to use accessible literary sources. But in selecting those most suitable for each section of his history, he tried conscientiously to strike a balance between opposed views, and to choose the authors who provided specialised knowledge on the events described. His technique of composition was to follow one source in building up his account of each event or scene, and then to provide the gist of any dissonant statements in other authorities consulted.[1]

For the third decade, this balance and specialised knowledge was sought from three main sources, the Greek Polybius, and the Romans L. Coelius Antipater and Valerius Antias. Polybius was certainly used for the Sicilian and Greek sections in the later books, but there is dispute about the extent to which Livy used him for Spanish and Italian events. The cause of this uncertainty is the fact that both Polybius and Coelius followed the same sources—Silenus, a Greek who accompanied Hannibal, for the Carthaginian viewpoint, and Fabius Pictor for the Roman. The situation can be described diagrammatically as follows:—

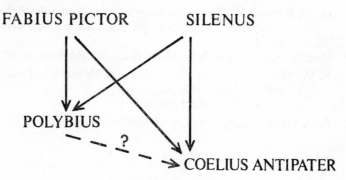

[1] On all this, see my *Livy*, ch. 5.

Moreover, it is likely that Coelius consulted Polybius directly. For these reasons, where Livy follows Coelius his account is extremely close to that of Polybius. The fact that he is not regularly following Polybius is demonstrable in the numerous places in Book XXI where he provides information different from, or more detailed than, that provided by Polybius [5.3 (Cartala/Althaea), 27.2, 31.6, 37.2, 39.4 and 10, 48.9, 55.2 and 4, nn.]. Note also that Coelius is cited three times in this book (38.7, 46.10, 47.4) and Polybius not at all, and that the account of Hannibal's dream derives from Coelius (22.6 n.). But in view of Livy's great knowledge of and respect for Polybius, we cannot dismiss the possibility that he has *consulted* the Greek historian throughout, and perhaps incorporated from him brief sections where Coelius had less detail.

Livy follows Coelius primarily for details of operations in Spain and Italy. But Coelius may not have incorporated sufficient evidence of Roman activity, and for this our historian turns to Valerius Antias and more occasionally to Claudius Quadrigarius. From these annalistic writers he obtained fuller detail of Roman administration and political activity in the capital. Livy's use of Antias is usually indicated by the annalistic structure, by the chauvinistic exaggerations of enemy losses and blatant pro-Roman distortion, by political bias against plebeian figures, by the heavy moralising veneer.

An approximate picture of Livy's alternating use of Coelius and Antias is given in the following table. In the sections ascribed to Coelius it is probable that he has consulted Polybius throughout, and in places incorporated Polybian material; in the sections ascribed to Antias, Claudius may also have been consulted.

1.1-2.2	Livy's Introduction.
2.3-6.2	Coelius.
6.3-6.8	Antias.
7.1-15.2	Coelius, contaminated by Antias' chronology.

BOOK XXI

Polybius was born at Megalopolis in Arcadia shortly before
200. A prominent politician there, he was one of those
important Achaeans deported to Italy after the Third
Macedonian War (168 B.C.) on suspicion of hostility to the
Roman regime. He there became friendly with Scipio
Aemilianus, in whose house he lodged and whom he accompanied on various journeys outside Italy. He was thus ideally
placed to write a universal history on the period 264-146, with
particular emphasis on the rise of Rome to world-dominion
between 220 and 168. Writing on a contemporary theme,
closely associated with a leading political family, experienced
in Greek affairs, a traveller to all the areas he describes, he

---

[1]The German scholar A. Klotz (*Livius und seine Vorgänger*, 119-136)
believes that Livy follows Coelius throughout the book except at 46.8,
47.6, 49.1-51.7, 57.1-4, 58.1-59.10, 61.4-10, 62.1-63.15.

can boast of that practical experience and personal investigation which he considers vital qualifications for a serious historian.

L. Coelius Antipater was the first to compose an historical monograph in Latin, taking the Hannibalic War as his theme. He began his work shortly after the death of C. Gracchus in 121 B.C. Well-known as a lawyer and literary man rather than as a politician, and writing a century after the event, he could not bring the personal investigations of a Polybius to bear, but his choice of good sources, and a much more impartial spirit than was the norm amongst Romans, made his work unusually objective and well-informed for his time. His great vice is to have been the victim of Greek predilections for dramatic and pathetic touches; hence the prominence given to the dream of Hannibal, and similar sensational themes later.

The two annalists Valerius Antias and Claudius Quadrigarius were armchair historians writing general histories of Rome, Antias from the foundation and Claudius from the Gallic sack. Composing their histories in the first half of the first century B.C., they wrote them in the framework of the *annales maximi*[1], setting down at the beginning of each year the documentary detail of elections, appointments, prodigies, etc. But having thus commenced each year with historically valuable documentation, they felt themselves free to distort subsequent details of military and political events in the interests of their city and their political prejudices. Livy is constantly taking Antias to task for "shameless lies" (XXVI.49.3, XXX.19.12), and most of the inaccuracies for which we pillory Livy can be ascribed to these later sources.

[1] The name given to the 80 books of Roman records taken from the tablets of the priests and published by Mucius Scaevola about 115 B.C.

Book XXI

SUGGESTIONS FOR FURTHER READING

Badian, E., "The Early Historians" in *Latin Historians* (ed. Dorey), ch. 1.

Ogilvie, R. M., *A Commentary on Livy Books* 1-5, Introduction.

Walbank, F. W., "Polybius" in *Latin Historians*, ch. 2.

Walbank, F. W., *Commentary on Polybius* I, Introduction.

Walsh, P. G., *Livy*, ch. 5.

T. LIVI
AB URBE CONDITA

LIBER XXI

In parte operis mei licet mihi praefari, quod in principio
summae totius professi plerique sunt rerum scriptores,
bellum maxime omnium memorabile quae unquam gesta
sint me scripturum, quod Hannibale duce Carthagin-
2 ienses cum populo Romano gessere. Nam neque
ualidiores opibus ullae inter se ciuitates gentesque
contulerunt arma neque his ipsis tantum unquam
uirium aut roboris fuit; et haud ignotas belli artes inter sese
sed expertas primo Punico conferebant bello, et adeo uaria
fortuna belli ancepsque Mars fuit ut propius periculum
3 fuerint qui uicerunt. Odiis etiam prope maioribus
certarunt quam uiribus, Romanis indignantibus quod
uictoribus uicti ultro inferrent arma, Poenis quod
superbe auareque crederent imperitatum uictis esse.
4 Fama est etiam Hannibalem annorum ferme nouem,
pueriliter blandientem patri Hamilcari ut duceretur in
Hispaniam, cum perfecto Africo bello exercitum eo
traiecturus sacrificaret, altaribus admotum tactis sacris
iure iurando adactum se cum primum posset hostem
5 fore populo Romano. Angebant ingentis spiritus uirum
Sicilia Sardiniaque amissae: nam et Siciliam nimis
celeri desperatione rerum concessam et Sardiniam inter
motum Africae fraude Romanorum, stipendio etiam
2 insuper imposito, interceptam. His anxius curis ita

se Africo bello quod fuit sub recentem Romanam pacem per quinque annos, ita deinde nouem annis in Hispania
2 augendo Punico imperio gessit ut appareret maius eum quam quod gereret agitare in animo bellum et, si diutius uixisset, Hamilcare duce Poenos arma Italiae inlaturos fuisse qui Hannibalis ductu intulerunt.
3 Mors Hamilcaris peropportuna et pueritia Hannibalis distulerunt bellum. Medius Hasdrubal inter patrem ac filium octo ferme annos imperium obtinuit, flore aetatis,
4 uti ferunt, primo Hamilcari conciliatus, gener inde ob aliam indolem profecto animi adscitus et, quia gener erat, factionis Barcinae opibus, quae apud milites plebemque plus quam modicae erant, haud sane uoluntate principum,
5 in imperio positus. Is plura consilio quam ui gerens, hospitiis magis regulorum conciliandisque per amicitiam principum nouis gentibus quam bello aut armis rem
6 Carthaginiensem auxit. Ceterum nihilo ei pax tutior fuit; barbarus eum quidam palam ob iram interfecti ab eo domini obtruncat; comprensusque ab circumstantibus haud alio quam si euasisset uoltu, tormentis quoque cum laceraretur, eo fuit habitu oris ut superante laetitia
7 dolores ridentis etiam speciem praebuerit. Cum hoc Hasdrubale, quia mirae artis in sollicitandis gentibus imperioque suo iungendis fuerat, foedus renouauerat populus Romanus ut finis utriusque imperii esset amnis Hiberus Saguntinisque mediis inter imperia duorum populorum libertas seruaretur.
3 In Hasdrubalis locum haud dubia res fuit quin⟨am successurus esset;⟩ praerogatiuam militarem qua extemplo iuuenis Hannibal in praetorium delatus imperatorque ingenti omnium clamore atque adsensu appellatus erat
2 fauor etiam plebis sequebatur. Hunc uixdum puberem Hasdrubal litteris ad se accersierat, actaque res etiam in

senatu fuerat. Barcinis nitentibus ut adsuesceret militiae Hannibal atque in paternas succederet opes, Hanno,
3 alterius factionis princeps, " Et aequum postulare uidetur" inquit, "Hasdrubal, et ego tamen non censeo
4 quod petit tribuendum." Cum admiratione tam ancipitis sententiae in se omnes conuertisset, "Florem aetatis" inquit, "Hasdrubal, quem ipse patri Hannibalis fruendum praebuit, iusto iure eum a filio repeti censet; nos tamen minime decet iuuentutem nostram pro militari rudimento
5 adsuefacere libidini praetorum. An hoc timemus ne Hamilcaris filius nimis sero imperia immodica et regni paterni speciem uideat et, cuius regis genero hereditarii sint relicti exercitus nostri, eius filio parum mature seruiamus?
6 Ego istum iuuenem domi tenendum sub legibus, sub magistratibus, docendum uiuere aequo iure cum ceteris censeo, ne quandoque paruus hic ignis incendium
4 ingens exsuscitet." Pauci ac ferme optimus quisque Hannoni adsentiebantur; sed, ut plerumque fit, maior pars meliorem uicit.

Missus Hannibal in Hispaniam primo statim aduentu
2 omnem exercitum in se conuertit; Hamilcarem iuuenem redditum sibi ueteres milites credere; eundem uigorem in uoltu uimque in oculis, habitum oris lineamentaque intueri. Dein breui effecit ut pater in se minimum
3 momentum ad fauorem conciliandum esset. Nunquam ingenium idem ad res diuersissimas, parendum atque imperandum, habilius fuit. Itaque haud facile discerneres
4 utrum imperatori an exercitui carior esset; neque Hasdrubal alium quemquam praeficere malle ubi quid fortiter ac strenue agendum esset, neque milites alio
5 duce plus confidere aut audere. Plurimum audaciae ad pericula capessenda, plurimum consilii inter ipsa pericula erat. Nullo labore aut corpus fatigari aut animus uinci

6 poterat. Caloris ac frigoris patientia par; cibi potionis-
que desiderio naturali, non uoluptate modus finitus;
uigiliarum somnique nec die nec nocte discriminata
7 tempora; id quod gerendis rebus superesset quieti
datum; ea neque molli strato neque silentio accersita;
multi saepe militari sagulo opertum humi iacentem inter
8 custodias stationesque militum conspexerunt. Vestitus
nihil inter aequales excellens: arma atque equi conspiciebantur. Equitum peditumque idem longe primus
erat; princeps in proelium ibat, ultimus conserto proelio
9 excedebat. Has tantas uiri uirtutes ingentia uitia
aequabant, inhumana crudelitas, perfidia plus quam
Punica, nihil ueri, nihil sancti, nullus deum metus,
10 nullum ius iurandum, nulla religio. Cum hac indole
uirtutum atque uitiorum triennio sub Hasdrubale
imperatore meruit, nulla re quae agenda uidendaque
magno futuro duci esset praetermissa.

5 Ceterum ex quo die dux est declaratus, uelut Italia ei
prouincia decreta bellumque Romanum mandatum esset,
2 nihil prolatandum ratus ne se quoque, ut patrem Hamilcarem, deinde Hasdrubalem, cunctantem casus aliquis
3 opprimeret, Saguntinis inferre bellum statuit. Quibus
oppugnandis quia haud dubie Romana arma mouebantur,
in Olcadum prius fines—ultra Hiberum ea gens in parte
magis quam in dicione Carthaginiensium erat—induxit
exercitum, ut non petisse Saguntinos sed rerum serie finitimis domitis gentibus iungendoque tractus ad id bellum
4 uideri posset. Cartalam, urbem opulentam, caput gentis
eius, expugnat diripitque; quo metu perculsae minores
ciuitates stipendio imposito imperium accepere. Victor
exercitus opulentusque praeda Carthaginem Nouam in
5 hiberna est deductus. Ibi large partiendo praedam
stipendioque praeterito cum fide exsoluendo cunctis ciuium

sociorumque animis in se firmatis uere primo in Vaccaeos
6 promotum bellum. Hermandica et Arbocala, eorum
urbes, ui captae. Arbocala et uirtute et multitudine
7 oppidanorum diu defensa; ab Hermandica profugi
exsulibus Olcadum, priore aestate domitae gentis, cum se
8 iunxissent, concitant Carpetanos adortique Hannibalem
regressum ex Vaccaeis haud procul Tago flumine agmen
9 graue praeda turbauere. Hannibal proelio abstinuit
castrisque super ripam positis, cum prima quies silentium-
que ab hostibus fuit, amnem uado traiecit ualloque ita
praeducto ut locum ad transgrediendum hostes haberent
10 inuadere eos transeuntes statuit. Equitibus praecepit ut,
cum ingressos aquam uiderent, adorirentur impeditum
agmen; in ripa elephantos—quadraginta autem erant—
11 disponit. Carpetanorum cum appendicibus Olcadum
Vaccaeorumque centum milia fuere, inuicta acies si aequo
12 dimicaretur campo. Itaque et ingenio feroces et multitudine freti et, quod metu cessisse credebant hostem, id
morari uictoriam rati quod interesset amnis, clamore
sublato passim sine ullius imperio qua cuique proximum
13 est in amnem ruunt. Et ex parte altera ripae uis ingens
equitum in flumen immissa, medioque alueo haudqua-
14 quam pari certamine concursum, quippe ubi pedes
instabilis ac uix uado fidens uel ab inermi equite, equo
temere acto, peruerti posset, eques corpore armisque
liber, equo uel per medios gurgites stabili, comminus
15 eminusque rem gereret. Pars magna flumine absumpta;
quidam uerticoso amni delati in hostes ab elephantis
16 obtriti sunt. Postremi, quibus regressus in suam ripam
tutior fuit, ex uaria trepidatione cum in unum colligeren-
tur, priusquam in tanto pauore reciperent animos,
Hannibal agmine quadrato amnem ingressus fugam ex
ripa fecit uastatisque agris intra paucos dies Carpetanos

17 quoque in deditionem accepit; et iam omnia trans
Hiberum praeter Saguntinos Carthaginiensium erant.

6 Cum Saguntinis bellum nondum erat; ceterum iam belli
causa certamina cum finitimis serebantur, maxime Turde-
2 tanis. Quibus cum adesset idem qui litis erat sator, nec
certamen iuris sed uim quaeri appareret, legati a Saguntinis Romam missi auxilium ad bellum iam haud dubie
3 imminens orantes. Consules tunc Romae erant P.
Cornelius Scipio et Ti. Sempronius Longus. Qui cum
legatis in senatum introductis de re publica rettulissent
placuissetque mitti legatos in Hispaniam ad res sociorum
4 inspiciendas, quibus si uideretur digna causa, et Hannibali
denuntiarent ut ab Saguntinis, sociis populi Romani,
abstineret et Carthaginem in Africam traicerent ac
5 sociorum populi Romani querimonias deferrent—hac
legatione decreta necdum missa, omnium spe celerius
Saguntum oppugnari allatum est. Tunc relata de
6 integro res ad senatum est; alii prouincias consulibus
Hispaniam atque Africam decernentes terra marique
rem gerendam censebant, alii totum in Hispaniam
7 Hannibalemque intenderant bellum; erant qui non
temere mouendam rem tantam exspectandosque ex
8 Hispania legatos censerent. Haec sententia, quae tutis-
sima uidebatur, uicit legatique eo maturius missi, P.
Valerius Flaccus et Q. Baebius Tampilus, Saguntum ad
Hannibalem atque inde Carthaginem si non absisteretur
bello ad ducem ipsum in poenam foederis rupti deposcendum.

7 Dum ea Romani parant consultantque, iam Saguntum
2 summa ui oppugnabatur. Ciuitas ea longe opulentissima
ultra Hiberum fuit, sita passus mille ferme a mari.
Oriundi a Zacyntho insula dicuntur mixtique etiam ab
3 Ardea Rutulorum quidam generis; ceterum in tantas

The Roman Theatre at Saguntum, with the Citadel behind.
(Photo: Ampliaciones y Reproducciones Mas, Barcelona.)

breui creuerant opes seu maritimis seu terrestribus
fructibus seu multitudinis incremento seu disciplinae
sanctitate qua fidem socialem usque ad perniciem suam
coluerunt.

4 Hannibal infesto exercitu ingressus fines, peruastatis
5 passim agris urbem tripertito adgreditur. Angulus muri
erat in planiorem patentioremque quam cetera circa
uallem uergens; aduersus eum uineas agere instituit per
6 quas aries moenibus admoueri posset. Sed ut locus
procul muro satis aequus agendis uineis fuit, ita haudquaquam prospere, postquam ad effectum operis uentum
7 est, coeptis succedebat. Et turris ingens imminebat et
murus, ut in suspecto loco, supra ceterae modum altitudinis emunitus erat, et iuuentus delecta ubi plurimum
periculi ac timoris ostendebatur ibi ui maiore obsistebant.

8 Ac primo missilibus summouere hostem nec quicquam
satis tutum munientibus pati; deinde iam non pro
moenibus modo atque turri tela micare, sed ad erumpendum etiam in stationes operaque hostium animus erat;
9 quibus tumultuariis certaminibus haud ferme plures
10 Saguntini cadebant quam Poeni. Vt uero Hannibal ipse,
dum murum incautius subit, aduersum femur tragula
grauiter ictus cecidit, tanta circa fuga ac trepidatio fuit
ut non multum abesset quin opera ac uineae desererentur.

8 Obsidio deinde per paucos dies magis quam oppugnatio
fuit dum uolnus ducis curaretur; per quod tempus ut
quies certaminum erat ita ab apparatu operum ac
2 munitionum nihil cessatum. Itaque acrius de integro
coortum est bellum pluribusque partibus, uix accipienti-
bus quibusdam opera locis, uineae coeptae agi admoueri-
3 que aries. Abundabat multitudine hominum Poenus—
ad centum enim quinquaginta milia habuisse in armis
4 satis creditur—: oppidani ad omnia tuenda atque

5 obeunda multifariam distineri coepti non sufficiebant. Itaque iam feriebantur arietibus muri quassataeque multae
partes erant; una continentibus ruinis nudauerat urbem;
tres deinceps turres quantumque inter eas muri erat cum
6 fragore ingenti prociderant. Captum oppidum ea ruina
crediderant Poeni, qua, uelut si pariter utrosque murus
7 texisset, ita utrimque in pugnam procursum est. Nihil
tumultuariae pugnae simile erat, quales in oppugnationi-
bus urbium per occasionem partis alterius conseri solent,
sed iustae acies, uelut patenti campo, inter ruinas muri
tectaque urbis modico distantia interuallo constiterant.
8 Hinc spes, hinc desperatio animos inritat, Poeno cepisse
iam se urbem si paulum adnitatur credente, Saguntinis
pro nudata moenibus patria corpora opponentibus nec
ullo pedem referente ne in relictum a se locum hostem im-
9 mitteret. Itaque quo acrius et confertim magis utrimque
pugnabatur, eo plures uolnerabantur nullo inter arma cor-
10 poraque uano intercidente telo. Phalarica erat Saguntinis missile telum hastili abiegno et cetera tereti praeterquam ad extremum unde ferrum exstabat; id, sicut in
pilo, quadratum stuppa circumligabant linebantque pice;
11 ferrum autem tres longum habebat pedes ut cum armis
transfigere corpus posset. Sed id maxime, etiamsi
12 haesisset in scuto nec penetrasset in corpus, pauorem
faciebat quod, cum medium accensum mitteretur
conceptumque ipso motu multo maiorem ignem ferret,
arma omitti cogebat nudumque militem ad insequentes
9 ictus praebebat. Cum diu anceps fuisset certamen et
Saguntinis quia praeter spem resisterent creuissent animi,
2 Poenus quia non uicisset pro uicto esset, clamorem repente
oppidani tollunt hostemque in ruinas muri expellunt,
inde impeditum trepidantemque exturbant, postremo
fusum fugatumque in castra redigunt.

3 Interim ab Roma legatos uenisse nuntiatum est; quibus
obuiam ad mare missi ab Hannibale qui dicerent nec tuto
eos adituros inter tot tam effrenatarum gentium arma nec
Hannibali in tanto discrimine rerum operae esse legationes
4 audire. Apparebat non admissos protinus Carthaginem
ituros. Litteras igitur nuntiosque ad principes factionis
Barcinae praemittit ut praepararent suorum animos ne
quid pars altera gratificari populo Romano posset.

10 Itaque, praeterquam quod admissi auditique sunt, ea
2 quoque uana atque inrita legatio fuit. Hanno unus aduersus senatum causam foederis magno silentio propter
3 auctoritatem suam, non cum adsensu audientium egit, per
deos foederum arbitros ac testes obtestans ne Romanum
cum Saguntino suscitarent bellum; monuisse, praedixisse
se ne Hamilcaris progeniem ad exercitum mitterent; non
manes, non stirpem eius conquiescere uiri, nec unquam
donec sanguinis nominisque Barcini quisquam supersit
4 quietura Romana foedera. "Iuuenem flagrantem cupi-
dine regni uiamque unam ad id cernentem si ex bellis
bella serendo succinctus armis legionibusque uiuat, uelut
materiam igni praebentes, ad exercitus misistis. Aluistis
5 ergo hoc incendium quo nunc ardetis. Saguntum uestri
circumsedent exercitus unde arcentur foedere; mox
Carthaginem circumsedebunt Romanae legiones ducibus
iisdem dis per quos priore bello rupta foedera sunt ulti.
6 Vtrum hostem an uos an fortunam utriusque populi
ignoratis? Legatos ab sociis et pro sociis uenientes bonus
imperator uester in castra non admisit; ius gentium
sustulit; hi tamen, unde ne hostium quidem legati
arcentur, pulsi, ad uos uenerunt. Res ex foedere
repetuntur; publica fraus absit: auctorem culpae et
7 reum criminis deposcunt. Quo lenius agunt, segnius in-
cipiunt, eo cum coeperint uereor ne perseuerantius

saeuiant. Aegates insulas Erycemque ante oculos pro-
ponite, quae terra marique per quattuor et uiginti annos
8 passi sitis. Nec puer hic dux erat sed pater ipse Hamilcar,
Mars alter, ut isti uolunt. Sed Tarento, id est Italia, non
abstinueramus ex foedere, sicut nunc Sagunto non absti-
9 nemus; uicerunt ergo di hominesque et, id de quo uerbis
ambigebatur uter populus foedus rupisset, euentus belli
uelut aequus iudex, unde ius stabat, ei uictoriam dedit.
10 Carthagini nunc Hannibal uineas turresque admouet:
Carthaginis moenia quatit ariete. Sagunti ruinae—
falsus utinam uates sim—nostris capitibus incident,
susceptumque cum Saguntinis bellum habendum cum
11 Romanis est. Dedemus ergo Hannibalem? dicet aliquis.
Scio meam leuem esse in eo auctoritatem propter paternas
inimicitias; sed et Hamilcarem eo perisse laetatus sum
quod, si ille uiueret, bellum iam haberemus cum Romanis,
et hunc iuuenem tamquam furiam facemque huius belli
12 odi ac detestor; nec dedendum solum id piaculum rupti
foederis, sed si nemo deposcit, deuehendum in ultimas
maris terrarumque oras, ablegandum eo unde nec ad nos
nomen famaque eius accedere neque ille sollicitare quietae
13 ciuitatis statum possit, ego ita censeo. Legatos extemplo
Romam mittendos qui senatui satisfaciant, alios qui Hannibali nuntient ut exercitum ab Sagunto abducat ipsum-
que Hannibalem ex foedere Romanis dedant, tertiam
legationem ad res Saguntinis reddendas decerno."
11 Cum Hanno perorasset, nemini omnium certare oratione
cum eo necesse fuit; adeo prope omnis senatus Hannibalis
erat, infestiusque locutum arguebant Hannonem quam
2 Flaccum Valerium, legatum Romanum. Responsum
inde legatis Romanis est bellum ortum ab Saguntinis, non
ab Hannibale esse; populum Romanum iniuste facere, si

Saguntinos uetustissimae Carthaginiensium societati praeponat.

3 Dum Romani tempus terunt legationibus mittendis, Hannibal, quia fessum militem proeliis operibusque habebat,
paucorum iis dierum quietem dedit stationibus ad
custodiam uinearum aliorumque operum dispositis.
Interim animos eorum nunc ira in hostes stimulando, nunc

4 spe praemiorum accendit; ut uero pro contione praedam
captae urbis edixit militum fore, adeo accensi omnes sunt
ut, si extemplo signum datum esset, nulla ui resisti

5 uideretur posse.   Saguntini ut a proeliis quietem habuer-
ant nec lacessentes nec lacessiti per aliquot dies, ita non
nocte, non die unquam cessauerant ab opere, ut nouum
murum ab ea parte qua patefactum oppidum ruinis erat

6 reficerent.   Inde oppugnatio eos aliquanto atrocior
quam ante adorta est, nec qua primum aut potissimum
parte ferrent opem, cum omnia uariis clamoribus streper-

7 ent, satis scire poterant.   Ipse Hannibal qua turris
mobilis, omnia munimenta urbis superans altitudine,
agebatur hortator aderat.   Quae cum admota catapultis
ballistisque per omnia tabulata dispositis muros defensori-

8 bus nudasset, tum Hannibal occasionem ratus, quingentos
ferme Afros cum dolabris ad subruendum ab imo murum
mittit; nec erat difficile opus, quod caementa non calce
durata erant sed interlita luto, structurae antiquae genere.

9 Itaque latius quam qua caederetur ruebat perque patentia
10 ruinis agmina armatorum in urbem uadebant.   Locum
quoque editum capiunt, conlatisque eo catapultis ballistisque ut castellum in ipsa urbe uelut arcem imminentem
haberent muro circumdant; et Saguntini murum

11 interiorem ab nondum capta parte urbis ducunt.   Vtrim-
que summa ui et muniunt et pugnant; sed interiora

12 tuendo minorem in dies urbem Saguntini faciunt.   Simul

crescit inopia omnium longa obsidione et minuitur
exspectatio externae opis, cum tam procul Romani, unica
13 spes, circa omnia hostium essent. Paulisper tamen
adfectos animos recreauit repentina profectio Hannibalis
in Oretanos Carpetanosque, qui duo populi, dilectus
acerbitate consternati, retentis conquisitoribus metum
defectionis cum praebuissent, oppressi celeritate Han-
12 nibalis omiserunt mota arma. Nec Sagunti oppugnatio
segnior erat Maharbale Himilconis filio—eum praefecerat
Hannibal—ita impigre rem agente ut ducem abesse
2 nec ciues nec hostes sentirent. Is et proelia aliquot
secunda fecit et tribus arietibus aliquantum muri discussit
strataque omnia recentibus ruinis aduenienti Hannibali
3 ostendit. Itaque ad ipsam arcem extemplo ductus
exercitus atroxque proelium cum multorum utrimque
caede initum et pars arcis capta est.

Temptata deinde per duos est exigua pacis spes, Alconem
4 Saguntinum et Alorcum Hispanum. Alco insciis Saguntinis, precibus aliquid moturum ratus, cum ad Hannibalem noctu transisset, postquam nihil lacrimae moue-
bant condicionesque tristes, ut ab irato uictore, ferebantur,
transfuga ex oratore factus apud hostem mansit, moritur-
um adfirmans qui sub condicionibus iis de pace ageret.
5 Postulabatur autem, redderent res Turdetanis traditoque
omni auro atque argento egressi urbe cum singulis
6 uestimentis ibi habitarent ubi Poenus iussisset. Has
pacis leges abnuente Alcone accepturos Saguntinos,
Alorcus, uinci animos ubi alia uincantur adfirmans, se
pacis eius interpretem fore pollicetur; erat autem tum
miles Hannibalis, ceterum publice Saguntinis amicus
7 atque hospes. Tradito palam telo custodibus hostium
transgressus munimenta ad praetorem Saguntinum—et
8 ipse ita iubebat—est deductus. Quo cum extemplo

concursus omnis generis hominum esset factus, submota cetera multitudine senatus Alorco datus est, cuius talis oratio fuit:

13 "Si ciuis uester Alco, sicut ad pacem petendam ad Hannibalem uenit, ita pacis condiciones ab Hannibale ad uos rettulisset, superuacaneum hoc mihi fuisset iter, quo nec

2 orator Hannibalis nec transfuga ad uos ueni; sed cum ille aut uestra aut sua culpa manserit apud hostem—sua, si metum simulauit: uestra, si periculum est apud uos uera referentibus—ego, ne ignoraretis esse et salutis aliquas et pacis uobis condiciones, pro uetusto hospitio quod mihi

3 uobiscum est ad uos ueni. Vestra autem causa me nec ullius alterius loqui quae loquor apud uos uel ea fides sit quod neque dum uestris uiribus restitistis neque dum auxilia ab Romanis sperastis pacis unquam apud uos

4 mentionem feci. Postquam nec ab Romanis uobis ulla est spes nec uestra uos iam aut arma aut moenia satis defendunt, pacem adfero ad uos magis necessariam quam

5 aequam. Cuius ita aliqua spes est, si eam, quemadmodum ut uictor fert Hannibal, sic uos ut uicti audiatis; si non id quod amittitur in damno, cum omnia uictoris sint, sed quidquid relinquitur pro munere habituri estis.

6 Vrbem uobis, quam ex magna parte dirutam, captam fere totam habet, adimit: agros relinquit, locum adsignaturus in quo nouum oppidum aedificetis. Aurum et argentum omne, publicum priuatumque, ad se iubet

7 deferri: corpora uestra coniugum ac liberorum uestrorum seruat inuiolata, si inermes cum binis uestimentis uelitis

8 ab Sagunto exire. Haec uictor hostis imperat; haec, quamquam sunt grauia atque acerba, fortuna uestra uobis suadet. Equidem haud despero, cum omnium potestas

9 ei facta sit, aliquid ex his rebus remissurum; sed uel haec patienda censeo potius quam trucidari corpora uestra,

rapi trahique ante ora uestra coniuges ac liberos belli iure sinatis.''

14 Ad haec audienda cum circumfusa paulatim multitudine permixtum senatui esset populi concilium, repente primores secessione facta priusquam responsum daretur argentum aurumque omne ex publico priuatoque in forum conlatum in ignem ad id raptim factum conicientes
2 eodem plerique semet ipsi praecipitauerunt. Cum ex eo pauor ac trepidatio totam urbem peruasisset, alius insuper tumultus ex arce auditur. Turris diu quassata prociderat, perque ruinam eius cohors Poenorum impetu facto cum signum imperatori dedisset nudatam stationibus custodiisque solitis hostium esse urbem, non cunctandum in tali
3 occasione ratus Hannibal, totis uiribus adgressus urbem momento cepit, signo dato ut omnes puberes interficerentur. Quod imperium crudele, ceterum prope necessar-
4 ium cognitum ipso euentu est; cui enim parci potuit ex iis qui aut inclusi cum coniugibus ac liberis domos super se ipsos concremauerunt aut armati nullum ante finem
15 pugnae quam morientes fecerunt? Captum oppidum est cum ingenti praeda. Quamquam pleraque ab dominis de industria corrupta erant et in caedibus uix ullum discrimen aetatis ira fecerat et captiui militum praeda
2 fuerant, tamen et ex pretio rerum uenditarum aliquantum pecuniae redactum esse constat et multam pretiosam supellectilem uestemque missam Carthaginem.
3 Octauo mense quam coeptum oppugnari captum Saguntum quidam scripsere; inde Carthaginem Nouam in hiberna Hannibalem concessisse; quinto deinde mense quam ab Carthagine profectus sit in Italiam peruenisse.
4 Quae si ita sunt, fieri non potuit ut P. Cornelius Ti. Sempronius consules fuerint, ad quos et principio oppugnationis legati Saguntini missi sint et qui in suo

magistratu cum Hannibale, alter ad Ticinum amnem,
5 ambo aliquanto post ad Trebiam pugnauerint. Aut omnia breuiora aliquanto fuere aut Saguntum principio anni, quo P. Cornelius Ti. Sempronius consules fuerunt,
6 non coeptum oppugnari est sed captum. Nam excessisse pugna ad Trebiam in annum Cn. Seruili et C. Flamini non potest, quia C. Flaminius Arimini consulatum iniit, creatus a Ti. Sempronio consule, qui post pugnam ad Trebiam ad creandos consules Romam cum uenisset comitiis perfectis ad exercitum in hiberna rediit.

16 Sub idem fere tempus et legati qui redierant ab Carthagine Romam rettulerunt omnia hostilia esse, et Sagunti
2 excidium nuntiatum est; tantusque simul maeror patres misericordiaque sociorum peremptorum indigne et pudor non lati auxilii et ira in Carthaginienses metusque de summa rerum cepit, uelut si iam ad portas hostis esset, ut tot uno tempore motibus animi turbati trepidarent magis
3 quam consulerent: nam neque hostem acriorem bellicosioremque secum congressum nec rem Romanam tam
4 desidem unquam fuisse atque imbellem. Sardos Corsosque et Histros atque Illyrios lacessisse magis quam exercuisse Romana arma et cum Gallis tumultuatum uerius
5 quam belligeratum: Poenum hostem ueteranum, trium et uiginti annorum militia durissima inter Hispanas gentes semper uictorem, duci acerrimo adsuetum, recentem ab
6 excidio opulentissimae urbis, Hiberum transire; trahere secum tot excitos Hispanorum populos; conciturum auidas semper armorum Gallicas gentes; cum orbe terrarum bellum gerendum in Italia ac pro moenibus Romanis esse.

17 Nominatae iam antea consulibus prouinciae erant; tum sortiri iussi. Cornelio Hispania, Sempronio Africa cum
2 Sicilia euenit. Sex in eum annum decretae legiones et

socium quantum ipsis uideretur et classis quanta parari
3 posset. Quattuor et uiginti peditum Romanorum milia
scripta et mille octingenti equites, sociorum quadraginta
milia peditum, quattuor milia et quadringenti equites;
naues ducentae uiginti quinqueremes, celoces uiginti
4 deducti. Latum inde ad populum uellent iuberent
populo Carthaginiensi bellum indici; eiusque belli
causa supplicatio per urbem habita atque adorati di, ut
bene ac feliciter eueniret quod bellum populus Romanus
5 iussisset. Inter consules ita copiae diuisae: Sempronio
datae legiones duae—ea quaterna milia erant peditum
et treceni equites—et sociorum sedecim milia peditum,
equites mille octingenti; naues longae centum sexaginta,
6 celoces duodecim. Cum his terrestribus maritimisque
copiis Ti. Sempronius missus in Siciliam, ita in Africam
transmissurus si ad arcendum Italia Poenum consul alter
7 satis esset. Cornelio minus copiarum datum, quia L.
Manlius praetor et ipse cum haud inualido praesidio in
8 Galliam mittebatur; nauium maxime Cornelio numerus
deminutus; sexaginta quinqueremes datae—neque enim
mari uenturum aut ea parte belli dimicaturum hostem
credebant—et duae Romanae legiones cum suo iusto
equitatu et quattuordecim milibus sociorum peditum,
9 equitibus mille sescentis. Duas legiones Romanas et
decem milia sociorum peditum, mille equites socios,
sescentos Romanos Gallia prouincia eodem uersa in
Punicum bellum habuit.

18 His ita comparatis, ut omnia iusta ante bellum fierent,
legatos maiores natu, Q. Fabium M. Liuium L. Aemilium
C. Licinium Q. Baebium in Africam mittunt ad percon-
tandos Carthaginienses publicone consilio Hannibal
2 Saguntum oppugnasset, et si id quod facturi uidebantur
faterentur ac defenderent publico consilio factum, ut

3 indicerent populo Carthaginiensi bellum. Romani postquam Carthaginem uenerunt, cum senatus datus esset et
Q. Fabius nihil ultra quam unum quod mandatum erat
percontatus esset, tum ex Carthaginiensibus unus:
4 "Praeceps uestra, Romani, et prior legatio fuit, cum
Hannibalem tamquam suo consilio Saguntum oppugnan-
tem deposcebatis; ceterum haec legatio uerbis adhuc
5 lenior est, re asperior. Tunc enim Hannibal et insimulabatur et deposcebatur; nunc ab nobis et confessio
culpae exprimitur et ut a confessis res extemplo repetun-
6 tur. Ego autem non priuato publicone consilio Saguntum
oppugnatum sit quaerendum censeam sed utrum iure an
7 iniuria; nostra enim haec quaestio atque animaduersio in
ciuem nostrum est quid nostro aut suo fecerit arbitrio:
uobiscum una disceptatio est licueritne per foedus fieri.
8 Itaque quoniam discerni placet quid publico consilio, quid
sua sponte imperatores faciant, nobis uobiscum foedus est
a C. Lutatio consule ictum in quo, cum caueretur utrorumque sociis, nihil de Saguntinis—necdum enim erant
9 socii uestri—cautum est. At enim eo foedere quod cum
Hasdrubale ictum est Saguntini excipiuntur. Aduersus
quod ego nihil dicturus sum nisi quod a uobis didici.
10 Vos enim, quod C. Lutatius consul primo nobiscum foedus
icit, quia neque auctoritate patrum nec populi iussu
ictum erat, negastis uos eo teneri; itaque aliud de
11 integro foedus publico consilio ictum est. Si uos non tenent
foedera uestra nisi ex auctoritate aut iussu uestro icta, ne
nos quidem Hasdrubalis foedus quod nobis insciis icit
12 obligare potuit. Proinde omittite Sagunti atque Hiberi
mentionem facere et quod diu parturit animus uester
13 aliquando pariat." Tum Romanus sinu ex toga facto,
"Hic" inquit, "uobis bellum et pacem portamus; utrum
placet sumite." Sub hanc uocem haud minus ferociter,

14 daret utrum uellet, succlamatum est; et cum is iterum sinu
effuso bellum dare dixisset, accipere se omnes responderunt et quibus acciperent animis iisdem se gesturos.

19 Haec derecta percontatio ac denuntiatio belli magis ex
dignitate populi Romani uisa est quam de foederum iure
uerbis disceptare, cum ante, tum maxime Sagunto excisa.

2 Nam si uerborum disceptationis res esset, quid foedus Hasdrubalis cum Lutati priore foedere, quod mutatum est,

3 comparandum erat, cum in Lutati foedere diserte additum
esset ita id ratum fore si populus censuisset, in Hasdrubalis
foedere nec exceptum tale quicquam fuerit et tot annorum
silentio ita uiuo eo comprobatum sit foedus ut ne mortuo

4 quidem auctore quicquam mutaretur? Quamquam, etsi
priore foedere staretur, satis cautum erat Saguntinis sociis
utrorumque exceptis; nam neque additum erat "iis qui

5 tunc essent" nec "ne qui postea adsumerentur". Et cum
adsumere nouos liceret socios, quis aequum censeret aut
ob nulla quemquam merita in amicitiam recipi aut
receptos in fidem non defendi, tantum ne Carthaginiensium socii aut sollicitarentur ad defectionem aut sua sponte
desciscentes reciperentur?

6 Legati Romani ab Carthagine, sicut iis Romae imperatum
erat, in Hispaniam ut adirent ciuitates ut in societatem

7 perlicerent aut auerterent a Poenis traiecerunt. Ad
Bargusios primum uenerunt, a quibus benigne excepti,
quia taedebat imperii Punici, multos trans Hiberum

8 populos ad cupidinem nouae fortunae erexerunt. Inde
est uentum ad Volcianos, quorum celebre per Hispaniam
responsum ceteros populos ab societate Romana auertit.
Ita enim maximus natu ex iis in concilio respondit:

9 "Quae uerecundia est, Romani, postulare uos uti uestram
Carthaginiensium amicitiae praeponamus, cum qui id
fecerunt [Saguntini] crudelius quam Poenus hostis

60

10 perdidit uos socii prodideritis? Ibi quaeratis socios
censeo ubi Saguntina clades ignota est; Hispanis populis
sicut lugubre, ita insigne documentum Sagunti ruinae
erunt ne quis fidei Romanae aut societati confidat."

11 Inde extemplo abire finibus Volcianorum iussi ab nullo
deinde concilio Hispaniae benigniora uerba tulere. Ita
nequiquam peragrata Hispania in Galliam transeunt.

20 In his noua terribilisque species uisa est, quod armati—ita
2 mos gentis erat—in concilium uenerunt. Cum uerbis
extollentes gloriam uirtutemque populi Romani ac magni-
tudinem imperii petissent ne Poeno bellum Italiae infer-
3 enti per agros urbesque suas transitum darent, tantus cum
fremitu risus dicitur ortus ut uix a magistratibus maiori-
4 busque natu iuuentus sedaretur; adeo stolida impudens-
que postulatio uisa est censere, ne in Italiam transmittant
Galli bellum, ipsos id auertere in se agrosque suos pro
5 alienis populandos obicere. Sedato tandem fremitu
responsum legatis est neque Romanorum in se meritum
esse neque Carthaginiensium iniuriam ob quae aut pro
6 Romanis aut aduersus Poenos sumant arma; contra ea
audire sese gentis suae homines agro finibusque Italiae
pelli a populo Romano stipendiumque pendere et
7 cetera indigna pati. Eadem ferme in ceteris Galliae
conciliis dicta auditaque, nec hospitale quicquam
pacatumue satis prius auditum quam Massiliam uenere.
8 Ibi omnia ab sociis inquisita cum cura ac fide cognita:
praeoccupatos iam ante ab Hannibale Gallorum animos
esse; sed ne illi quidem ipsi satis mitem gentem fore—
adeo ferocia atque indomita ingenia esse—ni subinde auro,
cuius auidissima gens est, principum animi concilientur.
9 Ita peragratis Hispaniae et Galliae populis legati Romam
redeunt haud ita multo post quam consules in prouincias
profecti erant. Ciuitatem omnem in exspectationem belli

erectam inuenerunt, satis constante fama iam Hiberum
Poenos tramisisse.

21 Hannibal Sagunto capto Carthaginem Nouam in hiberna
concesserat, ibique auditis quae Romae quaeque Carthagine acta decretaque forent, seque non ducem solum sed
2 etiam causam esse belli, partitis diuenditisque reliquiis
praedae nihil ultra differendum ratus, Hispani generis
3 milites conuocat. "Credo ego uos" inquit, "socii, et
ipsos cernere pacatis omnibus Hispaniae populis aut
finiendam nobis militiam exercitusque dimittendos esse
4 aut in alias terras transferendum bellum; ita enim hae
gentes non pacis solum sed etiam uictoriae bonis florebunt,
si ex aliis gentibus praedam et gloriam quaeremus.
5 Itaque cum longinqua ab domo instet militia incertumque
sit quando domos uestras et quae cuique ibi cara sunt
uisuri sitis, si quis uestrum suos inuisere uolt, com-
6 meatum do. Primo uere edico adsitis, ut dis bene
iuuantibus bellum ingentis gloriae praedaeque futurum
7 incipiamus." Omnibus fere uisendi domos oblata ultro
potestas grata erat, et iam desiderantibus suos et longius
8 in futurum prouidentibus desiderium. Per totum tempus
hiemis quies inter labores aut iam exhaustos aut mox
exhauriendos renouauit corpora animosque ad omnia de
integro patienda; uere primo ad edictum conuenere.
9 Hannibal cum recensuisset omnium gentium auxilia,
Gades profectus Herculi uota exsoluit nouisque se obligat
10 uotis, si cetera prospera euenissent. Inde partiens curas
simul ⟨in⟩ inferendum atque arcendum bellum, ne, dum
ipse terrestri per Hispaniam Galliasque itinere Italiam
peteret, nuda apertaque Romanis Africa ab Sicilia esset,
11 ualido praesidio firmare eam statuit; pro eo supplementum ipse ex Africa maxime iaculatorum leuium armis
petiit, ut Afri in Hispania, in Africa Hispani, melior

procul ab domo futurus uterque miles, uelut mutuis
12 pigneribus obligati stipendia facerent. Tredecim milia
octingentos quinquaginta pedites caetratos misit in
Africam et funditores Baliares octingentos septuaginta,
13 equites mixtos ex multis gentibus mille ducentos. Has
copias partim Carthagini praesidio esse, partim distribui
per Africam iubet. Simul conquisitoribus in ciuitates
missis quattuor milia conscripta delectae iuuentutis,
praesidium eosdem et obsides, duci Carthaginem iubet.
22 Neque Hispaniam neglegendam ratus, atque id eo minus
quod haud ignarus erat circumitam ab Romanis eam
2 legatis ad sollicitandos principum animos, Hasdrubali
fratri, uiro impigro, eam prouinciam destinat firmatque
eum Africis maxime praesidiis, peditum Afrorum undecim
milibus octingentis quinquaginta, Liguribus trecentis,
3 Baliaribus ⟨quingentis⟩. Ad haec peditum auxilia additi
equites Libyphoenices, mixtum Punicum Afris genus,
quadringenti ⟨quinquaginta⟩ et Numidae Maurique
accolae Oceani ad mille octingenti et parua Ilergetum
manus ex Hispania, ducenti equites, et, ne quod terrestris
4 deesset auxilii genus, elephanti uiginti unus. Classis
praeterea data tuendae maritimae orae, quia qua parte
belli uicerant ea tum quoque rem gesturos Romanos credi
poterat, quinquaginta quinqueremes, quadriremes duae,
triremes quinque; sed aptae instructaeque remigio
triginta et duae quinqueremes erant et triremes quinque.
5 Ab Gadibus Carthaginem ad hiberna exercitus rediit;
atque inde profectus praeter Onussam urbem ad Hiberum
6 maritima ora ducit. Ibi fama est in quiete uisum ab eo
iuuenem diuina specie qui se ab Ioue diceret ducem in
Italiam Hannibali missum; proinde sequeretur neque
7 usquam a se deflecteret oculos. pauidum primo, nusquam circumspicientem aut respicientem, secutum;

deinde cura ingenii humani cum, quidnam id esset quod
respicere uetitus esset, agitaret animo, temperare oculis
8 nequiuisse; tum uidisse post sese serpentem mira magnitudine cum ingenti arborum ac uirgultorum strage ferri
9 ac post insequi cum fragore caeli nimbum. tum quae
moles ea quidue prodigii esset quaerentem, audisse
uastitatem Italiae esse; pergeret porro ire nec ultra
inquireret sineretque fata in occulto esse.

23 Hoc uisu laetus tripertito Hiberum copias traiecit, praemissis qui Gallorum animos, qua traducendus exercitus
erat, donis conciliarent Alpiumque transitus specularen-
tur. Nonaginta milia peditum, duodecim milia equitum
2 Hiberum traduxit. Ilergetes inde Bargusiosque et Ausetanos et Lacetaniam, quae subiecta Pyrenaeis montibus
est, subegit oraeque huic omni praefecit Hannonem, ut
fauces quae Hispanias Galliis iungunt in potestate essent.
3 Decem milia peditum Hannoni ad praesidium obtinendae
4 regionis data et mille equites. Postquam per Pyrenaeum
saltum traduci exercitus est coeptus rumorque per
barbaros manauit certior de bello Romano, tria milia inde
Carpetanorum peditum iter auerterunt. Constabat non
tam bello motos quam longinquitate uiae insuperabilique
5 Alpium transitu. Hannibal quia reuocare aut ui retinere
eos anceps erat, ne ceterorum etiam feroces animi
6 inritarentur, supra septem milia hominum domos remisit,
quos et ipse grauari militia senserat, Carpetanos quoque
24 ab se dimissos simulans. Inde, ne mora atque otium
animos sollicitaret, cum reliquis copiis Pyrenaeum
transgreditur et ad oppidum Iliberrim castra locat.
2 Galli quamquam Italiae bellum inferri audiebant, tamen,
quia ui subactos trans Pyrenaeum Hispanos fama erat
praesidiaque ualida imposita, metu seruitutis ad arma
consternati Ruscinonem aliquot populi conueniunt.

3 Quod ubi Hannibali nuntiatum est, moram magis quam
bellum metuens, oratores ad regulos eorum misit, conloqui
semet ipsum cum iis uelle; et uel illi propius Iliberrim
accederent uel se Ruscinonem processurum, ut ex propin-
4 quo congressus facilior esset; nam et accepturum eos in
castra sua se laetum nec cunctanter se ipsum ad eos
uenturum; hospitem enim se Galliae non hostem aduenisse, nec stricturum ante gladium, si per Gallos liceat,
5 quam in Italiam uenisset. Et per nuntios quidem haec;
ut uero reguli Gallorum castris ad Iliberrim extemplo
motis haud grauate ad Poenum uenerunt, capti donis
cum bona pace exercitum per fines suos praeter Ruscinonem oppidum transmiserunt.

25 In Italiam interim nihil ultra quam Hiberum transisse
Hannibalem a Massiliensium legatis Romam perlatum
2 erat, cum, perinde ac si Alpes iam transisset, Boii sollicitatis Insubribus defecerunt, nec tam ob ueteres in populum
Romanum iras quam quod nuper circa Padum Placentiam Cremonamque colonias in agrum Gallicum deductas
3 aegre patiebantur. Itaque armis repente arreptis, in eum
ipsum agrum impetu facto tantum terroris ac tumultus
fecerunt ut non agrestis modo multitudo sed ipsi triumuiri
Romani, qui ad agrum uenerant adsignandum, diffisi
Placentiae moenibus Mutinam confugerint, C. Lutatius,
4 C. Seruilius, M. Annius.—Lutati nomen haud dubium
est; pro Annio Seruilioque M'. Acilium et C. Herennium
habent quidam annales, alii P. Cornelium Asinam et
5 C. Papirium Masonem. Id quoque dubium est legati
ad expostulandum missi ad Boios uiolati sint, [incertum]
an in triumuiros agrum metantes impetus sit factus.
6 Mutinae cum obsiderentur et gens ad oppugnandarum
urbium artes rudis, pigerrima eadem ad militaria opera,
segnis intactis adsideret muris, simulari coeptum de pace

7 agi; euocatique ab Gallorum principibus legati ad conloquium non contra ius modo gentium sed uiolata etiam
quae data in id tempus erat fide comprehenduntur, neganti-
bus Gallis, nisi obsides sibi redderentur, eos dimissuros.

8 Cum haec de legatis nuntiata essent et Mutina praesidium-
que in periculo esset, L. Manlius praetor ira accensus
effusum agmen ad Mutinam ducit.

9 Siluae tunc circa uiam erant, plerisque incultis. Ibi inexplorato profectus in insidias praecipitat multaque cum

10 caede suorum aegre in apertos campos emersit. Ibi castra
communita et, quia Gallis ad temptanda ea defuit spes,
refecti sunt militum animi, quamquam ad ⟨quingentos⟩

11 cecidisse satis constabat. Iter deinde de integro coeptum
nec, dum per patentia loca ducebatur agmen, apparuit

12 hostis; ubi rursus siluae intratae, tum postremos adorti
cum magna trepidatione ac pauore omnium septingentos

13 milites occiderunt, sex signa ademere. Finis et Gallis
territandi et pauendi fuit Romanis ut ex saltu inuio atque
impedito euasere. Inde apertis locis facile tutantes agmen
Romani Tannetum, uicum propinquum Pado, conten-

14 dere. Ibi se munimento ad tempus commeatibusque
fluminis et Brixianorum etiam Gallorum auxilio aduersus

26 crescentem in dies multitudinem hostium tutabantur. Qui
tumultus repens postquam est Romam perlatus et Punicum insuper Gallico bellum auctum patres acceperunt,

2 C. Atilium praetorem cum una legione Romana et
quinque milibus sociorum, dilectu nouo a consule cons-
criptis, auxilium ferre Manlio iubent; qui sine ullo
certamine—abscesserant enim metu hostes—Tannetum
peruenit.

3 Et P. Cornelius, in locum eius quae missa cum praetore
erat scripta legione noua, profectus ab urbe sexaginta
longis nauibus praeter oram Etruriae Ligurumque et inde

The Rhône at Tarascon. (*Photo: Vue aérienne, Alain Perceval, Paris.*)

4 Saluum montes peruenit Massiliam et ad proximum
ostium Rhodani—pluribus enim diuisus amnis in mare
decurrit—castra locat, uixdum satis credens Hannibalem
5 superasse Pyrenaeos montes. Quem ut de Rhodani
quoque transitu agitare animaduertit, incertus quonam
ei loco occurreret necdum satis refectis ab iactatione
maritima militibus trecentos interim delectos equites
ducibus Massiliensibus et auxiliaribus Gallis ad exploranda omnia uisendosque ex tuto hostes praemittit.
6 Hannibal ceteris metu aut pretio pacatis iam in Volcarum
peruenerat agrum, gentis ualidae. Colunt autem circa
utramque ripam Rhodani; sed diffisi citeriore agro
arceri Poenum posse, ut flumen pro munimento haberent,
omnibus ferme suis trans Rhodanum traiectis ulteriorem
7 ripam [amnis] armis obtinebant. Ceteros accolas fluminis Hannibal et eorum ipsorum quos sedes suae tenuerant
simul perlicit donis ad naues undique contrahendas
fabricandasque; simul et ipsi traici exercitum leuarique
quam primum regionem suam tanta hominum urgente
8 turba cupiebant. Itaque ingens coacta uis nauium est
lintriumque temere ad uicinalem usum paratarum;
nouasque alias primum Galli incohantes cauabant ex
9 singulis arboribus, deinde et ipsi milites simul copia
materiae, simul facilitate operis inducti, alueos informes,
nihil dummodo innare aquae et capere onera possent
curantes, raptim quibus se suaque transueherent faciebant.
27 Iamque omnibus satis comparatis ad traiciendum terrebant ex aduerso hostes omnem ripam equites uirique
2 obtinentes. Quos ut auerteret, Hannonem Bomilcaris
filium uigilia prima noctis cum parte copiarum, maxime
3 Hispanis, aduerso flumine ire iter unius diei iubet et, ubi
primum possit quam occultissime traiecto amni, circum-
ducere agmen ut cum opus facto sit adoriatur ab tergo

4 hostes. Ad id dati duces Galli edocent inde milia quinque et uiginti ferme supra paruae insulae circumfusum amnem latiore ubi diuidebatur eoque minus alto
5 alueo transitum ostendere. Ibi raptim caesa materia ratesque fabricatae in quibus equi uirique et alia onera traicerentur. Hispani sine ulla mole in utres uestimentis coniectis ipsi caetris superpositis incubantes flumen
6 tranauere. Et alius exercitus ratibus iunctis traiectus, castris prope flumen positis, nocturno itinere atque operis labore fessus quiete unius diei reficitur, intento duce ad
7 consilium opportune exsequendum. Postero die profecti, ex loco edito fumo significant transisse et haud procul abesse; quod ubi accepit Hannibal, ne tempori deesset dat signum ad traiciendum.
8 Iam paratas aptatasque habebat pedes lintres, eques fere propter equos nantes †. . .†. Nauium agmen ad excipiendum aduersi impetum fluminis parte superiore transmittens tranquillitatem infra traicientibus lintribus
9 praebebat; equorum pars magna nantes loris a puppibus trahebantur, praeter eos quos instratos frenatosque ut extemplo egresso in ripam equiti usui essent imposuerant in
28 naues. Galli occursant in ripa cum uariis ululatibus cantuque moris sui, quatientes scuta super capita uibrantes-
2 que dextris tela, quamquam et ex aduerso terrebat tanta uis nauium cum ingenti sono fluminis et clamore uario nautarum militumque, et qui nitebantur perrumpere impetum fluminis et qui ex altera ripa traicientes suos
3 hortabantur. Iam satis pauentes aduerso tumultu terribilior ab tergo adortus clamor, castris ab Hannone captis. Mox et ipse aderat ancepsque terror circumstabat, et e nauibus tanta ui armatorum in terram euadente et ab
4 tergo improuisa premente acie. Galli postquam utroque uim facere conati pellebantur, qua patere uisum maxime

iter perrumpunt trepidique in uicos passim suos diffugiunt.
Hannibal ceteris copiis per otium traiectis spernens iam
Gallicos tumultus castra locat.

5 Elephantorum traiciendorum uaria consilia fuisse credo;
certe uariata memoria actae rei. Quidam congregatis ad
ripam elephantis tradunt ferocissimum ex iis inritatum ab
rectore suo, cum refugientem in aquam nantem sequeretur, traxisse gregem, ut quemque timentem altitudinem
destitueret uadum, impetu ipso fluminis in alteram

6 ripam rapiente. Ceterum magis constat ratibus traiectos;
id ut tutius consilium ante rem foret, ita acta re ad fidem

7 pronius est. Ratem unam ducentos longam pedes,
quinquaginta latam a terra in amnem porrexerunt, quam,
ne secunda aqua deferretur, pluribus ualidis retinaculis
parte superiore ripae religatam pontis in modum humo
iniecta construerunt ut beluae audacter uelut per solum

8 ingrederentur. Altera ratis aeque lata, longa pedes
centum, ad traiciendum flumen apta, huic copulata est;
tres tum elephanti per stabilem ratem tamquam uiam
praegredientibus feminis acti ubi in minorem adplicatam

9 transgressi sunt, extemplo resolutis quibus leuiter adnexa
erat uinculis, ab actuariis aliquot nauibus ad alteram
ripam pertrahitur; ita primis expositis, alii deinde repetiti

10 ac traiecti sunt. Nihil sane trepidabant, donec continenti
uelut ponte agerentur; primus erat pauor cum soluta ab

11 ceteris rate in altum raperentur. Ibi urgentes inter se,
cedentibus extremis ab aqua, trepidationis aliquantum
edebant donec quietem ipse timor circumspectantibus

12 aquam fecisset. Excidere etiam saeuientes quidam in
flumen; sed pondere ipso stabiles, deiectis rectoribus,
quaerendis pedetemptim uadis in terram euasere.

29 Dum elephanti traiciuntur, interim Hannibal Numidas
equites quingentos ad castra Romana miserat speculatum

2 ubi et quantae copiae essent et quid pararent. Huic alae equitum missi, ut ante dictum est, ab ostio Rhodani trecenti Romanorum equites occurrunt. Proelium atro-

3 cius quam pro numero pugnantium editur; nam praeter multa uolnera caedes etiam prope par utrimque fuit, fugaque et pauor Numidarum Romanis iam admodum fessis uictoriam dedit. Victores ad centum sexaginta, nec omnes Romani sed pars Gallorum, uicti amplius

4 ducenti ceciderunt. Hoc principium simul omenque belli ut summae rerum prosperum euentum, ita haud sane incruentam ancipitisque certaminis uictoriam Romanis portendit.

5 Vt re ita gesta ad utrumque ducem sui redierunt, nec Scipioni stare sententia poterat nisi ut ex consiliis coeptis-

6 que hostis et ipse conatus caperet, et Hannibalem, incertum utrum coeptum in Italiam intenderet iter an cum eo qui primus se obtulisset Romanus exercitus manus consereret, auertit a praesenti certamine Boiorum legatorum regulique Magali aduentus, qui se duces itinerum, socios periculi fore adfirmantes, integro bello nusquam ante libatis uiribus Italiam adgrediendam

7 censent. Multitudo timebat quidem hostem nondum oblitterata memoria superioris belli; sed magis iter immensum Alpesque, rem fama utique inexpertis horrendam, metuebat.

30 Itaque Hannibal, postquam ipsi sententia stetit pergere ire atque Italiam petere, aduocata contione uarie militum

2 uersat animos castigando adhortandoque: Mirari se quinam pectora semper impauida repens terror inuaserit. per tot annos uincentes eos stipendia facere neque ante Hispania excessisse quam omnes gentesque et terrae quas duo diuersa maria amplectantur Carthaginiensium essent.

3 indignatos deinde quod quicumque Saguntum obsedissent

uelut ob noxam sibi dedi postularet populus Romanus,
Hiberum traiecisse ad delendum nomen Romanorum
4 liberandumque orbem terrarum. tum nemini uisum id
longum, cum ab occasu solis ad exortus intenderent iter:
5 nunc, postquam multo maiorem partem itineris emensam
cernant, Pyrenaeum saltum inter ferocissimas gentes
superatum, Rhodanum, tantum amnem, tot milibus
Gallorum prohibentibus, domita etiam ipsius fluminis ui
traiectum, in conspectu Alpes habeant quarum alterum
latus Italiae sit, in ipsis portis hostium fatigatos subsistere,
6 quid Alpes aliud esse credentes quam montium altitud-
7 ines? fingerent altiores Pyrenaei iugis: nullas profecto
terras caelum contingere nec inexsuperabiles humano
generi esse. Alpes quidem habitari, coli, gignere atque
alere animantes; peruias paucis esse, esse et exercitibus.
8 eos ipsos quos cernant legatos non pinnis sublime elatos
Alpes transgressos. ne maiores quidem eorum indigenas
sed aduenas Italiae cultores has ipsas Alpes ingentibus
saepe agminibus cum liberis ac coniugibus migrantium
9 modo tuto transmisisse. militi quidem armato nihil
secum praeter instrumenta belli portanti quid inuium aut
inexsuperabile esse? Saguntum ut caperetur, quid per
octo menses periculi, quid laboris exhaustum esse?
10 Romam, caput orbis terrarum, petentibus quicquam adeo
asperum atque arduum uideri quod inceptum moretur?
11 cepisse quondam Gallos ea quae adiri posse Poenus
desperet; proinde aut cederent animo atque uirtute genti
per eos dies totiens ab se uictae aut itineris finem sperent
campum interiacentem Tiberi ac moenibus Romanis.

31 His adhortationibus incitatos corpora curare atque ad iter
2 se parare iubet. Postero die profectus aduersa ripa
Rhodani mediterranea Galliae petit, non quia rectior ad
Alpes uia esset, sed quantum a mari recessisset minus

3 obuium fore Romanum credens, cum quo priusquam in
Italiam uentum foret non erat in animo manus conserere.

4 Quartis castris ad Insulam peruenit. Ibi †Sarar† Rhod-
anusque amnis diuersis ex Alpibus decurrentes, agri
aliquantum amplexi confluunt in unum in mediis campis;

5 Insulae nomen inditum. Incolunt prope Allobroges,
gens iam inde nulla Gallica gente opibus aut fama

6 inferior. Tum discors erat. Regni certamine ambigebant fratres; maior et qui prius imperitarat, Braneus
nomine, minore a fratre et coetu iuniorum qui iure minus,

7 ui plus poterant, pellebatur. Huius seditionis peropportuna disceptatio cum ad Hannibalem delata esset,
arbiter regni factus, quod ea senatus principumque

8 sententia fuerat, imperium maiori restituit. Ob id
meritum commeatu copiaque rerum omnium, maxime
uestis, est adiutus, quam infames frigoribus Alpes

9 praeparari cogebant. Sedatis certaminibus Allobrogum
cum iam Alpes peteret, non recta regione iter instituit sed
ad laeuam in Tricastinos flexit; inde per extremam
oram Vocontiorum agri tendit in Trigorios, haud
usquam impedita uia priusquam ad Druentiam flumen

10 peruenit. Is et ipse Alpinus amnis longe omnium Galliae
fluminum difficillimus transitu est; nam cum aquae uim

11 uehat ingentem, non tamen nauium patiens est, quia nullis
coercitus ripis, pluribus simul neque iisdem alueis fluens,
noua semper ⟨per⟩ uada nouosque gurgites—et ob eadem
pediti quoque incerta uia est—ad hoc saxa glareosa

12 uoluens, nihil stabile nec tutum ingredienti praebet; et
tum forte imbribus auctus ingentem transgredientibus
tumultum fecit, cum super cetera trepidatione ipsi sua
atque incertis clamoribus turbarentur.

32 P. Cornelius consul, triduo fere postquam Hannibal a ripa
Rhodani mouit, quadrato agmine ad castra hostium

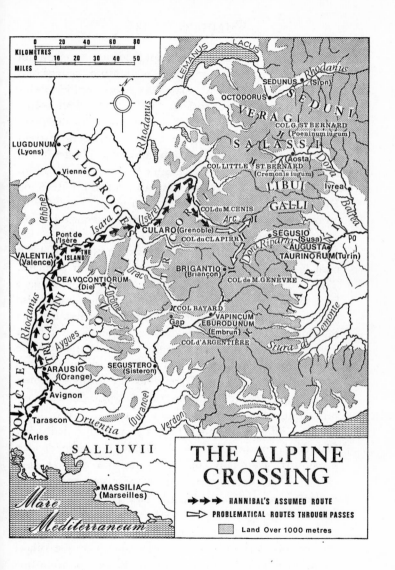

THE ALPINE
CROSSING

➤➤➤ HANNIBAL'S ASSUMED ROUTE

⟹ PROBLEMATICAL ROUTES THROUGH PASSES

▨ Land Over 1000 metres

73

2 uenerat, nullam dimicandi moram facturus; ceterum ubi deserta munimenta nec facile se tantum praegressos adsecuturum uidet, ad mare ac naues rediit, tutius faciliusque ita descendenti ab Alpibus Hannibali occur-

3 surus. Ne tamen nuda auxiliis Romanis Hispania esset, quam prouinciam sortitus erat, Cn. Scipionem fratrem cum maxima parte copiarum aduersus Hasdrubalem

4 misit, non ad tuendos tantummodo ueteres socios conciliandosque nouos sed etiam ad pellendum Hispania

5 Hasdrubalem. Ipse cum admodum exiguis copiis Genuam repetit, eo qui circa Padum erat exercitu Italiam defensurus.

6 Hannibal ab Druentia campestri maxime itinere ad Alpes cum bona pace incolentium ea loca Gallorum peruenit.

7 Tum, quamquam fama prius, qua incerta in maius uero ferri solent, praecepta res erat, tamen ex propinquo uisa montium altitudo niuesque caelo prope immixtae, tecta informia imposita rupibus, pecora iumentaque torrida frigore, homines intonsi et inculti, animalia inanimaque omnia rigentia gelu, cetera uisu quam dictu foediora

8 terrorem renouarunt. Erigentibus in primos agmen cliuos apparuerunt imminentes tumulos insidentes montani, qui, si ualles occultiores insedissent, coorti ad pugnam repente ingentem fugam stragemque dedissent.

9 Hannibal consistere signa iussit; Gallisque ad uisenda loca praemissis, postquam comperit transitum ea non esse, castra inter confragosa omnia praeruptaque quam

10 extentissima potest ualle locat. Tum per eosdem Gallos, haud sane multum lingua moribusque abhorrentes, cum se immiscuissent conloquiis montanorum, edoctus interdiu tantum obsideri saltum, nocte in sua quemque dilabi tecta, luce prima subiit tumulos, ut ex aperto atque

11 interdiu uim per angustias facturus. Die deinde simulando aliud quam quod parabatur consumpto, cum
12 eodem quo constiterant loco castra communissent, ubi primum degressos tumulis montanos laxatasque sensit custodias, pluribus ignibus quam pro numero manentium in speciem factis impedimentisque cum equite relictis et
13 maxima parte peditum, ipse cum expeditis, acerrimo quoque uiro, raptim angustias euadit iisque ipsis tumulis quos hostes tenuerant consedit.

33 Prima deinde luce castra mota et agmen reliquum incedere
2 coepit.   Iam montani signo dato ex castellis ad stationem solitam conueniebant, cum repente conspiciunt alios arce occupata sua super caput imminentes, alios uia transire
3 hostes. Vtraque simul obiecta res oculis animisque immobiles parumper eos defixit; deinde, ut trepidationem in angustiis suoque ipsum tumultu misceri agmen uidere,
4 equis maxime consternatis, quidquid adiecissent ipsi terroris satis ad perniciem fore rati, peruersis rupibus
5 iuxta inuia ac deuia adsueti decurrunt.   Tum uero simul ab hostibus, simul ab iniquitate locorum Poeni oppugnabantur plusque inter ipsos, sibi quoque tendente ut periculo primus euaderet, quam cum hostibus certaminis
6 erat.   Et equi maxime infestum agmen faciebant, qui et clamoribus dissonis quos nemora etiam repercussaeque ualles augebant territi trepidabant, et icti forte aut uolnerati adeo consternabantur, ut stragem ingentem simul hominum ac sarcinarum omnis generis facerent;
7 multosque turba, cum praecipites deruptaeque utrimque angustiae essent, in immensum altitudinis deiecit, quosdam et armatos; et ruinae maxime modo iumenta
8 cum oneribus deuoluebantur.   Quae quamquam foeda uisu erant, stetit parumper tamen Hannibal ac suos
9 continuit, ne tumultum ac trepidationem augeret; deinde,

postquam interrumpi agmen uidit periculumque esse,
ne exutum impedimentis exercitum nequiquam incolu-
mem traduxisset, decurrit ex superiore loco et, cum
impetu ipso fudisset hostem, suis quoque tumultum auxit.

10 Sed is tumultus momento temporis, postquam liberata
itinera fuga montanorum erant, sedatur, nec per otium

11 modo sed prope silentio mox omnes traducti. Castellum
inde, quod caput eius regionis erat, uiculosque circum-
iectos capit et capt⟨o c⟩ibo ac pecoribus per triduum
exercitum aluit; et, quia nec montanis primo perculsis
nec loco magno opere impediebantur, aliquantum eo
triduo uiae confecit.

34 Peruentum inde ad frequentem cultoribus alium, ut inter
montanos, populum. Ibi non bello aperto sed suis artibus,

2 fraude et insidiis, est prope circumuentus. Magno natu
principes castellorum oratores ad Poenum ueniunt, alienis
malis, utili exemplo, doctos memorantes amicitiam malle

3 quam uim experiri Poenorum; itaque oboedienter
imperata facturos; commeatum itinerisque duces et ad

4 fidem promissorum obsides acciperet. Hannibal nec
temere credendum nec † asperandos †⟨ratus⟩, ne repudiati
aperte hostes fierent, benigne cum respondisset, obsidibus
quos dabant acceptis et commeatu quem in uiam ipsi
detulerant usus, nequaquam ut inter pacatos composito

5 agmine duces eorum sequitur. Primum agmen elephanti
et equites erant; ipse post cum robore peditum circum-

6 spectans sollicitus omnia incedebat. Vbi in angustiorem
uiam et ex parte altera subiectam iugo insuper imminenti
uentum est, undique ex insidiis barbari a fronte ab tergo
coorti, comminus eminus petunt, saxa ingentia in agmen

7 deuoluunt. Maxima ab tergo uis hominum urgebat.
In eos uersa peditum acies haud dubium fecit quin, nisi
firmata extrema agminis fuissent, ingens in eo saltu

Grenoble and the Alps. (*Photo: Vue aérienne, Alain Perceval, Paris.*)

8 accipienda clades fuerit. Tunc quoque ad extremum
periculi ac prope perniciem uentum est; nam dum
cunctatur Hannibal demittere agmen in angustias, quia
non, ut ipse equitibus praesidio erat, ita peditibus quic-
9 quam ab tergo auxilii reliquerat, occursantes per obliqua
montani interrupto medio agmine uiam insedere, noxque
una Hannibali sine equitibus atque impedimentis acta est.

35 Postero die iam segnius intercursantibus barbaris iunctae
copiae saltusque haud sine clade, maiore tamen iument-
2 orum quam hominum pernicie, superatus. Inde montani
pauciores iam et latrocinii magis quam belli more concursabant modo in primum, modo in nouissimum agmen,
utcumque aut locus opportunitatem daret aut progressi
3 moratiue aliquam occasionem fecissent. Elephanti sicut
per artas [praecipites] uias magna mora agebantur, ita
tutum ab hostibus quacumque incederent, quia insuetis
adeundi propius metus erat, agmen praebebant.
4 Nono die in iugum Alpium peruentum est per inuia pleraque et errores, quos aut ducentium fraus aut, ubi fides iis
non esset, temere initae ualles a coniectantibus iter facie-
5 bant. Biduum in iugo statiua habita fessisque labore ac
pugnando quies data militibus; iumentaque aliquot, quae
prolapsa in rupibus erant, sequendo uestigia agminis in
6 castra peruenere. Fessis taedio tot malorum niuis etiam
casus, occidente iam sidere Vergiliarum, ingentem
7 terrorem adiecit. Per omnia niue oppleta cum signis
prima luce motis segniter agmen incederet pigritiaque et
desperatio in omnium uoltu emineret, praegressus signa
8 Hannibal in promunturio quodam, unde longe ac late
prospectus erat, consistere iussis militibus Italiam ostentat
subiectosque Alpinis montibus Circumpadanos campos,
9 moeniaque eos tum transcendere non Italiae modo sed
etiam urbis Romanae; cetera plana, procliuia fore;

uno aut summum altero proelio arcem et caput Italiae in
10 manu ac potestate habituros. Procedere inde agmen
coepit iam nihil ne hostibus quidem praeter parua furta
per occasionem temptantibus. Ceterum iter multo quam
in adscensu fuerat—ut pleraque Alpium ab Italia sicut
11 breuiora ita arrectiora sunt—difficilius fuit; omnis enim
12 ferme uia praeceps, angusta, lubrica erat, ut neque sustinere
se ab lapsu possent nec qui paulum titubassent haerere adflicti uestigio suo, aliique super alios et iumenta in homines
occiderent.

36 Ventum deinde ad multo angustiorem rupem atque ita
rectis saxis ut aegre expeditus miles temptabundus mani-
busque retinens uirgulta ac stirpes circa eminentes demit-
2 tere sese posset. Natura locus iam ante praeceps recenti
lapsu terrae in pedum mille admodum altitudinem
3 abruptus erat. Ibi cum uelut ad finem uiae equites
constitissent, miranti Hannibali quae res moraretur
4 agmen nuntiatur rupem inuiam esse. Digressus deinde
ipse ad locum uisendum. Haud dubia res uisa quin per
inuia circa nec trita antea, quamuis longo ambitu,
5 circumduceret agmen. Ea uero uia insuperabilis fuit;
nam cum super ueterem niuem intactam noua modicae
altitudinis esset, molli nec praealtae facile pedes ingred-
6 ientium insistebant; ut uero tot hominum iumentorumque incessu dilapsa est, per nudam infra glaciem fluentem-
7 que tabem liquescentis niuis ingrediebantur. Taetra ibi
luctatio erat, [ut a lubrica] glacie non recipiente uestigium et in prono citius pedes fallente, ut, seu manibus in
adsurgendo seu genu se adiuuissent, ipsis adminiculis
prolapsis iterum corruerent; nec stirpes circa radicesue ad
quas pede aut manu quisquam eniti posset erant; ita in
8 leui tantum glacie tabidaque niue uolutabantur. Iumenta
secabant interdum etiam infimam ingredientia niuem et

37 prolapsa iactandis grauius in conitendo ungulis penitus perfringebant, ut pleraque uelut pedica capta haererent in dura et alta concreta glacie. Tandem nequiquam iumentis atque hominibus fatigatis castra in iugo posita, aegerrime ad id ipsum loco purgato; tantum niuis fodiendum atque egerendum fuit.

2 Inde ad rupem muniendam per quam unam uia esse poterat milites ducti, cum caedendum esset saxum, arboribus circa immanibus deiectis detruncatisque struem ingentem lignorum faciunt eamque, cum et uis uenti apta faciendo igni coorta esset, succendunt ardentiaque saxa

3 infuso aceto putrefaciunt. Ita torridam incendio rupem ferro pandunt molliuntque anfractibus modicis cliuos ut non iumenta solum sed elephanti etiam deduci possent.

4 Quadriduum circa rupem consumptum, iumentis prope fame absumptis; nuda enim fere cacumina sunt et, si

5 quid est pabuli, obruunt niues. Inferiora uallis apricos quosdam colles habent riuosque prope siluas et iam

6 humano cultu digniora loca. Ibi iumenta in pabulum missa et quies muniendo fessis hominibus data. Triduo inde ad planum descensum et iam locis mollioribus et accolarum ingeniis.

38 Hoc maxime modo in Italiam peruentum est quinto mense a Carthagine Noua, ut quidam auctores sunt, quinto

2 decimo die Alpibus superatis. Quantae copiae transgresso in Italiam Hannibali fuerint nequaquam inter auctores constat. Qui plurimum, centum milia peditum, uiginti equitum fuisse scribunt; qui minimum, uiginti

3 milia peditum, sex equitum. L. Cincius Alimentus, qui captum se ab Hannibale scribit, maxime auctor moueret, nisi confunderet numerum Gallis Liguribusque additis;

4 cum his octoginta milia peditum, decem equitum adducta; —in Italia magis adfluxisse ueri simile est et ita quidam

5 auctores sunt;—ex ipso autem audisse Hannibale, postquam Rhodanum transierit triginta sex milia hominum
ingentemque numerum equorum et aliorum iumentorum
amisisse. Taurini Semigalli proxima gens erat in Italiam
6 degresso. Id cum inter omnes constet, eo magis miror
ambigi quanam Alpes transierit et uolgo credere Poenino
—atque inde nomen ei iugo Alpium inditum—trans-
7 gressum, Coelium per Cremonis iugum dicere transisse;
qui ambo saltus eum non in Taurinos sed per Salassos
8 montanos ad Libuos Gallos deduxerint. Nec ueri simile
est ea tum ad Galliam patuisse itinera; utique quae ad
Poeninum ferunt obsaepta gentibus semigermanis fuissent.
9 Neque hercule ⟨nomen⟩ montibus his, si quem forte id
mouet, ab transitu Poenorum ullo Sedunoueragri,
incolae iugi eius, norint inditum sed ab eo quem in
summo sacratum uertice Poeninum montani appellant.

39 Peropportune ad principia rerum Taurinis, proximae
genti, aduersus Insubres motum bellum erat. Sed armare
exercitum Hannibal ut parti alteri auxilio esset, in
reficiendo maxime sentientem contracta ante mala, non
2 poterat; otium enim ex labore, copia ex inopia, cultus ex
inluuie tabeque squalida et prope efferata corpora uarie
3 mouebat. Ea P. Cornelio consuli causa fuit, cum Pisas
nauibus uenisset, exercitu a Manlio Atilioque accepto
tirone et in nouis ignominiis trepido ad Padum festinandi
4 ut cum hoste nondum refecto manus consereret. Sed cum
Placentiam consul uenit, iam ex statiuis mouerat Hannibal
Taurinorumque unam urbem, caput gentis eius, quia
uolentes in amicitiam non ueniebant, ui expugnarat;
5 iunxissetque sibi non metu solum sed etiam uoluntate
Gallos accolas Padi, ni eos circumspectantes defectionis
6 tempus subito aduentu consul oppressisset. Et Hannibal
mouit ex Taurinis, incertos quae pars sequenda esset

7 Gallos praesentem secuturos esse ratus. Iam prope in
conspectu erant exercitus conuenerantque duces sicuti
inter se nondum satis noti, ita iam imbutus uterque
8 quadam admiratione alterius. Nam Hannibalis et apud
Romanos iam ante Sagunti excidium celeberrimum
nomen erat, et Scipionem Hannibal eo ipso quod
aduersus se dux potissimum lectus esset praestantem
9 uirum credebat; et auxerant inter se opinionem, Scipio,
quod relictus in Gallia obuius fuerat in Italiam transgresso
Hannibali, Hannibal et conatu tam audaci traiciendarum
10 Alpium et effectu. Occupauit tamen Scipio Padum
traicere et ad Ticinum amnem motis castris, priusquam
educeret in aciem, adhortandorum militum causa talem
orationem est exorsus.

40 "Si eum exercitum, milites, educerem in aciem quem in
2 Gallia mecum habui, supersedissem loqui apud uos; quid
enim adhortari referret aut eos equites qui equitatum
hostium ad Rhodanum flumen egregie uicissent, aut eas
legiones cum quibus fugientem hunc ipsum hostem
secutus confessionem cedentis ac detractantis certamen
3 pro uictoria habui? Nunc quia ille exercitus, Hispaniae
prouinciae scriptus, ibi cum fratre Cn. Scipione meis
auspiciis rem gerit ubi eum gerere senatus populusque
4 Romanus uoluit, ego, ut consulem ducem aduersus
Hannibalem ac Poenos haberetis, ipse me huic uoluntario
certamini obtuli, nouo imperatori apud nouos milites
5 pauca uerba facienda sunt. Ne genus belli neue hostem
ignoretis, cum iis est uobis, milites, pugnandum quos terra
marique priore bello uicistis, a quibus stipendium per
uiginti annos exegistis, a quibus capta belli praemia
6 Siciliam ac Sardiniam habetis. Erit igitur in hoc certamine is uobis illisque animus qui uictoribus et uictis esse
solet. Nec nunc illi quia audent sed quia necesse est

pugnaturi sunt, qui plures paene perierint quam super-
7 sint; nisi creditis, qui exercitu incolumi pugnam detractauere, eos duabus partibus peditum equitumque in
8 transitu Alpium amissis plus spei nactos esse. At enim
pauci quidem sunt sed uigentes animis corporibusque,
quorum robora ac uires uix sustinere uis ulla possit.
9 Effigies immo, umbrae hominum, fame, frigore, inluuie,
squalore enecti, contusi ac debilitati inter saxa rupesque;
ad hoc praeusti artus, niue rigentes nerui, membra torrida
gelu, quassata fractaque arma, claudi ac debiles equi.
10 Cum hoc equite, cum hoc pedite pugnaturi estis; reliquias
extremas hostis, non hostem habetis, ac nihil magis
uereor quam ne cui, uos cum pugnaueritis, Alpes uicisse
11 Hannibalem uideantur. Sed ita forsitan decuit, cum
foederum ruptore duce ac populo deos ipsos sine ulla
humana ope committere ac profligare bellum, nos, qui
secundum deos uiolati sumus, commissum ac profligatum
conficere.

41 Non uereor ne quis me haec uestri adhortandi causa
magnifice loqui existimet, ipsum aliter animo adfectum
2 esse. Licuit in Hispaniam, prouinciam meam, quo iam
profectus eram, cum exercitu ire meo, ubi et fratrem
consilii participem ac periculi socium haberem et
Hasdrubalem potius quam Hannibalem hostem et
3 minorem haud dubie molem belli; tamen, cum prae-
terueherer nauibus Galliae oram, ad famam huius hostis
in terram egressus, praemisso equitatu ad Rhodanum
4 moui castra. Equestri proelio, qua parte copiarum
conserendi manum fortuna data est, hostem fudi; peditum
agmen, quod in modum fugientium raptim agebatur,
quia adsequi terra non poteram, [neque] regressus ad
naues [erat] quanta maxime potui celeritate tanto maris
terrarumque circuitu, in radicibus prope Alpium huic

5 timendo hosti obuius fui. Vtrum, cum declinarem
certamen, improuidus incidisse uideor an occurrere in
uestigiis eius, lacessere ac trahere ad decernendum?

6 Experiri iuuat utrum alios repente Carthaginienses per
uiginti annos terra ediderit an iidem sint qui ad Aegates
pugnauerunt insulas et quos ab Eryce duodeuicenis

7 denariis aestimatos emisistis, et utrum Hannibal hic sit
aemulus itinerum Herculis, ut ipse fert, an uectigalis
stipendiariusque et seruus populi Romani a patre relictus.

8 Quem nisi Saguntinum scelus agitaret, respiceret profecto,
si non patriam uictam, domum certe patremque et foedera

9 Hamilcaris scripta manu, qui iussus ab consule nostro
praesidium deduxit ab Eryce, qui graues impositas uictis
Carthaginiensibus leges fremens maerensque accepit, qui
decedens Sicilia stipendium populo Romano dare pactus
est.

10 Itaque uos ego, milites, non eo solum animo quo aduersus
alios hostes soletis, pugnare uelim, sed cum indignatione
quadam atque ira, uelut si seruos uideatis uestros arma re-

11 pente contra uos ferentes. Licuit ad Erycem clausos
ultimo supplicio humanorum, fame interficere; licuit
uictricem classem in Africam traicere atque intra paucos

12 dies sine ullo certamine Carthaginem delere; ueniam
dedimus precantibus, emisimus ex obsidione, pacem cum
uictis fecimus, tutelae deinde nostrae duximus, cum Africo

13 bello urgerentur. Pro his impertitis furiosum iuuenem
sequentes oppugnatum patriam nostram ueniunt. Atque
utinam pro decore tantum hoc uobis et non pro salute

14 esset certamen! Non de possessione Siciliae ac Sardiniae,
de quibus quondam agebatur, sed pro Italia uobis est

15 pugnandum. Nec est alius ab tergo exercitus qui, nisi
nos uincimus, hosti obsistat, nec Alpes aliae sunt, quas
dum superant, comparari noua possint praesidia; hic est

83

obstandum, milites, uelut si ante Romana moenia pug-
16 nemus. Vnusquisque se non corpus suum sed coniugem
ac liberos paruos armis protegere putet; nec domesticas
solum agitet curas sed identidem hoc animo reputet
nostras nunc intueri manus senatum populumque Roman-
17 um: qualis nostra uis uirtusque fuerit, talem deinde
fortunam illius urbis ac Romani imperii fore."

42 Haec apud Romanos consul. Hannibal rebus prius quam
uerbis adhortandos milites ratus, circumdato ad spectaculum exercitu captiuos montanos uinctos in medio statuit
armisque Gallicis ante pedes eorum proiectis interrogare
interpretem iussit, ecquis, si uinculis leuaretur armaque et
2 equum uictor acciperet, decertare ferro uellet. Cum ad
unum omnes ferrum pugnamque poscerent et deiecta in
id sors esset, se quisque eum optabat quem fortuna in id
3 certamen legeret, et, ⟨ut⟩ cuiusque sors exciderat, alacer,
inter gratulantes gaudio exsultans, cum sui moris tripudiis
4 arma raptim capiebat. Vbi uero dimicarent, is habitus
animorum non inter eiusdem modo condicionis homines
erat sed etiam inter spectantes uolgo, ut non uincentium
43 magis quam bene morientium fortuna laudaretur. Cum
sic aliquot spectatis paribus adfectos dimisisset, contione
inde aduocata ita apud eos locutus fertur.
2 "Si, quem animum in alienae sortis exemplo paulo ante
habuistis, eundem mox in aestimanda fortuna uestra
habueritis, uicimus, milites; neque enim spectaculum
modo illud sed quaedam ueluti imago uestrae condicionis
3 erat. Ac nescio an maiora uincula maioresque necessi-
tates uobis quam captiuis uestris fortuna circumdederit.
4 Dextra laeuaque duo maria claudunt nullam ne ad
effugium quidem nauem habentes; circa Padus amnis,
maior [Padus] ac uiolentior Rhodano, ab tergo Alpes
5 urgent, uix integris uobis ac uigentibus transitae. Hic

uincendum aut moriendum, milites, est, ubi primum
hosti occurristis. Et eadem fortuna, quae necessitatem
pugnandi imposuit, praemia uobis ea uictoribus proponit
quibus ampliora homines ne ab dis quidem immortalibus
6 optare solent. Si Siciliam tantum ac Sardiniam parenti-
bus nostris ereptas nostra uirtute reciperaturi essemus,
satis tamen ampla pretia essent: quidquid Romani tot
triumphis partum congestumque possident, id omne
7 uestrum cum ipsis dominis futurum est; in hanc tam
opimam mercedem, agite dum, dis bene iuuantibus
8 arma capite. Satis adhuc in uastis Lusitaniae Celtiberiaeque montibus pecora consectando nullum emolumentum
9 tot laborum periculorumque uestrorum uidistis; tempus
est iam opulenta uos ac ditia stipendia facere et magna
operae pretia mereri, tantum itineris per tot montes
10 fluminaque et tot armatas gentes emensos. Hic uobis
terminum laborum fortuna dedit; hic dignam mercedem
11 emeritis stipendiis dabit. Nec, quam magni nominis
bellum est, tam difficilem existimaritis uictoriam fore;
saepe et contemptus hostis cruentum certamen edidit et
incliti populi regesque perleui momento uicti sunt.
12 Nam dempto hoc uno fulgore nominis Romani, quid est
13 cur illi uobis comparandi sint? Vt uiginti annorum
militiam uestram cum illa uirtute, cum illa fortuna
taceam, ab Herculis columnis, ab Oceano terminisque
ultimis terrarum per tot ferocissimos Hispaniae et Galliae
14 populos uincentes huc peruenistis; pugnabitis cum
exercitu tirone, hac ipsa aestate caeso, uicto, circumsesso
a Gallis, ignoto adhuc duci suo ignorantique ducem.
15 An me in praetorio patris, clarissimi imperatoris, prope
natum, certe eductum, domitorem Hispaniae Galliaeque,
uictorem eundem non Alpinarum modo gentium sed
ipsarum, quod multo maius est, Alpium, cum semenstri

16 hoc conferam duce, desertore exercitus sui? cui si quis
demptis signis Poenos Romanosque hodie ostendat,
ignoraturum certum habeo utrius exercitus sit consul.

17 Non ego illud parui aestimo, milites, quod nemo est uestrum
cuius non ante oculos ipse saepe militare aliquod ediderim
facinus, cui non idem ego uirtutis spectator ac testis
notata temporibus locisque referre sua possim decora.

18 Cum laudatis a me miliens donatisque, alumnus prius
omnium uestrum quam imperator, procedam in aciem
aduersus ignotos inter se ignorantesque.

44 Quocumque circumtuli oculos, plena omnia uideo animorum ac roboris, ueteranum peditem, generosissimarum

2 gentium equites frenatos infrenatosque, uos socios fidelis-
simos fortissimosque, uos, Carthaginienses, cum ob

3 patriam, tum ob iram iustissimam pugnaturos. Inferi-
mus bellum infestisque signis descendimus in Italiam,
tanto audacius fortiusque pugnaturi quam hostis, quanto
maior spes, maior est animus inferentis uim quam arcentis.

4 Accendit praeterea et stimulat animos dolor, iniuria,
indignitas. Ad supplicium depoposcerunt me ducem
primum, deinde uos omnes qui Saguntum oppugnassetis;

5 deditos ultimis cruciatibus adfecturi fuerunt. Crudelissima ac superbissima gens sua omnia suique arbitrii facit;
cum quibus bellum, cum quibus pacem habeamus, se
modum imponere aequum censet. Circumscribit in-
cluditque nos terminis montium fluminumque, quos
non excedamus, neque eos, quos statuit, terminos

6 obseruat: 'Ne transieris Hiberum; ne quid rei tibi sit
cum Saguntinis.' Ad Hiberum est Saguntum? 'Nus-

7 quam te uestigio moueris.' Parum est quod ueterrimas
prouincias meas, Siciliam ac Sardiniam, ⟨ademisti?⟩
Adimis etiam Hispanias et, si inde cessero, in Africam

transcendes. ⟨Transcendes⟩ autem? Transcendisse di-
co. Duos consules huius anni, unum in Africam, alterum
in Hispaniam miserunt. Nihil usquam nobis relictum
8 est nisi quod armis uindicarimus. Illis timidis et ignauis
esse licet, qui respectum habent, quos sua terra, suus ager
per tuta ac pacata itinera fugientes accipient: uobis
necesse est fortibus uiris esse et, omnibus inter uictoriam
mortemue certa desperatione abruptis, aut uincere aut,
si fortuna dubitabit, in proelio potius quam in fuga
9 mortem oppetere. Si hoc [bene fixum] omnibus destinatum in animo est, iterum dicam, uicistis; nullum contemptu m⟨ortis incitamentum⟩ ad uincendum homini ab
dis immortalibus acrius datum est."

45 His adhortationibus cum utrimque ad certamen accensi
militum animi essent, Romani ponte Ticinum iungunt
tutandique pontis causa castellum insuper imponunt:
2 Poenus hostibus opere occupatis Maharbalem cum ala
Numidarum, equitibus quingentis, ad depopulandos
3 sociorum populi Romani agros mittit; Gallis parci quam
maxime iubet principumque animos ad defectionem
sollicitari. Ponte perfecto traductus Romanus exercitus
in agrum Insubrium quinque milia passuum ab Victum-
4 ulis consedit. Ibi Hannibal castra habebat; reuocatoque
propere Maharbale atque equitibus cum instare certamen
cerneret, nihil unquam satis dictum praemonitumque ad
cohortandos milites ratus, uocatis ad contionem certa
5 praemia pronuntiat in quorum spem pugnarent: agrum
sese daturum esse in Italia, Africa, Hispania, ubi quisque
uelit, immunem ipsi qui accepisset liberisque; qui
pecuniam quam agrum maluisset, ei se argento satis-
6 facturum; qui sociorum ciues Carthaginienses fieri uellent,
potestatem facturum; qui domos redire mallent, daturum
se operam ne cuius suorum popularium mutatam secum

87

7 fortunam esse uellent. Seruis quoque dominos prosecutis
libertatem proponit binaque pro his mancipia dominis se
8 redditurum. Eaque ut rata scirent fore, agnum laeua
manu, dextra silicem retinens, si falleret, Iouem ceterosque
precatur deos ita se mactarent quemadmodum ipse agnum
mactasset, et secundum precationem caput pecudis saxo
9 elisit. Tum uero omnes, uelut dis auctoribus in spem
suam quisque acceptis, id morae quod nondum pugnarent
ad potienda sperata rati, proelium uno animo et uoce una
poscunt.

46 Apud Romanos haudquaquam tanta alacritas erat, super
2 cetera recentibus etiam territos prodigiis; nam et lupus in-
trauerat castra laniatisque obuiis ipse intactus euaserat,
⟨et⟩ examen apum in arbore praetorio imminente consed-
3 erat. Quibus procuratis Scipio cum equitatu iaculatori-
busque expeditis profectus ad castra hostium exque
propinquo copias, quantae et cuius generis essent,
speculandas obuius fit Hannibali et ipsi cum equitibus
4 ad exploranda circa loca progresso. Neutri alteros primo
cernebant; densior deinde incessu tot hominum ⟨et⟩ equorum oriens puluis signum propinquantium hostium fuit.
Consistit utrumque agmen et ad proelium sese expedie-
5 bant. Scipio iaculatores et Gallos equites in fronte locat,
Romanos sociorumque quod roboris fuit in subsidiis;
Hannibal frenatos equites in medium accipit, cornua
6 Numidis firmat. Vixdum clamore sublato iaculatores
fugerunt inter subsidia ac secundam aciem. Inde equitum certamen erat aliquamdiu anceps; dein quia turba-
bant equos pedites intermixti, multis labentibus ex equis
aut desilientibus ubi suos premi circumuentos uidissent,
7 iam magna ex parte ad pedes pugna abierat, donec
Numidae qui in cornibus erant circumuecti paulum ab
tergo se ostenderunt. Is pauor perculit Romanos,

auxitque pauorem consulis uolnus periculumque inter-
8 cursu tum primum pubescentis filii propulsatum. Hic
erit iuuenis penes quem perfecti huiusce belli laus est,
Africanus ob egregiam uictoriam de Hannibale Poenisque
9 appellatus. Fuga tamen effusa iaculatorum maxime fuit
quos primos Numidae inuaserunt; alius confertus
equitatus consulem in medium acceptum, non armis
modo sed etiam corporibus suis protegens, in castra
10 nusquam trepide neque effuse cedendo reduxit. Seruati
consulis decus Coelius ad seruum natione Ligurem
delegat; malim equidem de filio uerum esse, quod et
plures tradidere auctores et fama obtinuit.

47 Hoc primum cum Hannibale proelium fuit; quo facile
apparuit et equitatu meliorem Poenum esse et ob id
campos patentes, quales sunt inter Padum Alpesque, bello
2 gerendo Romanis aptos non esse. Itaque proxima nocte
iussis militibus uasa silentio colligere castra ab Ticino
mota festinatumque ad Padum est ut ratibus, quibus
iunxerat flumen, nondum resolutis sine tumultu atque
3 insectatione hostis copias traiceret. Prius Placentiam
peruenere quam satis sciret Hannibal ab Ticino profectos;
tamen ad sescentos moratorum in citeriore ripa Padi
segniter ratem soluentes cepit. Transire pontem non
potuit, ut extrema resoluta erant tota rate in secundam
4 aquam labente. Coelius auctor est Magonem cum
equitatu et Hispanis peditibus flumen extemplo tranasse,
ipsum Hannibalem per superiora Padi uada exercitum
traduxisse, elephantis in ordinem ad sustinendum
5 impetum fluminis oppositis. Ea peritis amnis eius uix
fidem fecerint; nam neque equites armis equisque saluis
tantam uim fluminis superasse ueri simile est—ut iam
Hispanos omnes inflati trauexerint utres—, et multorum
dierum circuitu Padi uada petenda fuerunt qua exercitus

6 grauis impedimentis traduci posset. Potiores apud me
auctores sunt qui biduo uix locum rate iungendo flumini
inuentum tradunt; ea cum Magone equites ⟨et⟩ His-
7 panorum expeditos praemissos. Dum Hannibal, circa
flumen legationibus Gallorum audiendis moratus, traicit
grauius peditum agmen, interim Mago equitesque ab
transitu fluminis diei unius itinere Placentiam ad hostes
8 contendunt. Hannibal paucis post diebus sex milia a
Placentia castra communiuit et postero die in conspectu
hostium acie directa potestatem pugnae fecit.

48 Insequenti nocte caedes in castris Romanis, tumultu
tamen quam re maior, ab auxiliaribus Gallis facta est.
2 Ad duo milia peditum et ducenti equites uigilibus ad
portas trucidatis ad Hannibalem transfugiunt; quos
Poenus benigne adlocutus et spe ingentium donorum
accensos in ciuitates quemque suas ad sollicitandos
3 popularium animos dimisit. Scipio caedem eam signum
defectionis omnium Gallorum esse ratus contactosque
eo scelere uelut iniecta rabie ad arma ituros, quamquam
4 grauis adhuc uolnere erat, tamen quarta uigilia noctis
insequentis tacito agmine profectus, ad Trebiam fluuium
iam in loca altiora collesque impeditiores equiti castra
5 mouet. Minus quam ad Ticinum fefellit; missisque
Hannibal primum Numidis, deinde omni equitatu
turbasset utique nouissimum agmen, ni auiditate praedae
6 in uacua Romana castra Numidae deuertissent. Ibi dum
perscrutantes loca omnia castrorum nullo satis digno
morae pretio tempus terunt, emissus hostis est de manibus;
et cum iam transgressos Trebiam Romanos metantesque
castra conspexissent, paucos moratorum occiderunt citra
7 flumen interceptos. Scipio, nec uexationem uolneris in
uia iactati ultra patiens et collegam—iam enim et
reuocatum ex Sicilia audierat—ratus exspectandum,

locum qui prope flumen tutissimus statiuis est uisus delec-
8 tum communiit. Nec procul inde Hannibal cum con-
sedisset, quantum uictoria equestri elatus, tantum anxius
inopia quae per hostium agros euntem, nusquam prae-
9 paratis commeatibus, maior in dies excipiebat, ad Clastidium uicum, quo magnum frumenti numerum conges-
serant Romani, mittit. Ibi cum uim pararent, spes facta
proditionis; nec sane magno pretio, nummis aureis
quadringentis, Dasio Brundisino praefecto praesidii
corrupto traditur Hannibali Clastidium. Id horreum
10 fuit Poenis sedentibus ad Trebiam. In captiuos ex
tradito praesidio, ut fama clementiae in principio rerum
colligeretur, nihil saeuitum est.

49 Cum ad Trebiam terrestre constitisset bellum, interim
circa Siciliam insulasque Italiae imminentes et a Sempronio consule et ante aduentum eius terra marique res
2 gestae. Viginti quinqueremes cum mille armatis ad
depopulandam oram Italiae a Carthaginiensibus missae;
nouem Liparas, octo ad insulam Volcani tenuerunt, tres
3 in fretum auertit aestus. Ad eas conspectas a Messana
duodecim naues ab Hierone rege Syracusanorum missae,
qui tum forte Messanae erat consulem Romanum
opperiens, nullo repugnante captas naues Messanam in
4 portum deduxerunt. Cognitum ex captiuis praeter
uiginti naues, cuius ipsi classis essent, in Italiam missas,
quinque et triginta alias quinqueremes Siciliam petere
5 ad sollicitandos ueteres socios; Lilybaei occupandi praeci-
puam curam esse; credere eadem tempestate qua ipsi
disiecti forent eam quoque classem ad Aegates insulas
6 deiectam. Haec, sicut audita erant, rex M. Aemilio
praetori, cuius Sicilia prouincia erat, perscribit monetque
7 [et] Lilybaeum firmo teneret praesidio. Extemplo et
circa a praetore ad ciuitates missi legati tribunique suos

ad curam custodiae intendere, et ante omnia Lilybaeum
8 tueri apparatu belli, edicto proposito ut socii nauales
decem dierum cocta cibaria ad naues deferrent et ubi
signum datum esset ne quis moram conscendendi faceret,

perque omnem oram qui ex speculis prospicerent aduen-
tantem hostium classem missis.
9 Itaque quamquam de industria morati cursum nauium
erant Carthaginienses ut ante lucem accederent Lilybaeum, praesensum tamen est quia et luna pernox erat et
10 sublatis armamentis ueniebant.   Extemplo datum signum

ex speculis et in oppido ad arma conclamatum est et in
naues conscensum; pars militum in muris portarumque
11 in stationibus, pars in nauibus erant. Et Carthaginienses,
quia rem fore haud cum imparatis cernebant, usque ad
lucem portu se abstinuerunt, demendis armamentis eo
12 tempore aptandaque ad pugnam classe absumpto. Vbi
inluxit, recepere classem in altum ut spatium pugnae esset
exitumque liberum e portu naues hostium haberent.
13 Nec Romani detractauere pugnam et memoria circa ea
ipsa loca gestarum rerum freti et militum multitudine ac
50 uirtute. Vbi in altum euecti sunt, Romanus conserere
2 pugnam et ex propinquo uires conferre uelle; contra
eludere Poenus et arte non ui rem gerere nauiumque
3 quam uirorum aut armorum malle certamen facere. Nam
ut sociis naualibus adfatim instructam classem, ita inopem
milite habebant et, sicubi conserta nauis esset, haudqua-
4 quam par numerus armatorum ex ea pugnabat. Quod
ubi animaduersum est, et Romanis multitudo sua auxit
5 animum et paucitas illis minuit. Extemplo septem naues
Punicae circumuentae: fugam ceterae ceperunt. Mille
et septingenti fuere in nauibus captis milites nautaeque, in
6 his tres nobiles Carthaginiensium. Classis Romana
incolumis, una tantum perforata naui sed ea quoque ipsa
reduce, in portum rediit.
7 Secundum hanc pugnam, nondum gnaris eius qui Messanae
erant Ti. Sempronius consul Messanam uenit. Ei fretum
8 intranti rex Hiero classem ornatam obuiam duxit, trans-
gressusque ex regia in praetoriam nauem, gratulatus
sospitem cum exercitu et nauibus aduenisse precatusque
9 prosperum ac felicem in Siciliam transitum, statum deinde
insulae et Carthaginiensium conata exposuit pollicitusque
est, quo animo priore bello populum Romanum iuuenis

10 adiuuisset, eo senem adiuturum; frumentum uestimenta-
que sese legionibus consulis sociisque naualibus gratis
praebiturum; grande periculum Lilybaeo maritimisque
ciuitatibus esse et quibusdam uolentibus nouas res fore.

11 Ob haec consuli nihil cunctandum uisum quin Lilybaeum
classe peteret. Et rex regiaque classis una profecti. Naui-
gantes inde pugnatum ad Lilybaeum fusasque et captas

51 hostium naues accepere. A Lilybaeo consul, Hierone cum
classe regia dimisso relictoque praetore ad tuendam
Siciliae oram, ipse in insulam Melitam, quae a Cartha-

2 giniensibus tenebatur, traiecit. Aduenienti Hamilcar
Gisgonis filius, praefectus praesidii, cum paulo minus
duobus milibus militum oppidumque cum insula traditur.
Inde post paucos dies reditum Lilybaeum captiuique et a
consule et a praetore, praeter insignes nobilitate uiros,

3 sub corona uenierunt. Postquam ab ea parte satis
tutam Siciliam censebat consul, ad insulas Volcani,
quia fama erat stare ibi Punicam classem, traiecit; nec

4 quisquam hostium circa eas insulas inuentus; iam forte
transmiserant ad uastandam Italiae oram depopulatoque

5 Vibonensi agro urbem etiam terrebant. Repetenti
Siciliam consuli escensio hostium in agrum Vibonensem
facta nuntiatur, litteraeque ab senatu de transitu in
Italiam Hannibalis et ut primo quoque tempore collegae

6 ferret auxilium missae traduntur. Multis simul anxius
curis exercitum extemplo in naues impositum Ariminum
mari supero misit, Sex. Pomponio legato cum uiginti
quinque longis nauibus Vibonensem agrum maritimam-

7 que oram Italiae tuendam attribuit, M. Aemilio praetori
quinquaginta nauium classem expleuit. Ipse compositis
Siciliae rebus decem nauibus oram Italiae legens Ariminum peruenit. Inde cum exercitu suo profectus ad
Trebiam flumen collegae coniungitur.

52 Iam ambo consules et quidquid Romanarum uirium erat Hannibali oppositum aut illis copiis defendi posse Romanum imperium aut spem nullam aliam esse satis declarabat.

2 Tamen consul alter, equestri proelio uno et uolnere suo comminutus, trahi rem malebat; recentis animi alter

3 eoque ferocior nullam dilationem patiebatur. Quod inter Trebiam Padumque agri est Galli tum incolebant, in duorum praepotentium populorum certamine per ambiguum fauorem haud dubie gratiam uictoris spectan-

4 tes. Id Romani, modo ne quid mouerent, aequo satis, Poenus periniquo animo ferebat, ab Gallis accitum se

5 uenisse ad liberandos eos dictitans. Ob eam iram, simul ut praeda militem aleret, duo milia peditum et mille equites, Numidas plerosque, mixtos quosdam et Gallos, populari omnem deinceps agrum usque ad Padi ripas

6 iussit. Egentes ope Galli, cum ad id dubios seruassent animos, coacti ab auctoribus iniuriae ad uindices futuros declinant legatisque ad consulem missis auxilium Romanorum terrae ob nimiam cultorum fidem in Romanos

7 laboranti orant. Cornelio nec causa nec tempus agendae rei placebat suspectaque ei gens erat cum ob infida multa facinora, tum, ut alia uetustate obsoleuissent, ob recen-

8 tem Boiorum perfidiam: Sempronius contra continendis in fide sociis maximum uinculum esse primos qui eguis-

9 sent ope defensos censebat. Tum collega cunctante equitatum suum, mille peditum, iaculatoribus ferme,

10 admixtis ad defendendum Gallicum agrum trans Trebiam mittit. Sparsos et incompositos, ad hoc graues praeda plerosque cum inopinato inuasissent, ingentem terrorem caedemque ac fugam usque ad castra stationesque hostium fecere; unde multitudine effusa pulsi, rursus subsidio

11 suorum proelium restituere. Varia inde pugna ⟨inter recedentes in⟩sequentesque, cumque ad extremum

aequassent certamen, maior tamen hostium ⟨cum caedes esset, penes⟩ Romanos fama uictoriae fuit.

53 Ceterum nemini omnium maior ea iustiorque quam ipsi consuli uideri; gaudio efferri, qua parte copiarum alter

2 consul uictus foret, ea se uicisse: restitutos ac refectos militibus animos nec quemquam esse praeter collegam qui dilatam dimicationem uellet; eum, animo magis quam corpore aegrum, memoria uolneris aciem ac tela horrere.

3 sed non esse cum aegro senescendum. quid enim ultra differri aut teri tempus? quem tertium consulem, quem

4 alium exercitum exspectari? castra Carthaginiensium in Italia ac prope in conspectu urbis esse. non Siciliam ac Sardiniam, uictis ademptas, nec cis Hiberum Hispaniam peti sed solo patrio terraque in qua geniti forent pelli

5 Romanos. "Quantum ingemiscant" inquit "patres nostri, circa moenia Carthaginis bellare soliti, si uideant nos, progeniem suam, duos consules consularesque exercitus, in media Italia pauentes intra castra, Poenum quod inter Alpes Appenninumque agri sit suae dicionis

6 fecisse?" Haec adsidens aegro collegae, haec in praetorio prope contionabundus agere. Stimulabat et tempus propinquum comitiorum, ne in nouos consules bellum differretur, et occasio in se unum uertendae gloriae, dum

7 aeger collega erat. Itaque nequiquam dissentiente Cornelio parari ad propinquum certamen milites iubet.

Hannibal cum quid optimum foret hosti cerneret, uix ullam spem habebat temere atque improuide quicquam

8 consules acturos; cum alterius ingenium, fama prius, deinde re cognitum, percitum ac ferox sciret esse ferociusque factum prospero cum praedatoribus suis certamine crederet, adesse gerendae rei fortunam haud diffidebat.

9 Cuius ne quod praetermitteret tempus, sollicitus intentusque erat, dum tiro hostium miles esset, dum meliorem ex

ducibus inutilem uolnus faceret, dum Gallorum animi
10 uigerent, quorum ingentem multitudinem sciebat segnius
11 secuturam quanto longius ab domo traherentur. Cum ob
haec taliaque speraret propinquum certamen et facere,
si cessaretur, cuperet speculatoresque Galli, ad ea
exploranda quae uellet tutiores quia in utrisque castris
militabant, paratos pugnae esse Romanos rettulissent,
54 locum insidiis circumspectare Poenus coepit. Erat in
medio riuus praealtis utrimque clausus ripis et circa
obsitus palustribus herbis et quibus inculta ferme uestiun-
tur, uirgultis uepribusque. Quem ubi equites quoque
tegendo satis latebrosum locum circumuectus ipse oculis
2 perlustrauit, "Hic erit locus" Magoni fratri ait "quem
teneas. Delige centenos uiros ex omni pedite atque
equite cum quibus ad me uigilia prima uenias; nunc
3 corpora curare tempus est." Ita praetorium missum.
Mox cum delectis Mago aderat. "Robora uirorum
cerno" inquit Hannibal; "sed uti numero etiam, non
animis modo ualeatis, singulis uobis nouenos ex turmis
manipulisque uestri similes eligite. Mago locum mon-
strabit quem insideatis; hostem caecum ad has belli artes
4 habetis." Ita ⟨cum⟩ mille equitibus Magone, mille
peditibus dimisso Hannibal prima luce Numidas equites
transgressos Trebiam flumen obequitare iubet hostium
portis iaculandoque in stationes elicere ad pugnam hostem,
iniecto deinde certamine cedendo sensim citra flumen
5 pertrahere. Haec mandata Numidis: ceteris ducibus
peditum equitumque praeceptum ut prandere omnes
iuberent, armatos deinde instratisque equis signum
exspectare.
6 Sempronius ad tumultum Numidarum primum omnem
equitatum, ferox ea parte uirium, deinde sex milia
peditum, postremo omnes copias ad destinatum iam ante

7 consilio auidus certaminis eduxit. Erat forte brumae
tempus et niualis dies in locis Alpibus Appenninoque
interiectis, propinquitate etiam fluminum ac paludum
8 praegelidis. Ad hoc raptim eductis hominibus atque
equis, non capto ante cibo, non ope ulla ad arcendum
frigus adhibita, nihil caloris inerat, et quidquid aurae
fluminis appropinquabant, adflabat acrior frigoris uis.
9 Vt uero refugientes Numidas insequentes aquam ingressi
sunt—et erat pectoribus tenus aucta nocturno imbri—
tum utique egressis rigere omnibus corpora ut uix armorum tenendorum potentia esset, et simul lassitudine et
procedente iam die fame etiam deficere. Hannibalis
interim miles ignibus ante tentoria factis oleoque per
manipulos, ut mollirent artus, misso et cibo per otium
capto, ubi transgressos flumen hostes nuntiatum est, alacer
animis corporibusque arma capit atque in aciem procedit.
2 Baliares locat ante signa ⟨ac⟩ leuem armaturam, octo
ferme milia hominum, dein grauiorem armis peditem,
quod uirium, quod roboris erat; in cornibus circumfudit
decem milia equitum et ab cornibus in utramque partem
3 diuersos elephantos statuit. Consul effuse sequentes
equites, cum ab resistentibus subito Numidis incauti
exciperentur, signo receptui dato reuocatos circumdedit
4 peditibus. Duodeuiginti milia Romani erant, socium
nominis Latini uiginti, auxilia praeterea Cenomanorum;
ea sola in fide manserat Gallica gens. Iis copiis concursum est.
5 Proelium a Baliaribus ortum est; quibus cum maiore
robore legiones obsisterent, diducta propere in cornua
leuis armatura est, quae res effecit ut equitatus Romanus
6 extemplo urgeretur. Nam cum uix iam per se resisterent
decem milibus equitum quattuor milia et fessi integris
plerisque, obruti sunt insuper uelut nube iaculorum a

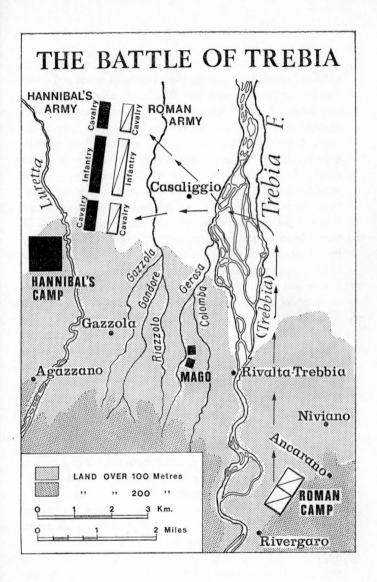

THE BATTLE OF TREBIA

HANNIBAL'S ARMY

ROMAN ARMY

Cavalry · Infantry · Cavalry

Cavalry · Infantry · Cavalry

Luretta

Casaliggio

Trebia F.

HANNIBAL'S CAMP

Gazzola

Gandore

Riazzolo

Gerosa

Colomba

(Trebbia)

Gazzola

Agazzano

MAGO

Rivalta-Trebbia

Niviano

Ancarano

ROMAN CAMP

Rivergaro

LAND OVER 100 Metres

  "   "   200   "

0   1   2   3 Km.

0   1   2 Miles

99

7 Baliaribus coniecta. Ad hoc elephanti eminentes ab
   extremis cornibus, equis maxime non uisu modo sed odore
8 insolito territis, fugam late faciebant. Pedestris pugna
   par animis magis quam uiribus erat, quas recentes
   Poenus paulo ante curatis corporibus in proelium attul-
   erat; contra ieiuna fessaque corpora Romanis et rigentia
   gelu torpebant. Restitissent tamen animis, si cum pedite
9 solum foret pugnatum; sed et Baliares pulso equite
   iaculabantur in latera et elephanti iam in mediam peditum aciem sese tulerant et Mago Numidaeque, simul
   latebras eorum improuida praeterlata acies est, exorti ab
10 tergo ingentem tumultum ac terrorem fecere. Tamen
   in tot circumstantibus malis mansit aliquamdiu immota
   acies, maxime praeter spem omnium aduersus elephantos.
11 Eos uelites ad id ipsum locati uerutis coniectis et auertere
   et insecuti auersos sub caudis, qua maxime molli cute
56 uolnera accipiunt, fodiebant. Trepidantesque et prope
   iam in suos consternatos e media acie in extremam ad
   sinistrum cornu aduersus Gallos auxiliares agi iussit
   Hannibal.
   Ibi extemplo haud dubiam fecere fugam; nouus quoque
   terror additus Romanis ut fusa auxilia sua uiderunt.
2 Itaque cum iam in orbem pugnarent, decem milia ferme
   hominum—cum alia euadere nequissent—media Afrorum acie quae Gallicis auxiliis firmata erat, cum ingenti
3 caede hostium perrupere et, cum neque in castra reditus
   esset flumine interclusis neque prae imbri satis decernere
   possent qua suis opem ferrent, Placentiam recto itinere
4 perrexere. Plures deinde in omnes partes eruptiones
   factae; et qui flumen petiere, aut gurgitibus absumpti
   sunt aut inter cunctationem ingrediendi ab hostibus
5 oppressi. Qui passim per agros fuga sparsi erant
   uestigia cedentis sequentes agminis Placentiam contendere;

aliis timor hostium audaciam ingrediendi flumen fecit,
6 transgressique in castra peruenerunt. Imber niue mixtus
et intoleranda uis frigoris et homines multos et iumenta et
7 elephantos prope omnes absumpsit. Finis insequendi
hostis Poenis flumen Trebia fuit, et ita torpentes gelu in
8 castra rediere ut uix laetitiam uictoriae sentirent. Itaque
nocte insequenti, cum praesidium castrorum et quod reliquum ⟨ex fuga semermium⟩ ex magna parte militum erat
9 ratibus Trebiam traicerent, aut nihil sensere obstrepente
pluuia aut, quia iam moueri nequibant prae lassitudine ac
uolneribus, sentire sese dissimularunt, quietisque Poenis
tacito agmine ab Scipione consule exercitus Placentiam est
perductus, inde Pado traiectus Cremonam, ne duorum
exercituum hibernis una colonia premeretur.

57 Romam tantus terror ex hac clade perlatus est ut iam ad
urbem Romanam crederent infestis signis hostem uenturum nec quicquam spei aut auxilii esse quo portis moeni-
2 busque uim arcerent: uno consule ad Ticinum uicto,
altero ex Sicilia reuocato, duobus consulibus, duobus
consularibus exercitibus uictis quos alios duces, quas alias
3 legiones esse quae arcessantur? Ita territis Sempronius
consul aduenit, ingenti periculo per effusos passim ad
praedandum hostium equites audacia magis quam consilio
aut spe fallendi resistendiue, si non falleret, transgressus.
4 Is, quod unum maxime in praesentia desiderabatur,
comitiis consularibus habitis in hiberna rediit. Creati
consules Cn. Seruilius et C. Flaminius.
5 Ceterum ne hiberna quidem Romanis quieta erant
uagantibus passim Numidis equitibus et, ⟨ut⟩ quaeque his
impeditiora erant, Celtiberis Lusitanisque. Omnes igitur
undique clausi commeatus erant, nisi quos Pado naues
6 subueherent. Emporium prope Placentiam fuit et opere
magno munitum et ualido firmatum praesidio. Eius

castelli oppugnandi spe cum equitibus ac leui armatura
profectus Hannibal, cum plurimum in celando incepto ad
effectum spei habuisset, nocte adortus non fefellit uigiles.
7 Tantus repente clamor est sublatus ut Placentiae quoque
audiretur.   Itaque sub lucem cum equitatu consul aderat
8 iussis quadrato agmine legionibus sequi. Equestre
interim proelium commissum; in quo, quia saucius
Hannibal pugna excessit, pauore hostibus iniecto defen-
9 sum egregie praesidium est.   Paucorum inde dierum
quiete sumpta et uixdum satis percurato uolnere, ad
10 Victumulas oppugnandas ire pergit. Id emporium
Romanis Gallico bello fuerat;   munitum inde locum
frequentauerant accolae mixti undique ex finitimis
populis, et tum terror populationum eo plerosque ex
11 agris compulerat.   Huius generis multitudo fama impigre
defensi ad Placentiam praesidii accensa armis arreptis
12 obuiam Hannibali procedit.   Magis agmina quam acies
in uia concurrerunt, et cum ex altera parte nihil
praeter inconditam turbam esset, in altera et dux
militi et duci miles fidens, ad triginta quinque milia
13 hominum a paucis fusa. Postero die deditione facta
praesidium intra moenia accepere; iussique arma
tradere cum dicto paruissent, signum repente uictoribus
14 datur, ut tamquam ui captam urbem diriperent; neque
ulla, quae in tali re memorabilis scribentibus uideri solet,
praetermissa clades est; adeo omne libidinis crudeli-
tatisque et inhumanae superbiae editum in miseros exemplum est.   Hae fuere hibernae expeditiones Hannibalis.

58 Haud longi inde temporis, dum intolerabilia frigora erant,
2 quies militi data est; et ad prima ac dubia signa ueris profectus ex hibernis in Etruriam ducit, eam quoque gentem,
sicut Gallos Liguresque, aut ui aut uoluntate adiuncturus.
3 Transeuntem Appenninum adeo atrox adorta tempestas

est, ut Alpium prope foeditatem superauerit. Vento mixtus imber cum ferretur in ipsa ora, primo, quia aut arma omittenda erant aut contra enitentes uertice intorti
4 adfligebantur, constitere; dein, cum iam spiritum includeret nec reciprocare animam sineret, auersi a uento
5 parumper consedere. Tum uero ingenti sono caelum strepere et inter horrendos fragores micare ignes; capti auribus et oculis metu omnes torpere; tandem effuso
6 imbre, cum eo magis accensa uis uenti esset, ipso illo quo deprensi erant loco castra ponere necessarium uisum est.
7 Id uero laboris uelut de integro initium fuit; nam nec explicare quicquam nec statuere poterant nec quod statutum esset manebat omnia perscindente uento et rapiente.
8 Et mox aqua leuata uento cum super gelida montium iuga concreta esset, tantum niuosae grandinis deiecit ut omnibus omissis procumberent homines tegminibus suis
9 magis obruti quam tecti; tantaque uis frigoris insecuta est ut ex illa miserabili hominum iumentorumque strage cum se quisque attollere ac leuare uellet, diu nequiret, quia torpentibus rigore neruis uix flectere artus poterant.
10 Deinde, ut tandem agitando sese mouere ac recipere animos et raris locis ignis fieri est coeptus, ad alienam
11 opem quisque inops tendere. Biduum eo loco uelut obsessi mansere; multi homines, multa iumenta, elephanti quoque ex iis qui proelio ad Trebiam facto superfuerant septem absumpti.

59 Degressus Appennino retro ad Placentiam castra mouit et ad decem milia progressus consedit. Postero die duodecim milia peditum, quinque equitum aduersus hostem
2 ducit; nec Sempronius consul—iam enim redierat ab Roma—detractauit certamen. Atque eo die tria milia
3 passuum inter bina castra fuere; postero die ingentibus animis uario euentu pugnatum est. Primo concursu

adeo res Romana superior fuit ut non acie uincerent
solum sed pulsos hostes in castra persequerentur, mox
4 castra quoque oppugnarent. Hannibal paucis propugnatoribus in uallo portisque positis, ceteros confertos in
media castra recepit intentosque signum ad erumpendum
5 exspectare iubet. Iam nona ferme diei hora erat, cum
Romanus nequiquam fatigato milite, postquam nulla spes
6 erat potiundi castris, signum receptui dedit. Quod ubi
Hannibal accepit laxatamque pugnam et recessum a
castris uidit, extemplo equitibus dextra laeuaque emissis
in hostem ipse cum peditum robore mediis castris erupit.
7 Pugna raro magis ulla saeua aut utriusque partis pernicie
clarior fuisset, si extendi eam dies in longum spatium
8 siuisset; nox accensum ingentibus animis proelium dire-
mit. Itaque acrior concursus fuit quam caedes et, sicut
aequata ferme pugna erat, ita clade pari discessum est.
Ab neutra parte sescentis plus peditibus et dimidium eius
9 equitum cecidit; sed maior Romanis quam pro numero
iactura fuit, quia equestris ordinis aliquot et tribuni
militum quinque et praefecti sociorum tres sunt interfecti.
10 Secundum eam pugnam Hannibal in Ligures, Sempronius
Lucam concessit. Venienti in Ligures Hannibali per
insidias intercepti duo quaestores Romani, C. Fuluius et
L. Lucretius, cum duobus tribunis militum et quinque
equestris ordinis, senatorum ferme liberis, quo magis
ratam fore cum iis pacem societatemque crederet,
traduntur.

60 Dum haec in Italia geruntur, Cn. Cornelius Scipio in His-
2 paniam cum classe et exercitu missus, cum ab ostio
Rhodani profectus Pyrenaeosque montes circumuectus
3 Emporias appulisset classem, exposito ibi exercitu orsus a
Laeetanis omnem oram usque ad Hiberum flumen partim

renouandis societatibus partim nouis instituendis Roman-
4 ae dicionis fecit.   Inde conciliata clementiae fama non ad
maritimos modo populos sed in mediterraneis quoque ac
montanis ad ferociores iam gentes ualuit; nec pax modo
apud eos sed societas etiam armorum parta est, ualidaeque
5 aliquot auxiliorum cohortes ex iis conscriptae sunt. Hannonis cis Hiberum prouincia erat; eum reliquerat Hannibal ad regionis eius praesidium. Itaque priusquam
alienarentur omnia obuiam eundum ratus, castris in
6 conspectu hostium positis in aciem eduxit. Nec Romano
differendum certamen uisum, quippe qui sciret cum
Hannone et Hasdrubale sibi dimicandum esse malletque
aduersus singulos separatim quam aduersus duos simul
7 rem gerere. Nec magni certaminis ea dimicatio fuit.
Sex milia hostium caesa, duo capta cum praesidio castrorum; nam et castra expugnata sunt atque ipse dux cum
aliquot principibus capiuntur; et Cissis, propinquum
8 castris oppidum, expugnatur. Ceterum praeda oppidi
parui pretii rerum fuit, supellex barbarica ac uilium
9 mancipiorum; castra militem ditauere, non eius modo
exercitus qui uictus erat sed et eius qui cum Hannibale in
Italia militabat, omnibus fere caris rebus, ne grauia
impedimenta ferentibus essent, citra Pyrenaeum relictis.
61 Priusquam certa huius cladis fama accideret, trangressus
Hiberum Hasdrubal cum octo milibus peditum, mille
equitum, tamquam ad primum aduentum Romanorum
occursurus, postquam perditas res ad Cissim amissaque
2 castra accepit, iter ad mare conuertit. Haud procul
Tarracone classicos milites naualesque socios uagos
palantesque per agros, quod ferme fit ut secundae res
neglegentiam creent, equite passim dimisso cum magna
3 caede, maiore fuga ad naues compellit; nec diutius circa
ea loca morari ausus, ne ab Scipione opprimeretur, trans

4 Hiberum sese recepit. Et Scipio raptim ad famam
nouorum hostium agmine acto, cum in paucos praefectos
nauium animaduertisset, praesidio Tarracone modico
5 relicto Emporias cum classe rediit. Vixdum digresso
eo Hasdrubal aderat et Ilergetum populo, qui obsides
Scipioni dederat, ad defectionem impulso cum eorum
ipsorum iuuentute agros fidelium Romanis sociorum
6 uastat; excito deinde Scipione hibernis toto cis Hiberum
rursus cedit agro. Scipio relictam ab auctore defectionis
Ilergetum gentem cum infesto exercitu inuasisset, compulsis omnibus Atanagrum urbem, quae caput eius populi
7 erat, circumsedit, intraque dies paucos pluribus quam
ante obsidibus imperatis Ilergetes pecunia etiam multatos
8 in ius dicionemque recepit. Inde in Ausetanos prope
Hiberum, socios et ipsos Poenorum, procedit atque urbe
eorum obsessa Lacetanos auxilium finitimis ferentes nocte
haud procul iam urbe, cum intrare uellent, excepit
9 insidiis. Caesa ad duodecim milia; exuti prope omnes
armis domos passim palantes per agros diffugere; nec
obsessos alia ulla res quam iniqua oppugnantibus hiemps
10 tutabatur. Triginta dies obsidio fuit, per quos raro unquam nix minus quattuor pedes alta iacuit adeoque
pluteos ac uineas Romanorum operuerat ut ea sola
ignibus aliquotiens coniectis ab hoste etiam tutamentum
11 fuerit. Postremo cum Amusicus princeps eorum ad
Hasdrubalem profugisset, uiginti argenti talentis pacti
deduntur. Tarraconem in hiberna reditum est.

62 Romae aut circa urbem multa ea hieme prodigia facta
aut, quod euenire solet motis semel in religionem animis,
2 multa nuntiata et temere credita sunt, in quis ingenuum
3 infantem semenstrem in foro holitorio triumphum clamasse, et ⟨in⟩ foro boario bouem in tertiam contignationem
sua sponte escendisse atque inde tumultu habitatorum

4 territum sese deiecisse, et nauium speciem de caelo
adfulsisse, et aedem Spei, quae est in foro holitorio,
fulmine ictam, et Lanuui hastam se commouisse et
coruum in aedem Iunonis deuolasse atque in ipso
5 puluinari consedisse, et in agro Amiternino multis locis
hominum specie procul candida ueste uisos nec cum ullo
congressos, et in Piceno lapidibus pluuisse, et Caere sortes
extenuatas, et in Gallia lupum uigili gladium ex uagina
6 raptum abstulisse. Ob cetera prodigia libros adire
decemuiri iussi; quod autem lapidibus pluuisset in
Piceno, nouendiale sacrum edictum; et subinde aliis
7 procurandis prope tota ciuitas operata fuit. Iam
primum omnium urbs lustrata est hostiaeque maiores
8 quibus editum est dis caesae, et donum ex auri pondo
quadraginta Lanuuium Iunoni portatum est et signum
aeneum matronae Iunoni in Auentino dedicauerunt, et
lectisternium Caere, ubi sortes attenuatae erant, impera-
9 tum, et supplicatio Fortunae in Algido; Romae quoque
et lectisternium Iuuentati et supplicatio ad aedem
Herculis nominatim, deinde uniuerso populo circa omnia
10 puluinaria indicta, et Genio maiores hostiae caesae quinque, et C. Atilius Serranus praetor uota suscipere iussus,
11 si in decem annos res publica eodem stetisset statu. Haec
procurata uotaque ex libris Sibyllinis magna ex parte
leuauerant religione animos.

63 Consulum designatorum alter Flaminius, cui eae legiones
quae Placentiae hibernabant sorte euenerant, edictum et
litteras ad consulem misit ut is exercitus idibus Martiis Ari-
2 mini adesset in castris. Hic in prouincia consulatum
inire consilium erat memori ueterum certaminum cum
patribus, quae tribunus plebis et quae postea consul prius
3 de consulatu qui abrogabatur, dein de triumpho habuerat,
inuisus etiam patribus ob nouam legem, quam Q.

CHAPTER 63

Claudius tribunus plebis aduersus senatum atque uno
patrum adiuuante C. Flaminio tulerat, ne quis senator
cuiue senator pater fuisset maritimam nauem, quae plus
4 quam trecentarum amphorarum esset, haberet. Id
satis habitum ad fructus ex agris uectandos; quaestus
omnis patribus indecorus uisus. Res per summam
contentionem acta inuidiam apud nobilitatem suasori
legis Flaminio, fauorem apud plebem alterumque inde
5 consulatum peperit. Ob haec ratus auspiciis ementiendis
Latinarumque feriarum mora et consularibus aliis
impedimentis retenturos se in urbe, simulato itinere
6 priuatus clam in prouinciam abiit. Ea res ubi palam
facta est, nouam insuper iram infestis iam ante patribus
mouit: non cum senatu modo sed iam cum dis immortali-
7 bus C. Flaminium bellum gerere. consulem ante
inauspicato factum reuocantibus ex ipsa acie dis atque hominibus non paruisse; nunc conscientia spretorum et
Capitolium et sollemnem uotorum nuncupationem fugisse,
8 ne die initi magistratus Iouis optimi maximi templum
adiret, ne senatum inuisus ipse et sibi uni inuisum uideret
consuleretque, ne Latinas indiceret Iouique Latiari
9 sollemne sacrum in monte faceret, ne auspicato profectus
in Capitolium ad uota nuncupanda, paludatus inde cum
lictoribus in prouinciam iret. lixae modo sine insignibus,
sine lictoribus profectum clam, furtim, haud aliter quam si
10 exsilii causa solum uertisset. magis pro maiestate
uidelicet imperii Arimini quam Romae magistratum
initurum et in deuersorio hospitali quam apud penates
11 suos praetextam sumpturum. Reuocandum uniuersi
retrahendumque censuerunt et cogendum omnibus prius
praesentem in deos hominesque fungi officiis quam ad
12 exercitum et in prouinciam iret. In eam legationem—
legatos enim mitti placuit—Q. Terentius et M. Antistius

profecti nihilo magis eum mouerunt quam priore consul-
13 atu litterae mouerant ab senatu missae. Paucos post
dies magistratum iniit, immolantique ei uitulus iam ictus
e manibus sacrificantium sese cum proripuisset, multos
14 circumstantes cruore respersit; fuga procul etiam maior
apud ignaros quid trepidaretur et concursatio fuit. Id a
15 plerisque in omen magni terroris acceptum. Legionibus
inde duabus a Sempronio prioris anni consule, duabus a
C. Atilio praetore acceptis in Etruriam per Appennini
tramites exercitus duci est coeptus.

Biographical Notes

Biographical Notes on some of the persons referred to in the General Introduction and the Introduction to Book XXI.

Appian, of Alexandria (early second century A.D.) wrote in Greek a history of the various Roman conquests in 24 books, of which nine survive complete and others in fragments, using as his immediate source an annalist of the time of Augustus or Tiberius. His work contains material of considerable value.

Cassius Dio, of Nicaea in Bithynia, b. A.D. 155, a senator and twice consul, wrote a history of Rome from the beginnings to A.D. 229 in 80 books, of which we have 19 in full and parts or epitomes of others. He draws on the annalistic sources, Polybius, Livy, etc. His work is most valuable for events of or near his own times, of which he had inside knowledge.

Drusus. Drusus Claudius Nero (38-9 B.C.), brother of Tiberius and step-son of Augustus. He was a popular general, campaigning mainly against the Germans. In 9 B.C., as consul, he reached the Elbe, but died during this campaign.

Fabius Maximus. Quintus Fabius Maximus "Cunctator" held five consulships between 233 and 209 B.C., and was the most prominent statesman and general in the Second Punic War until its last phase. He was appointed dictator after the Roman defeat at Lake Trasimene (217), and adopted a delaying policy (hence his nickname "Cunctator"), avoiding pitched battles, following Hannibal and wearing him down. After the disastrous battle of Cannae (216) this policy was renewed. He undoubtedly rendered the greatest services to Rome, but failed to see when it was time to go over to the offensive, and strongly opposed Scipio's policy of invading Africa.

Flaminius. Gaius Flaminius, a leader of the democratic opposition to the Senate, was elected consul for 217, and defeated and killed by Hannibal at Lake Trasimene.

Herodotus, of Halicarnassus (S.W. Asia Minor), c. 485 to after 430 B.C., the "father of history". He travelled over practically the whole world known to the Greeks, and wrote of all he saw and heard. His style is simple and flowing, eminently readable, and, though a work on this scale inevitably contains inaccuracies, he is invaluable as an authority.

Book XXI

Isocrates (436-338 B.C.), Athenian orator. He was a supreme stylist, and had an enormous influence on Greek and Latin prose writing. His most important works are speeches and essays on political subjects and on education.

Maecenas. Gaius Cilnius Maecenas (died 8 B.C.) was a close friend and minister of Augustus, and also a great patron of literature, especially of Virgil, who wrote the *Georgics* at his suggestion, and Horace, who often alludes to their friendship.

Messala. Valerius Messalla Corvinus (64 B.C.-A.D. 8), was distinguished as soldier, statesman, and orator under the principate of Augustus. He was also a great patron of literature, particularly of the poet Tibullus and his circle.

Pollio. Gaius Asinius Pollio (76 B.C.-A.D. 5) fought for Caesar and later Antony in the civil wars, but quarrelled with the latter, and withdrew from political activity. He wrote a history of the civil wars, besides tragedies and speeches, and was a friend and patron of many of the foremost writers of his time. Virgil's fourth eclogue is addressed to him.

Polybius (c. 203—c. 120 B.C.) took a prominent part in the Achaean League, in which he held high office. After the Third Macedonian War the Romans, dissatisfied at the lack of support they had received from the Achaeans, deported 1,000 of their leading men to Italy (168). Polybius was among these, and spent 17 years in Italy, where he became the friend of many prominent Romans and especially Scipio Aemilianus, whom he later accompanied on his campaigns to Spain (151) and Africa (147-6), and was present at the destruction of Carthage. He returned to Greece, then in the process of being annexed to Rome, where he used his influence to secure favourable conditions. He had a unique knowledge, gained from different points of view, of the main events of his time. His *Histories* are a major source for our knowledge of the period.

Pyrrhus (319-272 B.C.), King of Epirus, was a brilliant soldier, but though often victorious in battle, he never won a lasting success. He undertook various wars, first to liberate then to extend his kingdom even holding most of Macedonia for a short time, but was driven back and turned his attention to the West. At the invitation of Tarentum, a Greek colony in S. Italy, he invaded Italy in 280. He won two victories against the Romans (the first largely due to his use of elephants, which the Romans had never seen before), and advanced almost to Rome, but the Senate

NOTES

refused all terms, and he went off to Sicily. Here too he gained successes, but not decisive ones, and returning to Italy he was defeated by the Romans at Beneventum (275) and withdrew to Epirus. After more fighting against Macedonia he switched to the Peloponnese, and was killed in street fighting in Argos. The main effect of his exploits was to weaken Epirus by the constant drain on its man-power.

Sallust. Gaius Sallustius Crispus (86-c. 34 B.C.) was quaestor c. 59 and tribune in 52. He was expelled from the Senate by the censors in 50, but backed Caesar in the civil war, and was reinstated by him, becoming praetor in Africa and proconsular governor of Numidia. On his return to Rome he was threatened with prosecution and retired from politics. He wrote a history in five books, of which only fragments survive, and two monographs, the *Bellum Catilinae* and the *Bellum Iugurthinum*, which are extant. His views are anti-senatorial and he is at pains to point out the vices and corruption of the upper classes.

Scipio. Publius Cornelius Scipio Africanus (236-184 B.C.) is said to have saved his father's life at the Ticinus, the first battle of the Second Punic War (218). As military tribune he took part in the battle of Cannae (216), and rallied the survivors. In 210, though not in office, he was given the command in Spain, where his father and uncle had just been defeated and killed, as proconsul. He seized the Carthaginian base, New Carthage, by a brilliant stroke, and by 206 had completely expelled the Carthaginians from Spain. Elected consul for 205, he planned the invasion of Africa in spite of strong opposition from Fabius and his party, hitherto dominant in the Senate. He invaded Africa (204) and ended the war by his victory over Hannibal at Zama in 202. In 190 he crossed to Asia with his brother Lucius to fight Antiochus, but fell ill and was not present at the decisive battle of Magnesia. Later he fell victim to political opposition and accusations, and retired from Rome.

Tacitus. Cornelius Tacitus (his praenomen is unknown) was born c. A.D. 55. He followed a senatorial career, becoming consul for a part of 97 and proconsul of Asia, probably 112-13. He married the daughter of Agricola, best known as governor of Britain, 78-85. His historical works are the *Annales*, of which we have twelve books (one incomplete), and the *Histories*, of which we have four books and part of the fifth. Between them these covered the period from the death of Augustus to that of Domitian (A.D. 14-96). We also have a *Dialogue on Orators*, a life of Agricola, and the *Germania*, a description of the tribes and customs of the

Book XXI

Germans. Like Sallust and Livy, Tacitus is impressed by the decadence of his own times and regrets the "freedom" of the republic, but he is much more bitter than Livy, no doubt in part because he lived through the reign of terror of the latter years of Domitian. Abandoning the periodic structure of Cicero and Livy, he writes in sentences for the most part short, and striking in their epigrammatic phrases and unusual constructions.

Thucydides. Born c. 460-455, died c. 400 B.C. He was one of the Athenian generals in the Peloponnesian war, and was involved in the loss of the important Athenian colony of Amphipolis (424), for which he was exiled. He returned to Athens twenty years later, and died soon after. He wrote the history of the Peloponnesian war in eight books, of which book 8 is unfinished. He was the first "scientific" historian, ignoring myth, divine intervention, etc., and endeavouring to give the facts accurately and without prejudice or moral comment. The fact that his work (apart from the introductory chapters) covers a period of only 27 years, all within his own adult lifetime, and a limited area, and that, owing to his exile, he was able to get into touch with Peloponnesian sources made accuracy easier for him than for most other historians. He gave great prominence to set speeches in his history. These are sometimes accurate reports (*e.g.* Pericles's funeral speech), but are often invented to explain to the reader the feelings, motives, etc., of the speaker. This is a legitimate and effective device, but when imitated by lesser men increased dangerously the rhetorical element in history. In the time of Thucydides Attic prose style was not yet fully developed, and he is a difficult author, though with many fine passages.

Varro. Gaius Terentius Varro, a leader of the democratic party, was consul in 216 B.C., in which year he was defeated at the disastrous battle of Cannae.

Velleius. Gaius Velleius Paterculus (c. 19 B.C. to after A.D. 31), of an old Campanian family, served in the army, mainly under Tiberius, with considerable distinction, and on his retirement wrote a compendium of history in two books. The first (much of which is missing) stretches from the earliest times to the destruction of Carthage and Corinth in 146, the second from 146 B.C. to A.D. 30, becoming fuller as he reaches his own times. His work, both in style and selection and judgment, is somewhat amateurish, but he gives lively pictures of some of his heroes.

List of Roman Magistracies

Consuls. The two consuls were the highest regular magistrates. They held office for one year, presided over the Senate and at elections, and commanded the armies in time of war.

Praetors. The praetor urbanus and praetor peregrinus acted as judges, the former in lawsuits between Roman citizens, the latter in those between a Roman and a non-Roman. Additional praetors were appointed to govern the provinces of Sicily, Sardinia, and, from 197, the two provinces of Nearer and Further Spain. They often held army commands in less important theatres of war.

Aediles. The curule and plebeian aediles controlled the markets and open spaces of Rome, and in particular the corn-supply. They had some police and judicial powers. They were also in charge of public games (curule aediles of the Ludi Romani or Magni, plebeian aediles of the Ludi Plebeii), and in this capacity often endeavoured, by providing lavish attractions, to secure popularity, and therefore votes when they stood for higher office.

Quaestors. The quaestors acted as paymasters. Two of them were attached to the Treasury at Rome, while every governor or army commander had a quaestor on his staff.

Tribunes. The tribunes were the special officers of the plebs, whose interests they protected. They could veto an act of any magistrate or a decision by the Senate. It was a serious crime to resist, obstruct, or injure them.

Censors. Every four years (every five after 209 B.C.) a census was held and the list of senators and citizens revised. This was done by two censors, who could expel senators or degrade citizens if they had misbehaved.

Dictator. In times of emergency a dictator was appointed for six months. He took priority over all other magistrates, and his decisions were not subject to appeal or tribunician veto.

The curule magistrates (dictator, censors, consuls, praetors, and curule aediles) were originally patricians, and had special marks of distinction. In particular, they sat in an official ivory chair of state (*sella curulis*), and had the right to display in their houses waxen portraits of those of their ancestors who had held any of these offices.

Index of Proper Names

Acilius, M'., ?triumvir: 25.4.
Aegates Insulae, islands off N.W. Sicily: 10.7, 41.6, 49.5.
Aemilius Lepidus, M., praetor 218: 49.6, 51.7.
Aemilius Paullus, L., consul 219: 18.1.
Alco, Saguntine citizen: 12.3ff.
Allobroges, Gallic tribe: 31.5ff.
Alorcus, Spaniard: 12.3, 12.6ff.
Amiternum, Sabine town: 62.5.
Amusicus, Spanish chief: 61.11.
Annius, M., ?triumvir: 25.3.
Antistius, M., senatorial legate: 63.12.
Arbocala, Spanish town: 5.6.
Ardea, Rutulian town: 7.2.
Ariminum, Umbrian town: 15.6, 51.6f., 63.1, 63.10.
Atanagrum, Spanish town: 61.6.
Atilius Serranus, C., praetor 218: 26,2, 39.3, 62.10, 63.15.
Auentinus, Roman hill: 62.8.
Ausetani, Spanish tribe: 23.2, 61.8.

Baebius Tampilus, Q., Roman legate: 6.8, 18.1.
Baliares, Baliaric slingers: 21.12, 22.2, 55.2, 55.5f.
Barcines: family of Hannibal, 2.4, 10.3; political faction, 3.2, 9.4.
Bargusii, Spanish tribe: 19.7, 23.2.
Boii, Gallic tribe: revolt from Rome, 25.2ff., 52.7; delegates at Rhône, 29.6.
Braneus, Allobrogian: 31.6.
Brixiani, Gallic tribe: 25.14.

Caere, Etruscan town: 62.5, 62.8.
Carpetani, Spanish tribe: 5.8, 5.11, 5.16, 11.13, 23.4, 23.6.
Cartala, Spanish town: 5.4.
Carthago: debates at, 3.2ff., 10.1ff.; Roman legates at, 18.1ff.
Carthago Nova, Carthaginian town in Spain: 5.4, 15.3, 21.1, 22.5, 38.1.
Celtiberi/Celtiberia, Spanish tribe/region: 43.8, 57.5.
Cenomani, Gallic tribe: 55.4.
Cincius Alimentus, L., Roman historian: 38.3.
Cissis, Spanish town: 60.7, 61.1.
Clastidium, town in Cisalpine Gaul: 48.9.
Claudius, Q., tribune: 63.3.

NOTES

Coelius Antipater, L., Roman historian: 38.7, 46.8, 47.4.
Cornelius Scipio Asina, P., consul 221: 25.4.
Cornelius Scipio, Cn., consul 222: 32.3, 40.3; in Spain, 60.1ff.
Cornelius Scipio, P., the elder, consul 218: 6.3, 15.4f.; Spain as province,
  17.1, 17.7f.; leaves Italy, 26.3; at Rhône, 29.5; prepares return to
  Italy, 32.1ff.; at Pisa, 39.3; speech at Ticinus, 39.10ff.; at battle of
  Ticinus, 46.3ff.; moves to Trebia, 48.3ff.; strategy at Trebia, 52.7ff.,
  53.7.
Cornelius Scipio, P., the younger (**Africanus**): 46.8ff.
Corsica/Corsi: 16.4.
Cremona, town in Cisalpine Gaul: 25.2.
Cremonis iugum, Little St Bernard Pass: 38.7.

Dasius, garrison-commander at Clastidium: 48.9.
Druentia, river, mod. Durance: 31.9, 32.6.

Emporiae, Spanish town: 60.2, 61.4.
Emporium, town near Placentia: 57.6ff.
Eryx, mountain in N. W. Sicily: 10.7, 41.6, 41.9, 41.11.
Etruria: 26.3, 58.3, 63.15.

Fabius Maximus Cunctator, Q., consul 233: 18.1, 18.3.
Flaminius, C., consul 223/217: 15.6, 57.4, 63.1ff.
Fortuna, Roman goddess: 62.8.
Fulvius, C., quaestor 218: 59.10.

Gades, Spanish town: 21.9, 22.4.
Galli/Gallia, Cisalpine Gaul: 16.4, 16.6, 17.7f., 25.7ff., 38.3, 39.4ff.,
  43.14, 45.3, 48.1ff., 52.3ff., 58.2, 62.5; Transalpine Gaul, 19.11, 20.4,
  20.7ff., 23.1, 24.2ff., 26.5ff., 31.2, 31.10.
Genius populi Romani, deity: 62.10.
Genua, Italian town: 32.5.

Hamilcar, father of Hannibal: 1.4, 3.4; general in Sicily, 10.8, 41.8;
  general in Africa, 2.1; in Spain, 2.1f.; death, 2.3, 5.2.
Hamilcar, son of Gisgo, 51.2.
Hannibal: 1.1; boyhood, 1.4, 2.3; in Spain, 4.1ff.; character-sketch of,
  4.3ff.; under Hasdrubal, 4.4, 4.10; general in Spain, 5.1ff.; attacks
  Saguntum, 7.4ff.; at New Carthage, 21.1ff., 22.5; at Gades, 21.9;
  dream, 22.5ff.; crosses Ebro, 23.1; in Transalpine Gaul, 24.1ff.;
  crosses Rhône, 27.1ff.; Alpine crossing, 30.1ff.; in Italy, 39.1ff.; speech
  at Ticinus, 43.1ff.; at battle of Ticinus, 46.3ff.; at Trebia, 53.7ff.;

NOTES

Lutatius, C., consul 242: 18.10, 19.2-3.
Lutatius Catulus, C., consul 220: 25.3-4.
Magalus, Boian chief: 29.6.
Mago, brother of Hannibal: 47.4ff., 54.2ff., 55.9.
Maharbal, deputy of Hannibal: 12.1, 45.2ff.
Manlius Vulso, L., praetor 218: 17.7, 25.8, 39.3, 45.2.
Mars, Roman god: 10.8.
Massilia, town in Transalpine Gaul: 20.7, 25.1, 26.3ff.
Mauri, African tribe inhabiting Morocco: 22.3.
Melita (Malta): 51.1.
Messana, Sicilian town: 49.3, 50.7.
Mutina, town in Cisalpine Gaul: 25.3, 25.6ff.

Numidae, African people: 22.3; cavalry of, 29.1ff., 45.2ff., 46.5ff., 48.5, 52.5, 54.4ff., 55.9, 57.5.

Oceanus = Atlantic: 22.3, 43.13.
Olcades, Spanish tribe: 5.2f., 5.7, 5.11, 11.13.
Onussa, Spanish town: 22.5.

Padus, river, mod. Po: 25.2, 32.5, 39.3ff., 43.4, 47.1ff., 52.3ff., 56.9.
Papirius Maso, C., consul 231: 25.4.
Picenum, area of N. E. Italy: 62.5f.
Placentia, town of Cisalpine Gaul: 25.2f., 39.4, 47.3, 47.7f., 56.3, 56.9, 57.6ff., 59.1, 63.1.
Poeninum iugum, Great St Bernard Pass: 38.6, 38.8f.
Pomponius, Sex., legate of Sempronius: 51.6.
Pyrenaei montes/Pyrenaeus saltus: 23.2, 23.4, 24.1f., 26.4, 30.5f., 60.2.

Rhodanus, river (Rhône): 26.4ff., 30.5, 40.2, 41.3, 60.2.
Rome: Saguntines at, 6.3ff.; reaction at fall of Saguntum, 16.1ff.; after Trebia defeat, 57.1ff.; prodigies at, 62.1ff.
Ruscino, town in Pyrenees, 24.2ff.
Rutuli, Italian people S. of Rome: 7.2.

Saguntum/Saguntini, Spanish town S. of Ebro: 7.2; origins of, 7.2; Hannibal's designs on, 5.2f., 6.1ff.; attack on, 6.5, 7.1ff., 18.2, 18.6, 18.12, 19.10, 30.3, 30.9, 41.8, 44.4ff.; capture of, 15.1; chronology of, 15.3ff.; and treaties between Rome and Carthage, 19.1, 19.4.
Salassi, tribe in Cisalpine Gaul: 38.7.
Sarar, river (?Isère): 31.4.
Sardi/Sardinia: as cause of war, 1.5, 16.4, 40.5, 41.14, 43.6, 44.7, 53.4.
Scipio, see Cornelius.

Book XXI

Sedunoveragri, Alpine people: 38.9.
Sempronius Longus, Ti., consul 218: 6.3, 15.4ff.; gets province of Africa, 17.1, 17.6; operations in Sicily, 49.1ff., 50.7ff.; at Trebia, 51.7ff., 52.8ff., 54.6ff.; at Rome after Trebia, 57.3; at Placentia, 59.2; at Luca, 59.10; hands over legions, 63.15.
Servilius Geminus, C., praetor ?220: 25.3.
Servilius Geminus, Cn., consul 217: 15.6, 57.4.
Sibyllini libri: 62.11.
Sicilia: as cause of war, 1.5, 40.5, 41.14, 43.6, 44.7, 53.4; quitted by Hamilcar, 41.9; operations in, 49.1ff.
Spes, Roman goddess: 62.4.
Syracusae/Syracusani, Sicilian town/population: 49.3.

Tagus, Spanish river: battle at, 5.8ff.
Tannetum, village in Cisalpine Gaul: 25.13, 26.2.
Tarentum, S. Italian town: 10.8.
Tarraco, Spanish town: 61.2ff., 61.11.
Taurini Semigalli, tribe of Cisalpine Gaul: 38.5, 38.7, 39.1, 39.4ff.
Terentius, Q.: 63.12.
Tiberis, river of Rome: 30.11.
Ticinus, river in Cisalpine Gaul: 15.4, 39.10ff., 45.1, 47.2f., 48.5, 57.2.
Trebia, river in Cisalpine Gaul: 15.4, 15.6, 48.4ff., 51.7ff., 54.4, 56.7ff., 58.11.
Tricastini, tribe in Transalpine Gaul: 31.9.
Trigorii (or Tricorii), Gallic tribe: 31.9.
Turdetani, Spanish tribe: 6.1, 12.5.

Vaccaei, Spanish tribe: 5.8, 5.11.
Valerius Flaccus, P., legate to Hannibal and Carthage: 6.8, 11.2.
Vergiliae, constellation (= Pleiades): 35.6.
Vibonensis ager, territory in S. W. Italy: 51.4, 51.6.
Victumulae, town in Cisalpine Gaul: 45.3, 57.9.
Vocontii, Gallic tribe: 31.9.
Volcae, Gallic tribe: 26.6.
Volciani, Spanish tribe: 19.8, 19.11.
Vulcani insulae, islands off N. Sicily: 49.2, 51.3.

Zacynthus, Greek island off Elis: 7.2.

Notes

ABBREVIATIONS

Broughton	T. R. S. Broughton, *The Magistrates of the Roman Republic* (New York 1952)
De Beer	Sir Gavin de Beer, *Alps and Elephants* (London 1955)
De Sanctis	G. De Sanctis, *Storia dei Romani* (Turin 1907-)
Dimsdale	M. Dimsdale, Pitt Press edition of Livy XXI
Handford	S. A. Handford, *The Latin Subjunctive* (London 1947)
Jullian	C. Jullian, *Histoire de la Gaule* (Paris 1909-26)
Klotz	A. Klotz, *Livius und seine Vorgänger* (Leipzig 1940)
Kühnast	L. Kühnast, *Die Hauptpunkte der livianischen Syntax* (Berlin 1872)
Kühner-Stegmann	*Ausführliche Grammatik der lateinischen Sprache* (repr. Darmstadt 1962)
Madvig, *E. L.*	J. N. Madvig, *Emendationes Livianae* (1860)
Mikkola	E. Mikkola, *Die Konzessivität bei Livius* (Helsinki 1957)
Ogilvie	R. M. Ogilvie, *A Commentary on Livy Books* 1-5 (Oxford 1965)
Packard	D. W. Packard, *A Concordance to Livy* (Cambridge, Mass. 1968)
Riemann	O. Riemann, *Etudes sur la langue et la grammaire de Tite-Live* (Paris 1885)
Walbank	F. W. Walbank, *A Historical Commentary on Polybius I* (Oxford 1957)
Weissenborn-Müller	*T. Livi Ab urbe condita* (repr. Berlin 1962)
Woodcock	E. C. Woodcock, *A New Latin Syntax* (London 1959)

1.1-4.10. *The causes of the war. Carthaginian Operations in Spain, 236-221*

Chapter 1.

1. **In parte operis mei:** After his Preface, Livy wrote fresh introductions at apposite points; *e.g.* at the beginning of Books VI, XXI, and XXXI. He planned his history with the pentad and the decade as basic units, and this introduction serves for the whole decade.

NOTES

summae totius: *totius* is tautologous, for *summa* means the whole of a literary work; cf. Quint. IV.2.41.

professi plerique: Not only Thucydides (1.1: ἐλπίσας μέγαν τε ἔσεσθαι καὶ ἀξιολογώτατον, etc.) but also Sallust (*Cat.* 4.4; cf. *Jug.* 5.1).

2. neque validiores opibus . . . neque his ipsis: Making in reverse order precisely the points made by Thuc.: ἀκμάζοντές τε ἦσαν ἐς αὐτὸν ἀμφότεροι παρασκευῇ τῇ πάσῃ . . . κίνησις γὰρ αὕτη δὴ μεγίστη τοῖς Ἕλλησιν ἐγένετο καὶ μέρει τινὶ τῶν βαρβάρων.

virium aut roboris: Perhaps physical strength and mental vigour, as 40.8 indicates, not offensive and defensive power; but elsewhere (55.2) no clear distinction is drawn between the two words.

belli artes . . . conferebant: A phrase not paralleled elsewhere, and the reading of *CMDA*, *conserebant*, is not impossible; but cf. 50.1, *conserere pugnam et . . . vires conferre.*

ancepsque Mars: Also at VII.29.2, but not earlier in extant prose, where *communis Mars* is regular.

propius periculum: "closer to defeat". The alliteration dictates the choice of noun. *prope, propius, proxime* are used as prepositions in Caesar (e.g. *B.G.* I. 46.1) and Cicero (*Phil.* 6.5, 10.26).

3. ultro: A partisan Roman judgment; Introduction, p. 27.

superbe avareque imperitatum: Note that such anti-Roman judgments are attributed to others rather than voiced by the historian. The frequentative, which does not appear earlier in extant prose, may here have its full force, referring to the terms of 241 and 237.

crederent: This illogical subjunctive (for *imperitatum esset* or *imperitatum esse credebant*) is common at all times; see Woodcock, § 242 n.2. The balancing *inferrent* encouraged a second subjunctive here.

4. fama est: The story appears in Polybius III. 11.5-7, Nepos, *Hann.* II.3-4, and Appian, *Ib.* 9. It should not be dismissed as myth; Hannibal himself is said to have recounted it to Antiochus in 193 in exile (Livy XXXV.19.3). But the variations between Livy and Polybius are noteworthy. Polybius states that Hamilcar took the initiative in asking his son to go to Spain; in Livy, Hannibal's plea characterises him as a militarist from his early years. Secondly, the oath taken is in Pol.'s words μηδέποτε Ῥωμαίοις εὐνοήσειν and this is echoed by Livy at XXXV.19.3: *nunquam amicum fore populi Romani.* There is all the difference in the world between this and swearing to be an enemy *cum primum posset.* Livy's claim that the oath was a cause of the war is tendentious and invalid. Since Appian has Livy's version, it is likely that the distortion goes back to Valerius Antias (Introduction, p. 41).

Book XXI

annorum ferme novem: Genitive of quality without substantive is frequent in Livy. See Woodcock, § 85(*b*).

blandientem: "persuading by coaxing", a commoner sense than L. & S. suggests (cf. XXXII.40.11 and the new *Oxford Latin Dictionary*, s.v.). The following *ut* is uncommon, but cf. Plaut. *Cas.* 883, Sen. *Ep.* 46.1.

perfecto Africo bello: 2.1 n.

traiecturus: The predicative use of the future participle to express purpose (17.6, 21.11, 32. 1 and 2, 32.10, 44.3, 52.6, 58.2, 61.1) is rare in earlier prose. Cf. Cic. *Verr.* II.1.56; Woodcock, § 92.

sacrificaret: Of the two main Carthaginian deities, Tanit Pené Baal ("Tanit face of Baal") held predominance over her consort Baal Hammon. Shrines unearthed at Carthage contain numerous stelae commemorating ritual sacrifice of children and animals. See, *e.g.*, Harden, *The Phoenicians*, ch. 7.

5. angebant ingentis spiritus virum: The prominence lent to Hamilcar's anger reflects the tradition that this was the first cause of the war; cf. Pol. III.9.6 (with Walbank's note). The ensuing *oratio obliqua* is Livy's characteristic method of psychological depiction of leading figures. **Sardiniam ... stipendio ... imposito interceptam** ("snatched by robbery"; cf. III.71.7). For the indemnity of 3200 talents, see Pol. III.27.5; for the chronology, Walbank on Pol. I.88.8.

Chapter 2.

1. quod fuit per quinque annos (*fuit* = "lasted", a favourite expression of Livy's). Polybius says the war lasted 3 years 4 months (early 240-spring 237). Livy inaccurately computes the entire period from the end of the 1st Punic War to Hamilcar's crossing into Spain (early 241-summer 237). Diodorus 25.6 gives a period of 4 years 4 months, either by error or by reckoning the revolt from the return of the mercenaries in 241.

sub recentem pacem: "beginning about the time of the recent peace with Rome"—cf. *sub noctem, sub tempus,* etc., a common usage in Livy.

novem annis: The ablative is sometimes used for duration of *completed* action (cf. Cic. *De Or.* 3.138), and Livy uses it here for variation after *per* with the accusative. The nine years are summer 237-winter 229; for the date of Hamilcar's death, "ten years before the beginning of the Second War", see Pol. III.10.7.

augendo Punico imperio: Livy commonly uses the instrumental ablative with gerund(ive) with a force equivalent to a present participle or *dum*-clause (III.65.4, VIII.17.1; cf. Woodcock, § 207. 4).

NOTES

Carthage had long had a foothold at Gades (Cadiz), probably the earliest Phoenician foundation in the western Mediterranean, dating from 850 if not earlier; see below, 21.9 n. Hamilcar established Carthaginian control in the southern coastal area. Cf. Appian. *Ib.* 2; Diod. 25.10.

2. intulerunt: Though the *qui* clause stands within the *oratio obliqua* introduced by *appareret*, the indicative is used because in strict logic Hannibal's troops could not have been in men's minds a decade earlier.

Hasdrubal in Spain (229-221 B.C.)

According to the biased Roman tradition inaugurated by Fabius Pictor (Pol. III.8), Hasdrubal's rapacity and love of power, which sought control in Spain independent of the Carthaginian government, was a cause of the Second War. The good sense of Livy (and his source Coelius) excises this.

3. Mors Hamilcaris: *ad Castrum Album* (XXIV.41.3). Diodorus 25.10 is our main authority. Having subdued many cities, Hamilcar founded Leuke Akra (Castrum Album); he then besieged Helike. But the king of the Orissoi (Oretani) came to the aid of the town, and defeated Hamilcar by treachery. Hamilcar was drowned trying to escape. Leuke Akra has been speculatively identified with Lucentum (modern Alicante), where there is such a "white promontory"; and only 13 miles inland is Elche, which can be identified with Helike. Sumner's arguments against these identifications (*HSCP*, 1968, 208 ff.), are not convincing; Leuke Akra will surely be a coastal town, and not on the Upper Baetis.

pueritia: Since Hannibal was 9 in 237 (1.4), he was now 17.

octo ferme annos: So also Pol. II.36.1 (229-221 B.C.).

flore aetatis, uti ferunt: Polybius has no mention of such homosexual practices, and the phrase of qualification (*ut ferunt*) contrasted with *profecto* in the next phrase reflects Livy's scepticism. Such charges were a staple calumny in Roman historiography; cf. Sallust, *Cat.* 14.7.

4. factionis Barcinae ... apud milites plebemque: The suggestion that the Barcids had popular support but opposition from Carthaginian political leaders has little to commend it at this time (Warmington, 169), and may reflect the situation after the Second War.

ob aliam indolem animi: *animi* is usually taken as explanatory genitive, but *indoles* is inclusive of such traits as the complaisance just mentioned (cf. 4.10), and the genitive is simply possessive.

5. plura consilio quam vi: Hasdrubal plays Numa to Hamilcar's Romulus.

BOOK XXI

6. nihilo ei pax tutior: i.e. *quam bellum Hamilcari*, but Livy has unfortunately omitted to state that Hamilcar died in war-operations.
barbarus: The word was doubtless used by Livy because the assassin is variously identified as a Spanish slave (Justinus 44.5) and a Celt (Pol. II.36.1).
ridentis: The indeterminate sense of the present participle is a feature of Livy's style (VI.14.11, XXVII.2.5, etc.; see Riemann, 87). This type of information, the courage of a patriot under torture, is included for the moral lesson it teaches.

7. mirae artis: 1.4 n.
foedus: The Ebro treaty, the source of much modern controversy; see Walbank on Pol. II.13.7. The date was probably winter 226-5, and the Roman motives for making it were mainly their desire to concentrate on the Gallic danger (Pol. II.13.3 ff.) and their apprehension, prompted by the Massilians, that Hasdrubal's foundation of New Carthage would soon be followed by Carthaginian dominance over the whole eastern coastline.

According to Polybius, the sole stipulation was that the Carthaginians should not cross the Ebro to make war. Rome may not have bound herself by a similar clause not to make war south of the Ebro, because she had no military presence in Spain. We may assume that the Carthaginians believed that the treaty empowered them to exploit the eastern coastal area south of the Ebro, but that the formulation did not guarantee this. Livy's clause, *ut finis utriusque imperii esset amnis Hiberus*, is wholly anachronistic; the treaty was not concerned with Spain as a whole, and the Romans had no imperium in the area.

Livy's second clause, *Saguntinisque ... libertas servaretur*, is both geographically tendentious (Saguntum lies 100 miles south of the Ebro) and chauvinistic forgery reproduced from annalistic sources; Polybius has no mention of it. Yet Rome was probably in alliance with Saguntum at the time of the Ebro treaty, for such a connexion went back "several years" before 221 (Pol. III.30.1), and was probably made by the Roman embassy which visited Hamilcar in 231. Saguntum could have been totally omitted from the terms of the Ebro agreement because Rome was solely concerned to demarcate the area of the coast north of the Ebro not to be approached by Carthaginian arms.

One attempt to resolve this difficulty is the suggestion that the Hiberus of the treaty was not the modern Ebro. Carcopino's suggestion (*REA*, 1953, 258 ff., *CRAI*, 1960, 341 ff.) that it was the Sucro (modern Jucar) raises more problems than it solves. Why was the Roman protest to Carthage not directly referred to the Ebro treaty? Why were the ancillary operations of Hannibal not condemned? Why were Polybius and Livy in ignorance of the two Ebros? Moreover, Carcopino's arguments that the Sucro bore the name Hiberus have now been demolished by Sumner (*HSCP*, 1968). Sumner, however, is convinced that the Hiberus is not the Ebro, and argues for the possible existence of another river of the same name near the Cape de la Nao. But such speculation is not helpful; the line of demarcation must have been readily identifiable by the interested parties. It seems best to accept the Hiberus as the Ebro, and to posit the view that Rome, though allied to Saguntum, did not guarantee her freedom in the Ebro treaty. Livy's second clause, echoed in Appian (*Ib.* 7) and Zon. (8.21), derives from the fabrication of an earlier historian, probably Valerius Antias, who sought to justify Roman policies and Roman *fides*.

Hannibal takes over (221 B.C.); debate at Carthage

Chapter 3.

1. **In Hasdrubalis locum:** Here Livy presents one of his rounded episodes, introduced as regularly with pluperfects setting the scene (*accersierat . . . acta fuerat*). It is rounded off by a short concluding sentence expressing the outcome (4.1). The episode stresses as moral the dangers of autocratic government.

quin<am successurus esset>: This is Walters' ingenious solution to fill out an obvious lacuna in the text. For the historical fact, see Pol. III.13.3-5.

praerogativam: Technically the adjective used of the centuria voting first at the Roman elections (III.51.8, V.18.1, etc.). As often, Livy describes the procedures of foreign assemblies in terms familiar to his readers. Translate: "The prior choice of the soldiers."

2. **vixdum puberem:** A word more precise and evocative than *adulescens* or *iuvenis* (which are applicable to men of 40); it is common as collective singular but rare in this sense of "stripling" (cf. I.32.12).

litteris accersierat: A dubious version, contradicting Livy's own statement elsewhere (XXX.37.9) that after crossing to Spain with Hamilcar Hannibal had never returned to Africa. Livy reproduces from his source more discrediting gossip about the Barcids on the familiar topic of homosexuality.

Book XXI

in senatu: The debate was recorded in Coelius (frr. 5-6 Peter) on whose account Livy's version of Hanno's speech may be based. By *senatu* Livy means not the *gerousia* of 30, which he calls *consilium* (XXX.16.3) but the *sunkletos* of 300. It is worth noting how slight Livy's information is on Carthaginian politics. Apart from this passage and ch. 10 below, there is little detail before Book XXX (but cf. XXIII.11-13, XXIII.32, XXIX.3-4). Historians regard this debate with some scepticism; the arguments have been lent anachronistic colouring by events at Carthage after 200, when Hannibal became suffete with proposals for fiscal and constitutional reform, but was forced into exile. The mercantile and banking class had much to thank the Barcids for in 221, since they were opening up Spain for greater economic exploitation. Livy's general picture of virtually no opposition to Barcid leadership in Spain (4.1) must be true. Whether Hanno can be envisaged as the spokesman of the decent elements (*optimus quisque*, 4.1) is more dubious. He had been prominent as general thirty years before, capturing Hecatompylos (Theveste) about 247 (Diod. XXIV.10.2). During the Mercenary War, he quarrelled with Hamilcar, and though they were later reconciled, his was an obvious name to which to attribute anti-Barcid arguments; the words attributed to him here smack of Roman rather than Carthaginian political preoccupations (3.5 n.).

4. pro militari rudimento: "as if it were", cf. II.35.5, II.62.5, etc. The noun is not found before Livy and Virgil.

praetorum: Chosen here to achieve the Ciceronian clausula instead of *dux* or *imperator*, used elsewhere by Livy for foreign generals. Cf. Cicero, *Div.* 1.123.

5. cuius regis genero ... eius filio: "that we may not early enough become slaves to the son of that king whose son-in-law received our armies as his inheritance?" The elaborate balance of correlatives is typical of Cicero, who is Livy's model in speeches. The attribution of the title *regis* to Hamilcar, and the demand (§ 6) that Hannibal be kept *sub legibus sub magistratibus* is an echo of first-century political controversies at Rome surrounding Julius Caesar; Hanno is here credited with the Ciceronian-Livian political ideal, frequently expressed in the first decade, that no man should be above the law or the constitutional offices.

6. quandoque: This is the first extant use (and only here in Livy) as adverb of indefinite futurity.

ignis incendium exsuscitet: Of the limited range of extended metaphors in Livy's speeches, that of fire is the commonest; see Ullmann, *Étude sur le* *style des discours de Tite-Live* (Oslo, 1929). The verb appears here only in Livy, but for this metaphorical use see Ovid, *Fasti* 5.507.

Chapter 4.

1. optimus quisque: not "the aristocratic party" but the few right-minded citizens, as at Cic. *Sest.* 97: *quis ergo iste optimus quisque? omnes optimates sunt qui neque nocentes sunt nec natura improbi nec furiosi nec malis domesticis impediti.*

in se convertit: "attracted the attention of" as at 3.4, not "won over", which the following sentences show to be premature.

2. For the character-sketch, Livy adopts the pithy Latinity of Sallust. Catiline's portrait (*Cat.* 14-16) is the model. The structure is paratactic; notable are the use of historic infinitives (§ § 2, 4; cf. *Cat.* 14.6, 16.2), the omission of verbs (§ § 6, 8; *Cat.* 15.5), alliterative effects (§ § 2, 8, 9; *Cat.* 14.1, 16.2, etc.), and anaphora (§ 9; *Cat.* 15.1).

vigorem: Not in extant prose before Livy.

3. parendum atque imperandum: Livy is fond of this *adnominatio;* cf. *perdere quam perire* (IX.14.15) *hostis pro hospite* (I.58.8), etc. The omission of a preposition here and at XXII.8.5 is un-Ciceronian—see Madvig on Cic. *Fin.* 2.40.

haud facile discerneres: The phrase appears also in Sallust's character-sketch of Sempronia, *Cat.* 25.3. This is the regular use of the imperfect subjunctive in the can-potential originally restricted to a small group of verbs (especially *scire, videre, invenire*) but later extended. See Handford, § § 120 ff.

4. ubi agendum esset: Frequentative subjunctives after *ubi* and *ut* become common in extant prose in Livy. In Cicero and Caesar such subjunctives are found in *cum*-clauses (Cic. *Verr.* II.4.48; Caes. *B.C.* II.41.6), *si*-clauses (Cic. *Rep.* 1.66), and occasional *ubi*-clauses (*B.C.* II.15.2). The use with *ut* and with *qua* (11.9) extends the usage. Only imperfect and pluperfect subjunctives are found, the tenses to which the *cum*-clauses in Cicero/Caesar are restricted. Handford, § 191; Kühner-Stegmann, 2.206 ff.

5. audaciae ... consilii: Livy's faithfulness to his sources (here Coelius) can be measured by Polybius' comment (III.47.7) that some historians praise Hannibal as ἀμίμητόν τινα ... στρατηγὸν καὶ τολμῇ καὶ προνοίᾳ.

6. desiderio naturali, non voluptate: Stoic terminology; see Cic. *Fin.* 2.27 (with Selem's note).

discriminata: Not elsewhere in Livy, but see Cic. *Phil.* 12.23: *Etruriam* *discriminat Cassia*—precisely the sense here, for the time of sleeping is not "demarcated" from that of waking.

7. accersita: A medical expression. Celsus 3.18: *somnum medicamentis arcessere.*

inter custodias stationesque: In the defensive arrangement of a Roman camp there were guard-posts both within and without (Pol. VI.35). No general in his senses would sleep outside; Hannibal is visualised as sleeping amongst the guard-posts and sentry-stations within the camp, not in the praetorium.

8. inter aequales: Compendious for *inter aequalium vestitum. Aequales* are not his "equals in rank"; as second-in-command and cavalry-commander (App. *Ib.* 23; Nep. *Hann.* 3) he has none. The sense is more vaguely "his fellows".

conspiciebantur: "singled him out", a frequent passive use in Livy; cf. I.47.5, II.5.5, V.23.5, and Sall. *Cat.* 7.6.

9. inhumana crudelitas: Historians of the country ravaged by the Second War are naturally emphatic about this; see 57.14, XXIV.45.13, XXVI.38.3, etc. Polybius however is more circumspect, as at IX.24.8, IX.26.11 (where it is suggested that only Romans regard him as notorious on this score).

perfidia: This too was proverbial at Rome (Cic. *Leg. Agr.* 2.95, Hor. *C.* IV.4.49, etc.), but again there are dissonant strands in the tradition; cf. XXIII.19.16, where he acts at Casilinum *summa cum fide.* Similarly the criticism *nihil sancti . . . nulla religio* is to be regarded suspiciously, for at 21.9 he pays vows to Hercules (Melqart) and at 45.8 prays to Jove and other gods.

10. triennio: (For the ablative, 2.1 n.). Hannibal had served continuously in Spain since Hamilcar's generalship, so these years either mark his period as second-in-command (224-221) or more probably continue the fiction that Hannibal came to Spain at Hasdrubal's instigation (3.2 n.).

5.1-6.8. Hannibal's operations, 221-219

Chapter 5.

1. velut: Cicero and Caesar write *velut si*, but Cicero has *tamquam* for *tamquam si* at *Verr.* II.4.49, and the abbreviated form reflects a natural development of the language.

bellum Romanum: 1.4 n.

NOTES

2. ne casus aliquis: The "rule" that *quis* and *qui* are used as indefinite pronoun and adjective after *si, nisi, num, ne, quanto, quo* is merely a convention often disregarded by Cicero, especially when conjunction and indefinite pronoun or adjective are not juxtaposed (*Leg.* 3.21: *De Or.* 2.38: Riemann, 165 ff.). *aliquis* is frequently adjectival; e.g. *Tusc.* 1.82.

3. arma movebantur: The phrase does not appear before Livy (Kühnast, 377). *quibus oppugnandis* is here equivalent to the protasis of a past unreal condition, and the logical apodosis remains unexpressed (*arma movebantur et mota essent*); cf. Woodcock, § 200. The abbreviation of the thought is perhaps affected by the framework of the *quia* clause.

Olcadum fines: The date is 221. Polybius' account is similar, but he calls the capital not Cartala but Althaea; Livy is following another authority with access to the same information, who will be Coelius, and who may have prefixed the name of the town with Cart-, the Punic for "city" as in Cart-hadasht, to give the Carthaginian version of the Iberian name. The readings of the manuscripts vary; Livy may in fact have written Cartalta or even Cartaltea.

Most scholars assume that the Olcades lived in the upper reaches of the modern Guadiana (so Kiepert, Weissenborn-Müller, and Walbank [cautiously] on Pol. III.14.5.) But since Hamilcar's conquests had been in the coastal areas of the south and south-east, and Hasdrubal had concentrated on developing New Carthage, there is a case for assuming, with Stephanus, that Hannibal's first campaign was in the coastal area north of New Carthage and Akra Leuke; there is an Altea 90 miles from New Carthage and not far from the Cape de la Nao. See Sumner, *HSCP* (1968), 216.

in parte magis: Livy is right to emphasise that little of the hinterland had been subdued by the Carthaginians; exploitation of coastal areas was their traditional colonising policy.

finitimis domitis gentibus: This interpretation, by which all the operations of 221-219 are visualised as the systematic subjugation of territory preliminary to the attack on Saguntum, reveals the tendentious nature of Livy's sources and exposes his geographical vagueness. The operations of 221-20 against Olcades, Vaccaei, Carpetani are a demonstration of Carthaginian power to ensure that her exploitation of southern and eastern areas can proceed safely. Saguntum is deliberately left in abeyance on Hamilcar's advice (Pol. III.14.10).

iungendoque, the best attested reading, and Gron.'s *vincendoque* are both open to the objection that neither action would "compel" Hannibal to go to war with Saguntum. Perhaps *iurgandoque* (cf. 6.1) should be read.

Book XXI

4. diripitque: Polybius mentions a tribute imposed, but no plundering.
in hiberna: for the winter of 221-220; cf. Pol. III.13.7.

5. stipendio praeterito: "arrears of pay"; I can find no parallel
for this curious phrase, perhaps a military expression.
in Vaccaeos: The region is revealed by the cities mentioned here
and in Polybius. Hermandica (Pol. Ἑλμαντική, Plut. *Mul. Virt.* 10
Σαλμαντική) is the modern Salamanca; Arbocala (Pol. Ἀρβουκάλη) is the
nearby Toro. See Schulten, *CAH* 7, 789. It should again be stressed
that the Carthaginians would never have thought of occupying territory
so far inland; the aim would be to terrorise and to exact tribute.

7. ab Hermandica: The use of *ab* with towns to express movement
recently undertaken is thoroughly Ciceronian (*Verr.* II.4.72, etc: Kühner-
Stegmann, 1.478), but Livy does not restrict its use in this way; *e.g.* 16.1,
19.6.

8. Carpetanos: Since Toletum (Toledo) is one of their towns (see
XXXIX.30.2) they dwelt in the eastern area of New Castile.
haud procul Tago: Always *procul a* in Cicero/Caesar; again the abbreviation reflects a natural development in language.

9. castrisque super ripam positis: Livy's battle-account is characteristically confused. Polybius makes it clear that Hannibal was attacked
after he had crossed south of the river. He retraces his steps and holds the
southern bank against the numerically superior enemy (III.14.5). But
according to Livy, he pitches camp on the *north* bank (for *super* meaning "on",
see XXVII.48.2, XXXII.30.4, XXXV.33.10, etc.), takes his army
secretly by night over to the south bank, raises a *vallum* (mysteriously,
because no camp is mentioned) and attacks the enemy as they cross.
Damsté's ingenious transposition of *castrisque positis* to after *traiecit* will not
do, because Livy's version of Hannibal's plan depends on the Spaniards'
not suspecting that he was going to cross. Witte (*RhM* [1910], 414)
contrasts the two accounts of Polybius and Livy—the one of the critical
historian, the other of the artistic narrator.
valloque ita praeducto: So Walters, but the manuscripts have *producto*,
which should have been retained. *Praeducto* would have been apposite
if Livy had been positing the defence of a camp on the southern bank.
producto ("extending the rampart in such a way as to allow . . .") can be
paralleled at XXXVII.40.7.

It is possible that Livy or his source mistranslated here. Polybius has
no mention of a *vallum*; he states that the river was used as a πρόβλημα.

Coelius or Livy may have misinterpreted his source (see Walbank on Pol. III.14.5).

11. appendicibus: This word is not used in the military sense before Livy, who favours it (IX.41.16, XXXIX.27.5).

centum milia: This number and that of the elephants are identical with Pol. III.14.5 and 8.

dimicaretur: In early Latin the imperfect subjunctive was the regular tense for past unreal conditions, and remains common in Cicero (Handford, § 139 f.). Woodcock (§ 199) implausibly suggests that the subjunctive here is one in *oratio obliqua*.

12. freti ... rati: The psychological explanation should be noted as characteristic. Livy uses ablative after *freti* here and at IX.35.3, but elsewhere the dative, which is found in no other author. See Kühner-Stegmann, 1.400.

sine ullius imperio: There is no trace of the phrase in Polybius; it is a moralising insertion to stress the importance of *disciplina*.

13. ex parte altera ripae: "on the other side of the river". For *ripa* in this sense of "course" or "waters" cf. 31.2n., Ovid, *Am.* II.17.31, Statius, *Silvae* II.3.17.

14. quippe ubi is equivalent to *quippe in quo:* ("since on the river bed . . .") not "since in that case" as at Lucr. I.617.

perverti: "brought down", a rare word perhaps adopted from Coelius, who uses it at fr. 11 Peter; cf. Plautus, *Stichus* 287.

corpore armisque: Ablatives of separation; "not having to bear the weight of their bodies and arms".

15. quidam in the sense of *nonnulli* is common in Livy; cf. 28.12, 33.7, 37.5, 52.5; Riemann, 188.

verticoso: The word (found only here in Livy; of the sea in Sall. *Hist.* IV.28 M.) dramatically exaggerates the force of the river current.

16. Postremi ...: Note how in this Livian period-sentence the end of the battle is economically combined with the winding-up of operations against the Carpetani. Livy has compressed all Hannibal's earlier operations into a single chapter before treating the Saguntum episode with dramatic detail.

in tanto pavore: The manuscripts have *tanto pavore*, and Heerwagen's *a tanto pavore* should be adopted as the common Livian idiom; see II.50.10 with Weissenborn-Müller's n. (Lewis and Short's citation of *e pavore animum recipere* is not authenticated by mss. readings.)

fugam fecit: 55.7 n.

Carpetanos quoque: As well as the Vaccaei.

Book XXI

Chapter 6.

1. nondum: That is, in autumn 220. Pol. III.15.3 states that the Carthaginians now returned to New Carthage, there being no further operations this year.

certamina serebantur: Between Saguntum and her neighbours. (This metaphorical use of *serere* is Ciceronian).

maxime Turdetanis: It is clear from the geographers (Strabo III.1.6 and 2.15, Ptolemy II.4.9ff.) that though Turdetani and Turduli were originally distinguished (e.g. by Polybius) they were neighbours both living in the region of Andalucia; by Livy's time they were not distinguished from each other (cf. XXXIV 17.1-4, 19.2, 20.2, clearly referring to operations in Hispania Ulterior). This passage and Appian, *Ib.* 10, putting Turdetani/Turduli close to Saguntum, are almost certainly in error.

2. quibus cum adesset: "But when the author of the dispute actually appeared before Saguntum". (Note the extension of the metaphor).

legati a Saguntinis: This sentence marks the beginning of the authorised Roman version of events at Saguntum—a version which falsifies the historical facts to mask Rome's failure to intervene effectively to save her ally, and which seeks to make Hannibal the transgressor responsible for the war. It is clear from Polybius III.15.1 that the Saguntines had sent repeated messages (συνεχῶς) to Rome in 220-219, and that the Romans ignored these appeals (πλεονάκις αὐτῶν παρακηκόοτες).

3. P. Cornelius Scipio et Ti. Sempronius Longus: These are the consuls for 218. Livy is himself not responsible for this tendentious omission of more than a year, and it would be difficult to attach this shameless lie to Coelius Antipater, a diligent and honest historian (see Badian, *Latin Historians* ed. Dorey, 16). It is much more probable that Valerius Antias is the culprit; Livy elsewhere castigates him for shameless fiction (XXVI.49.3, XXX.19.11). Livy regularly turns to Antias for details of the Roman scene, which Coelius does not report in such detail; this change of sources will be the cause of the chronological chaos which now ensues in Livy's account. The debate dated here to 218 actually took place in 220; a legation visited Hannibal at New Carthage before the attack on Saguntum began (Pol. III.17) early in 219.

de republica: "Brought a motion before the senate on the state of the nation". For the priority accorded to this over other business, see Ogilvie, 468-9 (with references to XXII.11.1, XXVI.10.2).

4. ab Saguntinis abstineret: The verb is usually transitive (*me abstineo*) but cf. Caesar, *B.G.* I.22.3; Cic. *Off.* III.72, etc.

5. omnium spe celerius: The actual date of the arrival of this new embassy from Saguntum must have been May-June 219, shortly after Hannibal's attack on the city began.

6. intenderant: "Had mentally consigned". Walters' suggestion that *intendebant* should perhaps be read is misguided; the pluperfect represents a pre-existing attitude of mind, and Livy is fond of combining pluperfects with perfects or imperfects in similar contexts (cf. VI.38.8, VII.25.10, etc.). The technique is not restricted to Livy; see Kühner-Stegmann, 1.139.

7. exspectandosque: Since the legates had not yet gone according to this Livian version, the sense here is that they should send and await the return of the legates.

8. P. Valerius Flaccus et Q. Baebius Tampilus: On the orthography (not Tamphilus) see Walters' n. Valerius was a senior senatorial (cos. 227) but his colleague is unknown. The inclusion of the names (not in Pol.) reflects the usefulness of the annalistic tradition for such prosopographical documentation.

Saguntum: The embassy may have called at Saguntum en route, but they met Hannibal at New Carthage when he returned from campaigning against the Vaccaei (Pol. III.15.3 ff.) in autumn 220.

absisteretur: Not found before Livy in this sense of *desistere*.

ad ducem ... deposcendum: This task was originally the work of the *fetiales*, but by this time had been taken over by senatorial legates. See Walbank, *JRS*, 1937, 192 ff., *CP*, 1949, 15.

7.1-15.6. Siege and capture of Saguntum; reactions at Rome and Carthage

Chapter 7.

1. iam: Frequently used at the beginning of an episode to plunge the reader *in medias res*. The geographical and ethnological explanation which follows is also characteristic of Livy's techniques of introducing important events; see *e.g.* XXXIII.32.

2. civitas longe opulentissima: The city stood on the site of the modern Sagunto, formerly Murviedro. It was an Iberian town as the evidence of the coins shows. (See Schulten, *CAH* 8, 309). Its wealth lay chiefly in agriculture; cf. Pol. III.17.3: χώραν ... πάμφορον καὶ διαφέρουσαν ἀρετῇ πάσης τῆς Ἰβηρίας.

Book XXI

ultra Hiberum: "south of the Ebro". Livy nowhere makes the error committed even by Polybius (III.30.3 with Walbank's n.) of placing the town north of the river.

passus mille ferme: Pol. III.17.2: ὡς ἑπτὰ στάδια.

oriundi a Zacyntho ... ab Ardea: These suggestions are wholly false, being based on false etymologies, but they were widely held (*e.g.* Pliny, *N.H.* XVI.21.6). The connexion with Zacynthus is prompted by the Greek name for the Saguntines, οἱ Ζακανθαῖοι; perhaps the Iberian name for the town, Arsescen (*CIL* 2.511 f.) was the cause of the link with Ardea. See De Sanctis III.1.417, n. 74.

3. maritimis fructibus: Maritime trade, not fishing. The harbour was small, but so were Phoenician (cothons). Commercial trade with Massilia, rather than with Carthage, was responsible for such prosperity (Schulten, *Phil. Woch.*, 1927, 1582).

disciplinae sanctitate: *Disciplina* is one of the necessary attributes for a healthy community, and Livy lays great stress on its importance; see my *Livy*, 70 f.

fidem socialem: *Fides*, the determination to uphold obligations and promises, is another necessary moral virtue; see my *Livy*, 67 ff. *socialem* illustrates Livy's tendency to use the adjective as variation for the possessive genitive; it is found, for example, with *foedus, coetus, bellum, equitatus.*

4. Hannibal infesto exercitu: The account of the siege, which begins here, is artistically divided into three parts. First come the initial attacks (7.4-9.2); next the citadel is partly captured (11.3-12.3); and finally the town falls (14.1-15.2). As entr'actes we have the arrival of the Roman mission (9.3 ff.) and the speech of the Spaniard Alorcus (12.4 ff.). Suspense is thus maintained without wearying the reader with a continuous narration of the siege.

Polybius' brief account follows the Carthaginian viewpoint and must go back to Silenus (III.17). Livy has almost certainly used both Coelius (also dependent on Carthaginian viewpoints) and Antias, who is presumably responsible for much of the conventional colouring lacking a factual substratum, as at 7.8 ff.

tripertito: A favourite word of Caesar, whom Livy studied to some advantage for his battle-narratives; see my *Livy*, 203.

5. in planiorem patentioremque quam cetera circa vallem vergens: Such alliterative effects occur frequently in character-sketches (4.2 n.), in archaic and poetic contexts (VI.22.7, etc.), in comment of a studied kind (*e.g.* ch. 1) and in dramatic narrative as here.

erat ... vergens: No more than a periphrasis of *vergebat*; cf. XXVII.26.7, XXVII.42.10, etc.

per quas: Since a series of sheds was joined to allow the manipulators of the ram to manoeuvre beneath them (see Vegetius, *De re mil.* 4.15), *per* could mean literally "through" here.

6. aequus agendis vineis: The gerundival dative of work contemplated dependent on an adjective is rare in prose before Livy, who (like Tacitus later) uses it frequently. See 47.1, XXII.28.6, XXIX.31.9, etc.; Woodcock, § 207. 4.

ad effectum operis: i.e., *ad opus efficiendum.* Cf. 57.6.

haudquaquam coeptis succedebat: "The attempt was far from successful." The impersonal use of this verb with the dative is not found earlier in prose but is common in Livy.

7. ceterae altitudinis emunitus: "built up beyond the height of the rest of the wall". Livy is fond of the abstract for the concrete, as at XXVII.18.9; see Riemann, 63 ff. *emunire* is not found before the Augustan period; for the sense here, cf. XXIV.21.12.

8. primo ... deinde: Clear chronological sequence is a regular feature of Livy's graphic narratives of military action; the use of the historic infinitives should also be noted.

micare: connoting not merely brightness but also rapid movement; see IV.37.10, VI.12.9, etc.

9. tumultuariis: "irregular", a word not found before Livy.

haud ferme plures: not "as a rule not more" but "scarcely more"; cf. XXVII.28.14.

10. femur ictus: This Greek accusative of the part affected after adjectives and participles appears in Sallust and in the *Bellum Africanum* (78.10: *pilo caput ictus*), but not in Cicero or Caesar. Caesar writes: *T. Balventio utrumque femur tragula traicitur* (*B.G.* V.35.6). But by Quintilian's time this accusative appeared even in the *acta* (IX.3.17). Kühner-Stegmann, 1.291; Woodcock, § 19.

Chapter 8.

1. dum curaretur: This is the regular classical usage here, but elsewhere in Livy *dum* is frequently followed by a subjunctive in a purely temporal sense (*e.g.*, I.40.7, II.47.5, X.18.1; Madvig's emendation of these passages is rightly censured by Riemann, 298 ff.)

operum ac munitionum: There is no distinction of meaning between the two; they also connote defensive works.

Book XXI

2. vineae agi: The stock Caesarean expression (*B.G.* II.12.3, etc.).

3. Poenus ... oppidani: Livy often seeks *variatio* by such a combination of singular and plural (8.8, 9.1, 45.1, 55.8, etc.), a technique frequently employed by Tacitus (Dräger, *Synt. u. Stil.*, 55).

ad centum ... quinquaginta milia: (*ad* is adverbial in such expressions in the sense of "approximately"; it is found with the nominative at X.17.8 and the ablative at Caes. *B.G.* II.33.5). The figures are blatantly excessive; more reasonable is the figure of 68,000 offered by Diodorus 25.17.

4. non sufficiebant: Madvig (*E.L.* 210) punctuates: *non sufficiebant itaque. iam feriebantur* ... on the grounds that the second sentence is not a consequence of the first. In fact the onslaught on the walls is a result of the paucity of the defenders; the change is wholly unnecessary.

5. continentibus ruinis: "with a line of fallen masonry". This concrete sense of *ruinae* is not in Caesar/Cicero, but frequent in Livy (8.7, 9.2, 10.10, 11.9, etc.). The singular *ruina* is likewise concrete in sense at 14.2, but at 8.6 it has the abstract sense of "fall". The more regular sense of the singular in Livy is "destruction" or "catastrophe"; see Packard's *Concordance* for examples.

deinceps (= ἐφεξῆς), "one after another", a favourite word of Caesar's.

cum fragore ingenti: For examples of *cum* and adjective together in such ablatives of accompaniment, see Cic. *N.D.* 2.97; Woodcock, § 46 ff.

prociderant: Not found before the Augustan period; cf. 14.2. The manuscripts have *prociderunt*, which should have been retained; the following sentence likewise combines pluperfect and perfect. *Prociderunt* and *procursum est* both express momentary action. See 6.6 n.

7. nihil: "not at all", a colloquialism; Kühner-Stegmann, 1.818.

tumultuariae: 7.9 n.

per occasionem ...: "When one or other seizes an opportunity"; cf. XXIV.3.17.

patenti campo: The locatival ablative with an adjective is found in Caesar (*B.G.* III.26.5), but Livy uses *campo* without an adjective at XXII.4.6, and similarly *templo* (XXXI.12.6), *carpento* (I.34.8), etc.

8. hinc spes, hinc desperatio: In this graphic description of the first stage of the conflict, with its striking picture of the two armies facing each other between the fallen wall and the first lines of houses, the psychological emphasis is characteristic. Livy is especially fond of it in descriptions of sieges, where the feelings of the besieged under pressures of continual danger and fear are sympathetically portrayed. See my *Livy*, 192 ff.

Poeno ... Saguntinis: 8.3 n.

adnitatur: The present subjunctive is fully Ciceronian, since the preceding *credente* is the equivalent of a historic present tense; contrast 10.3.

9. nullo inter arma corporaque telo: *arma* is "protective armour" here and at 8.11 below. The meaning is that every weapon found a mark. Cf. XXII.5.4. Translate: "since no weapon fell ineffectually, without striking armour or person".

10. phalarica: Festus (p. 78 Lindsay) claims that *fala*, a siege-platform, (from which *phalarica* is derived—a missile launched from a *fala*) comes from the Etruscan *faladum*, sky. But more probably the word is Iberian. As Livy describes it, it is basically a *pilum* specially adapted.

abiegno: Before Livy a poetic adjective only (found in Ennius, Plautus, Catullus, Ovid). For fir-wood used for spears, see Virgil, *Aen.* XI.667.

cetera tereti: The adverbial accusative after an adjective is not found in Cicero/Caesar. Sallust (*Jug.* 19.7, etc.) is fond of it. It is a clear imitation of the Greek construction, and related to the accusative of specification (*genus, secus,* etc.). See Riemann, 262; Kühner-Stegmann, 1.286.

sicut in pilo: to be taken with *quadratum* alone. Polybius (VI.23.10) describes the length of the shaft as about 3 cubits (5 ft.), and the iron head riveted half-way along the shaft was of the same length; hence overall it was about 7½ ft. long. See Daremberg-Saglio, IV. 1, 481 ff.

stuppa . . . pice: Tow smeared with pitch, the resin from fir or pine trees (Pliny, *N.H.* XXIII.24.47), was frequently used in such operations—*e.g.*, for firing ships at Caesar, *B.C.* III.101.

11. haesisset . . . penetrasset: Frequentative subjunctives; 4.4 n.

12. medium: accusative of part affected; 7.10 n.

mitteretur: In this confined space the *phalarica* was thrown by hand, not catapulted, before the flame took hold. Cf. XXXIV.14.11.

conceptumque: *ignis conceptus* is fire which has caught and is ablaze. At XXXVII.11.3 Rhodian and Coan ships escape by bearing in front of them *multum conceptum ignem* in iron receptacles, at which the enemy give way *terrore flammae micantis*. Translate:—"When the missile was ignited at the centre and thrown, it carried a flame fanned to a larger blaze by its very motion."

insequentes ictus: *i.e.,* from other missiles.

Chapter 9.

1. Saguntinis . . . Poenus: 8.3 n.

resisterent . . . vicisset: The subjunctives express the reasons for elation and dejection from the standpoint of Saguntines and Carthaginians.

Book XXI

quia non vicisset pro victo esset: The epigram is almost Tacitean. For this use of *pro*, compare Cic. *Sest.* 81.

2. repente: Livy frequently emphasises the suddenness of an action dictated by emotional pressures on combatants' minds; for such use of *repente* and *subito*, see 14.1, 33.2, 57.7, XXIII.26.8, XXXI.18.6, etc. The historic presents add to the effect here.

ruinas: 8.5 n.

fusum fugatumque: A cliché in battle-descriptions not only in Livy but also in Sallust and Cicero.

3. interim: 6.8 n. The legates had actually met Hannibal at New Carthage in late 220 before the siege began. This purely fictitious visit to Saguntum allows the Roman chauvinistic tradition to claim that Hannibal had contravened the *ius gentium* by refusing to parley with the Roman legates (cf. 10.6).

ab Roma: 5.7 n.

effrenatarum: A favourite metaphor of Cicero's; *Cat.* 1.25, *Tusc.* 3.11, etc.

operae: "worth his while", labelled dative by Roby, § 1283, but in fact an abbreviation of *operae pretium*. The full expression as used by Cicero/ Caesar is found at *Praef.* 1, a more formal context; elsewhere not only *operae* but also *pretium* is found alone in the same sense. For *operae*, see I.24.6, IV.8.3, etc.; and in general Ogilvie on V.15.6.

4. non admissos: Causal.

litteras . . . nuntiosque: "written and verbal instructions".

Chapter 10.

1. admissi auditique: Polybius III.15.12 states that after meeting Hannibal at New Carthage in late 220 the Roman legates continued to Carthage to make the same representations which had cut no ice with Hannibal. Since Livy's account of this debate at Carthage presumes the siege of Saguntum to be in progress, it follows that in substance it is fictitious. The content of this eloquent speech ascribed to Hanno is probably derived from the imagination of Valerius Antias (6.3 n.). Coelius, fr. 5 P. (*tantum bellum suscitare conari adversarios contra bellosum genus*) may indeed be derived from an account of this debate of late 220, but there is no evidence to show that Coelius mendaciously introduced the unhistorical content found in Livy's version.

vana atque inrita: The two adjectives intensify the sense; "absolutely fruitless".

2. foederis: This is the treaty of 241, by which each side had agreed to refrain from attacking the allies of the other.

NOTES

magno silentio ... non cum adsensu: The manuscripts do not have *non*, and since their import is the opposite of the sense required Lipsius supplied it. Livy however does not write *cum adsensu* with a following genitive; Madvig's emendation, *magis silentio ... quam adsensu*, is attractive.

3. arbitros ac testes: irritating *congeries*; cf. XXXVIII.51.7-11.
non manes conquiescere: For the poetic phrase, cf. III.58.11.
donec: = "while", rarely in prose before Livy; Woodcock, § 218.
quisquam: Livy like Cicero uses this pronoun chiefly but not exclusively in negative expressions. Cf. XXIV.31.8 and *Tusc.* 5.22.
supersit: Present subjunctive in *oratio obliqua* after a historic introductory verb; for such *repraesentatio*, see Handford, § 167; Kühner-Stegmann, 2.194. Livy's systematic procedure in this technique favoured by the historians (cf. Caes. *B.G.* I.34.2, etc.) is to use a secondary subjunctive in the same sentence as the introductory historic verb (so here *suscitarent*); but subsequently, whenever the words actually spoken have a corresponding tense of the subjunctive, he retains that tense. So *monui ne mitteretis* becomes *monuisse ne mitterent*; *donec superest* becomes *donec supersit*. The formulation is well set out in Conway's edition of Book 2, App. 2; but the rule is not wholly hard and fast.

4. iuvenem ...: The regular medium for speeches in the annalistic historians was *oratio obliqua* (see the remark of Pompeius Trogus at Iustin. XXXVIII.3.11), yet Antias certainly used *oratio recta* on occasion (see Gell. IV.11.4). In Livy's early books there is four times as much *oratio obliqua* as *oratio recta*, but more *oratio recta* later, under the influence of Polybius and the Greek convention. The mixture of *oratio obliqua* and *oratio recta* allows Livy to heighten the dramatic effect of the denunciation of Hannibal by breaking into *oratio recta* at this point. For the figures of metaphor (§ 4), antithesis (§ 5), interrogatio (§ 6), irony (§ 6), asyndeton (§ 6), exempla (§ 7), anaphora (§ 10), simile (§§ 9,11), congeries verborum (§ 11), see my *Livy*, 237 ff. The clausulae are Ciceronian; double-spondee at §§ 6, 10, 13; spondee/trochee at §§ 4, 6, 8, 11. On the role of Livian speeches in general, and on the techniques of composition, see *Livy*, ch. 9.
flagrantem ... materiam igni ... incendium: 3.6 n.
viamque unam ... vivat: An open condition in *oratio obliqua*, with *viam unam* standing in place of the apodosis (= *se id consecuturum . . .*) and *vivat* being subjunctive in *oratio obliqua*.
succinctus armis legionibusque: For the metaphor, cf. Cic. *Agr.* 2.87. The *legiones* are the Carthaginian military units described after Livy's regular fashion in Roman terms (cf. XXII.39.5).

Book XXI

5. ducibus iisdem dis: The sentiment is thoroughly Roman. The gods do not interfere in human affairs directly (cf. V.11.16, VI.18.9) but favour states which exhibit *iustitia* and *fides*. So Roman disasters are traditionally explained as the outcome of the abnegation of such virtues; *e.g.*, the Allia (V.36.6 ff.) and Caudium (IX.1.6 ff.). In such disasters the failure to follow *virtus* and to cooperate with Providence is visualised in a theological framework which is a synthesis of Roman religious tradition and Stoicism. See *AJP* (1958), 355 ff.

rupta foedera: In 272 when the Romans were besieging Tarentum, held by a lieutenant of Pyrrhus, a Carthaginian fleet entered the harbour but sailed out without an action (Livy *Per.* 14, Dio fr. 43.1, etc.). This incident has been inflated by earlier Roman historians into a contravention of a treaty. They sought to demonstrate Carthage's hostile intentions in 264. Quite apart from the fact that the Carthaginians did not land, it is improbable that any such approach was forbidden by a treaty-provision at this date; see Pol. III.26. And the lapse of eight years before the declaration of war shows how unimportant the incident was as a *casus belli*.

6. fortunam utriusque populi: The notion of a race's allotted fate under providential design is already in Cicero (*Cat.* 1.15) and Sallust (*Cat.* 41.3), but Livy and Virgil respond to the Augustan *Zeitgeist* by laying stronger emphasis on Rome's ineluctable destiny (II.40.13, III.7.1, VI.30.6, etc.) which dictates the fate of her enemies like the Hernici (VII.8.4), the Samnites (VIII.37.5), and the Carthaginians (XXVII.51.12).

bonus: For irony as a staple of Livy's speeches, see V.4.12, XXXII.21.8, etc.; Canter, *AJP* (1917), 125 ff.; Ullmann (3.6 n.).

ius gentium sustulit: For the *ius inter gentes*, cf. Pol. II.58.6: τοὺς κοινοὺς τῶν ἀνθρώπων νόμους. In international law the duties and privileges of ambassadors were closely governed. They were not allowed to bear arms (cf. V.36.6). Their persons and their right to deliver their instructions were sacrosanct.

res ex foedere repetuntur: Throughout his speech, Hanno is made to echo the Roman version of events in Spain. We have seen (2.7 n.) that there are no grounds for believing that the freedom of the Saguntines was safeguarded in the Ebro treaty; in any case the legates were at Carthage before the attack on Saguntum began, and no such demand for reparations was relevant to the situation.

publica fraus: consists in the acquiescence by the government in the illegal act of its representative. For *fraus* in this sense, cf. *Digest* I.3.29 f.;

publica fraus, cf. XXX.25.5. The emendation of Perizonius, *repetunt ut publica fraus absit*, should be adopted here.

7. Aegates insulas Erycemque: These rhetorical *exempla* recall the final operations of the First War off north-west Sicily and the last land-engagement at Mt Eryx (San Giuliano). Hamilcar Barca had seized the town lying between the summit and the foot in 244, and the Romans ended the war when Lutatius Catulus cut off Hamilcar's army (Pol. I.58 f.).

8. puer: Hannibal was now 27; cf. 1.4.
Tarento: 10.5 n.

9. di hominesque: So the manuscripts, rightly retained here. Madvig (*E.L.* 211), supported by Weissenborn-Müller and Conway, prefers *di homines*, "the gods prevailed over mortals". But the gods work through men (10.5 n.), and at V.49.5 there is a precise parallel, *iam deorum opes humanaque consilia rem Romanam adiuvabant.*

id de quo ambigebatur: *id*, which points forward to the *uter*-clause, is best regarded as a pronominal ("internal") accusative after *dedit.* "In the verbal dispute seeking to establish which people had broken the treaty, the outcome of the war conferred victory . . ."

unde: i.e., *a qua parte;* cf. XXV.15.13.

10. ruinae: 8.5 n.

11. in eo: "so far as he is concerned"; cf. Woodcock, § 52 n.2.
paternas inimicitias: 3.2 n.

furiam facemque: The bold alliterative phrase conveys a vivid image of the torch-bearing furies, symbols of the destructive power he wields. Cf. Cicero's description of Clodius at *Sest.* 33, and *Fam.* I.9.15.

12. id piaculum: The manuscript-reading *ad* should have been retained; cf. XLV.10.13 *ad piaculum noxae.* For *piaculum* in a personal sense, however, cf. X.28.13.

deposcit: Hanno has just stated (§ 6) that the Romans do so demand Hannibal; hence *deposcat, deposceret, depoposcerit* have all been proposed. The only possible defence of the manuscript reading is the assumption that Livy is thoroughly confused in face of his two irreconcilable versions—Coelius', containing no such demand, and Antias', continuing the fabrication begun at 6.8. But such an explanation rings hollow.

13. ego ita censeo: Walters' punctuation is perverse. The last or penultimate sentences of speeches in the *genus deliberativum* regularly commence in this way; cf. VI.18.14, XXII.60.27, XXXIV.4.20. Hence a full stop after *possit* (which is a potential subjunctive) and a semicolon after *dedant* are required.

Book XXI

Chapter 11.

1. nemini necesse fuit: Wölfflin complains that Livy has suppressed a speech expressing the Barcine viewpoint, as at App. *Ib.* 11 and Zon. 8.21. But in the later debate in ch. 18 Livy records only the anti-Roman sentiment in a speech which economically balances that of Hanno here.

adeo: "to such an extent"; a usage not in Cicero or Caesar but frequent in Livy (II.27.3, etc.).

Flaccum Valerium: The full name having been given earlier (6.8), the cognomen as regularly precedes the nomen for readier identification. See Weissenborn-Müller on XXVI.22.13.

2. vetustissimae societati: Allegedly dating from 509-8, the first treaty has been much disputed; see the bibliographical discussion of Walbank on Pol. III.22. The recent discoveries at Pyrgi (J. Heurgon, *JRS* 1966, 1 ff.) add credence to the traditional date.

praeponat: 10.3 n.

3. dum Romani ...: Note the skilful variation of tenses. Hannibal's preliminary operations are described with a string of perfects (§§ 3-4), Saguntine activities retrospectively with pluperfects (§ 5). The initial attack now made has a perfect (§ 6), the defenders' state of mind the imperfect (§ 6). The undermining of the wall has a historic present, but the gradual fall of the masonry an apposite imperfect (§§ 8-9). The main operations are recounted with a string of historic presents (§§ 10-12); but with the retirement of Hannibal the slackening of the dramatic pressure is indicated by reversion to perfect (§ 13).

Hannibal ... Saguntini ... ipse Hannibal ... et Saguntini: Note the architecture of the episode, constructed with that alternation of standpoint between attackers and defenders which is a common feature of Livy's periodic style. See McDonald, *JRS* (1957), 155 ff.

aliorum: in the sense of *ceterorum* is found in Cicero/Caesar (*B.G.* I.41.4, *Rep.* VI.18.18, etc.), but the colloquialism is much commoner in Livy; cf. 27.5 and 6, I.12.9, etc. and Riemann, 187.

ira ... stimulando: *in hostes stimulando* is usually regarded as explanatory, following closely on *ira* which is taken with *accendit*. But such parallels as I.22.2, *avita gloria animum stimulabat*, and XXX.11.3, *stimulabat aegrum amore uxor*, suggest that *animos* is governed by *stimulando* as well as by *accendit*; "Meanwhile, by rousing their minds with anger against the enemy and with hope of reward, he fired them".

4. pro contione: "In front of the crowd of soldiers".

5. novum murum ... reficerent: Tautologous.

NOTES

6. omnia ... streperent: Livy is fond of this neuter plural in dramatic descriptions (32.7, I.29.2, etc.), and the effect is heightened by the poetic verb (cf. Virg. *Aen.* VI.709; *strepit omnis murmure campus*).

7. turris mobilis: Brought up on wheels or rollers, it could in Caesar's time have as many as ten storeys or *tabulata* (*B.G.* VIII.41.5). Archers and slingers were posted on the upper tiers, and sappers below. See Kromayer-Veith, *Heerwesen und Kriegführung der Griechen und Römer*, 44.

8. muros defensoribus nudasset: This phrase, and *subruere murum* below, both appear in the same chapter of Caesar (*B.G.* II.6.2.)

occasionem ratus: A strange expression, but cf. VI.28.2.

cum dolabris: The pick-axe was a regular issue to some sections of the Roman infantry; Kromayer-Veith, 44.

caementa non calce durata: "rough stones not set fast with mortar". *durata* is nominative, though strictly it is the *calx* (mixed with sand, or *harenata*, Cato, *R.R.* 18.7) which hardens.

structurae: abstract, "as in the manner of primitive building".

9. caederetur: For the subjunctive, 4.4 n. The word is often used for demolishing walls because the mortar is chipped out.

11. tuendo: Participial in force; it is not by defending but whilst defending that their city daily becomes smaller. The usage occurs in Cicero (*Or.* 228, etc.: Riemann, 308) but much more commonly in Livy (II.32.4, etc.).

13. adfectos: "languishing", often of bodily ailments in Cicero.

Oretanos Carpetanosque: For the Carpetani, 5.8 n. The Oretani (Orissi, Oretes) dwelt further south around the Baetis and Anas, extending as far as Malaca (Strabo III.163; Walbank on Pol. III.33.9).

consternati: Not "dismayed" or "terrified" but "outraged", "roused to madness" (cf. 24.2; *B.G.* VII.30.4).

metum defectionis praebuissent: "Having caused Hannibal to fear revolt".

celeritate: Calling to the minds of first-century readers the *celeritas Caesaris*.

mota arma: 5.3 n.

Chapter 12.

1. Maharbale: He is later to be prominent as a cavalry commander in Italy; cf. 45.2 and XXII.6.11, on which see Walbank's note on Pol. III.84.14.

nec cives nec hostes: Livy almost invariably looks at sieges from the view-point of the besieged. Even the Romans are called *hostes* when they are the attackers; cf. V.21.12, XXXVI.23.6, etc.

3. Alconem Saguntinum et Alorcum Hispanum: The racial distinction is falsely made because of Livy's mistaken notion of the provenance of the Saguntines; 7.2 n.

4. precibus aliquid moturum: The accusative (*se*) is omitted with the future infinitive, as often (cf. 13.8, Cic. *Verr.* II.1.97, etc.). It is probable that this is a survival of the originally indeclinable neuter verbal noun in *-urum* (cf. Gell. 1.7; Woodcock, § 104).

ferebantur: "were being proposed".

mansit: The tense reflects the moment of decision.

sub condicionibus iis: A regular Livian expression; Cicero would have written *his condicionibus* (Kühnast, 367).

5. redderent res Turdetanis: Whatever the truth about Hannibal's machinations (6.1), this passage proves that the Saguntines had inflicted damage on their neighbours, on whom see 6.1 n.

cum singulis vestimentis: Contrast *binis* at 13.7. The explanations offered for the inconsistency smack of desperation; "Ober- und Unterkleid" (Weissenborn-Müller), one on and one carried (Franchi). Livy has absent-mindedly conflated the differing versions of his sources.

6. alia: This reading of the manuscripts is rightly retained; 11.3 n.

amicus atque hospes: 10.3 n., though *hospes* indicates that Alorcus is a regular visitor to Saguntum.

7. tradito palam telo: 10.6 n. *palam* suggests that he hands over his weapon to the Carthaginian guards (*hostium*, 12.1 n.) in the sight of the Saguntines.

praetorem: Used regularly by Livy to denote the chief magistrate of foreign nations; XXXI.24.6 (Athenians), XXIX.12.11, XXV.29.1, etc.

ipse: Alorcus.

8. senatus Alorco datus est: The procedural description in Roman terms for a Roman audience is characteristic of Livy.

talis: The word indicates a stylistic remodelling of the version of his source; see my *Livy*, 237. The speech is constructed according to the conventions of the deliberative genre (Quint. III.8.10 ff.):—

13.1-3: Exordium (*principium a nostra persona*): I come to lend assistance.

    4-8: Theme and tractatio. The peace proposed is necessary rather than just (*necessarium/iustum*).

      9: Conclusio. Compliance is preferable to extinction.

NOTES

Chapter 13.

1. si ... rettulisset: The hypothetical condition is a stock beginning. See 40.1, Cic. *Phil.* 14, *Pro Caelio*, etc.

sicut ... ad Hannibalem ... ita ... ab Hannibale: The Ciceronian antithesis is conspicuous throughout the speech.

supervacaneum: Note that the Ciceronian word is used in speeches (XXII.39.1, X.24.12) and *supervacuus* restricted to narrative (II.37.8).

2. ad vos veni: The identical clausula as in § 1, deliberately repeated to emphasise his sympathetic role.

3. vel ea fides sit: "This at any rate should guarantee ..."

4. postquam: Causal; rare in earlier prose (but cf. Cic. *Verr.* II.5.103) but frequent in Livy (III.60.4, V.10.11, etc.).

necessariam quam aequam: It is the job of the orator in a deliberative assembly to discuss an issue by laying down what is *honestum, utile, necessarium* (Quint. III.8.22, who prefers *possibile* to *necessarium* as the third category, argues from the case of the Saguntines that no course is ever absolutely necessary). The *aequum* is one facet of the *honestum* (Quint. III.8.26).

5. si non: The reading is clearly right; see Conway's Praefatio to XXI-XXV, 78. The sense would be clarified by substituting a comma for the semicolon after *audiatis*. "There is some hope of that peace if you give ear to it as conquered men ... and if you do not regard all deprivation as loss ..."

6. adsignaturus: 1.4 n.

7. corpora vestra coniugum ac liberorum: This section of the speech (§§ 6-7) is staccato in tone since it reproduces Hannibal's flat demands; hence *corpora* is not repeated before *coniugum*.

servat ... si velitis: *servat* contains the offer or guarantee of Hannibal, and *velitis* is subjunctive in *oratio obliqua*, since this is a condition of his offer.

ab Sagunto: 5.7 n.

8. omnium: neuter; cf. 11.12.

9. potius quam sinatis: The subjunctive is potential. There is implicit in the early development of such expressions a repudiating question with a potential subjunctive as reply; e.g. *rapine ... coniuges sinamus? omnia potius patienda sint.* See Handford, § 87.

Chapter 14.

1. ad haec: In this period-sentence, the basic structure of alternating participial phrases and subordinate clauses follows the pattern as in Caesar:

Book XXI

ad haec audienda cum/circumfusa paulatim multitudine/permixtum senatui esset populi concilium,/repente primores, secessione facta,/ priusquam responsum daretur,/ argentum aurumque omne ex publico privatoque in forum conlatum in ignem ad id raptim factum conicientes,/eodem plerique semet ipsi praecipitaverunt.

There is a slightly illogical shift of subject from *primores* to *plerique* here, caused by Livy's attempt to contain the whole dramatic incident in a single sentence. Cf. 5.16 n.

repente: 9.2 n.

primores: Not in prose before Livy (Kühnast, 337).

daretur: The classical construction; 8.1 n.

2. turris diu quassata: After a brief intervening sentence, the capture of the city is described in a second period-sentence which details the action of the Carthaginians. The whole of this final episode is thus economically presented in a carefully balanced structure.

None of this detail appears in Polybius, who is content with the bald statement that Hannibal captured the town after eight months' hardship and anxiety (III.17.9).

3. signo dato . . .: This *imperium crudele* is not in Polybius, and may well come from Antias as part of the "beastly Hannibal" portrayal. See 15.1 n.

4. domos ... concremaverunt: *concremare*, a favourite word of Livy's, is not found before the Augustan period. For similarly affecting descriptions of the citizens' *rabies* at the fall of a town, see XXVIII.23, XXXI.17; and in general Quintilian's remarks (VIII.3.67 ff.).

Chapter 15.

1. cum ingenti praeda: In other authors divergent versions appear. Polybius (following Silenus) omits mention of the massive destruction of their property by the Saguntines, and says that Hannibal obtained vast moneys, slaves, and property. Diodorus (25.15) records frenzied destruction and claims there was no booty. Livy combines two dissonant traditions; probably his account of the destruction of property is from Antias, that of the massive booty from Coelius or Polybius, to whose version this section (15.1-2) is very close.

2. supellectilem vestemque: Combined also at XXVI.21.8. *supellex* is always singular in Latin.

3. octavo mense: Livy now subjoins the correct chronology from Coelius or Polybius or both, making nonsense of his previous narrative. Livy's compositional method, the *exaedificatio* of a description on the basis of a single source, frequently leads to such contradictions. Though

146

subsequently he assumes that this second version is correct, he does not trouble to go back over his account to make corrections in the light of this realisation.

Though the exact months of the siege cannot be declared with certainty, it is reasonable to assume that Hannibal began it in early May (see Pol. III.17.1) and captured it in late December 219 or early January (§ 5; *principio anni*) 218. See Sumner, *PACA* (1966), 6 ff.

quinto deinde mense: The declaration of war was made by Rome in April 218 (and no earlier: see 18.1) and Hannibal may have awaited the result of the Roman embassy before leaving New Carthage. Hence the months are May to September.

ab Carthagine (New Carthage): 5.7 n.

4. fieri non potuit ut P. Cornelius, etc. Contradicting 6.3; the consuls of 219, when the attack began, were L. Aemilius Paullus and M. Livius Salinator. Cornelius Scipio, father of the great Africanus, is to play a prominent part in the Italian and Spanish campaigns until he is killed in 211; Sempronius Longus, a member of a prominent plebeian gens, retires into obscurity after his disastrous generalship at the Trebia.

alter ad Ticinum: Cornelius Scipio; cf. 46.3.

aliquanto post: 54.7 n.

5. principio anni: This is the truth, or something very near it.

6. excessisse: "cannot have been protracted into 217".

Arimini: 63.1-2.

creatus ... ad creandos: The technical expression for presiding at the election of the consuls is *creare* (Cic. *N.D. 2.*10).

16.1-19.5. Roman reactions; the declaration of war

Chapter 16.

1. sub idem fere tempus, etc. 16.1-6 is a superb example of Livy's psychological approach—his attempt to penetrate the facts of the historical situation in order to probe the attitudes and emotions of the participants. The dangers of such an approach are well illustrated here, since the Roman fear and panic are unhistorical (16.2 n.). The use of *oratio obliqua* to portray such attitudes is a technique worthy of study. See §§ 3-6.

One feels that the chronology is deliberately vague. In fact, since the ambassadors had visited Spain and Carthage in the winter of 220-19

Book XXI

(10.1 n.), they must have returned to Rome long before the attack on Saguntum began.

ab Carthagine: 5.7 n.

omnia hostilia: 11.6 n.

Sagunti excidium: Hannibal, *religione inductus*, spared the shrine of Diana (Pliny, *N.H.* XVI.216) and the city is not deserted in 217 (Livy XXII.22.4). Appian, *Ib.* 12 is wrong in his statement that it was colonised by the Carthaginians.

2. maeror ... misericordiaque ... et pudor: 8.8 n.

peremptorum: "slaughtered", used in this sense previously only in poetry.

de summa rerum: "The whole situation" (cf. 29.4) rather than "the situation of the state".

trepidarent magis quam consulerent: The exaggeration here is revealed by the actual decisions taken by the Senate (ch. 17), which are offensive in strategy. Pol. III.20.3 criticises those historians who describe the dejection of the Roman senate after the fall of Saguntum, and states that none of this is likely or true. Clearly therefore Livy is reproducing a version which goes back to Fabius Pictor, and the effect of sensationalist Hellenistic historiography on the Roman tradition is marked.

3. nam neque hostem: Note how, in this psychological portrayal of Roman apprehensions through oratio obliqua, the antithesis between Carthaginian preparation and Roman unreadiness is stylistically marked by balance of adjectives and length of clauses.

desidem: The word does not appear before Livy; Kühnast, 340.

4. Sardos Corsosque et Histros atque Illyrios: The varying copulatives indicate that Livy is closely associating the first pair and likewise the second pair; cf. VIII.10.4; *memores patriae parentumque et coniugum ac liberorum. -que* and *ac (atque)* are used to link the associated words to each other, whereas *et* is employed to combine the groups. See also IX.38.8; Kühner-Stegmann, 2.37 n.*b*.

Sardinia was annexed by Rome probably in 237 (see Walbank on Pol. I.88.8). In the following six years systematic attempts were made to reduce the natives not only of Sardinia but also of Corsica (where Aleria had been seized by L. Cornelius Scipio as early as 258). About 227 the islands became a Roman province, after which a new Sardinian revolt was repressed by 225. Rome's Adriatic operations were mounted with the intention of securing her rear in the event of a war with Carthage (Pol. III.16.1). Two expeditions were made against Istria in 221 and 220, and a force was sent into Illyria under the two consuls L. Aemilius Paullus and

NOTES

M. Livius Salinator in 219 "to censure and punish" Demetrius of Pharos for his anti-Roman policies. It is notable that the Romans embarked on this campaign in full knowledge of the attack on Saguntum; their apparent indifference to events in the Spanish theatre is to be explained by their desire to secure the position in the east before confronting the Carthaginians. This aim was achieved by the settlement in Illyria later in 219.

cum Gallis: Five small-scale expeditions against the Ligurians were mounted between 238 and 230, culminating in the adhesion of Pisa to the Roman confederacy. But the main Roman preoccupation was with the Boii, Insubres, and Gaesati, who banded together and invaded the territory of Etruria with 50,000 infantry and 20,000 cavalry in 225. The Romans suffered a heavy reverse near Faesulae (Pol. II.25.6) or Montepulciano (so De Sanctis and Walbank), losing 6,000 men. Later in the year two Roman armies converged on the Gauls who were defeated with 40,000 dead (so Pol. II.31.1, doubtless a greatly exaggerated tally). There were further campaigns against the Boii in 224 and the Insubres in 223-2, in the last of which Mediolanum (Milan) was captured. Livy plays down these large-scale engagements to emphasise the danger from Carthage, whereas according to Polybius they were "inferior to none in history in the madness and daring of the participants, in the battles fought, and in the numbers who engaged and died." (II.35.2).

tumultuatum verius quam belligeratum: The collateral active form of the deponent verb *tumultuari* is found earlier in Caesar in this impersonal passive (*B.G.* VII.61.3). *Belligerare*, an archaic and poetic verb not found elsewhere in Livy, is employed here to achieve an artistic syllabic balance with *tumultuatum*.

5. **trium et viginti annorum:** Since Hamilcar had landed in Spain in 237, there were only 19 years of operations *inter Hispanas gentes*. Livy has made a crude error by taking as his starting-point the end of the First War.

recentem ab: Like the English "fresh from", "immediately after"; cf. Cic. *N.D.* 3.11; Varro, *R. R.* II.8.2. It should of course be noted that there was no prospect of an invasion by Hannibal in January 218; only after the Roman declaration of war in April was Hannibal's final decision taken, and only in May did he cross the Ebro.

6. **conciturum ... cum orbe terrarum:** Livy's view is here utterly retrospective, attributing to the Romans fears of events of which they could have had no inkling.

Book XXI

Chapter 17.

1. nominatae iam antea, etc. This clear, concise account of Roman commands and legionary dispositions reflects one of Livy's greatest merits as historian. His regular year-by-year survey of appointments and troops allotted to the various theatres of war gives us a clear picture of that Senatorial strategy and detailed planning which was the primary cause of Rome's eventual victory. These details probably go back to the much-maligned Valerius Antias, and ultimately to the *annales maximi* and the *acta senatus*; see my *Livy*, 110 ff. The style aimed at in this chapter is plain and paratactic, as is apposite for such administrative detail.

nominatae ... provinciae: At this date the Senate decided which the consular provinces should be; cf. XXXII.8.1, XXXIII.25.4, etc. Livy has not here anachronistically anticipated the *lex Sempronia* of 123 (as Franchi claims). That law enacted that the provinces be named before the election of consuls (Sall. *Jug.* 27); in the present case the consuls are already in office from March 15, 218, and the Senate later named the provinces for which the consuls draw lots (*sortiri*).

cum Sicilia: 49.6 n.

2. sex decretae legiones: Hitherto the regular number had been four (Pol. III.107.10), but the emergency demands an increase—two for each consular province and two for N. Italy. Two are enrolled later in the year (26.2-3). By 214 there are 18 in service, and by 213 there are 23.

socium: Frequently but not invariably (see § 3) used by Livy as the genitive plural of the Latin allies, as at XXII.27.11. Previously the form is restricted to the poets; Neue, *Formenlehre*, 1.112 f.

ipsis: i.e., *consulibus*.

3. quattuor et viginti peditum: This would make the legionary complement 4000 infantry and 300 cavalry. Pol. VI.20.8 states that the normal complement was 4,200 infantry, increased in time of crisis to 5,000 (see XXII.36.3), and 300 cavalry. Elsewhere (III.107.10) he uses the rough figure of 4,000 and states that 200 was the cavalry complement.

sociorum, etc. Orders were sent by the consuls to the Italian cities, stipulating the number required. Under the normal requirement the allied infantry was equal in number to the Roman legionary infantry, but the cavalry requisitioned was three times as large as the Roman cavalry (Pol. VI.21.4, 26.7).

ducentae viginti quinqueremes: The fleet which won the battle off the Aegates islands in 241 had been only 200 strong (Pol. I.59.8)—not necessarily all quinqueremes, for the Greek word (πεντήρεις) is used loosely also for smaller ships.

celoces: "cutters", much used by pirates for their speed and ease of handling; cf. XXXVII.27.4 ff. The word appears in Ennius and Plautus as feminine; Livy makes it masculine like κελής.

4. vellent iuberent: The formula was *velitis iubeatis;* these jussive subjunctives become *vellent iuberent* after *latum.* Note however at I.46.1 Livy writes *vellent iuberentne.*

Livy retains the archaic phraseology of the comitial procedure (cf. *"bene ac feliciter eveniret"* below) to lend authentic flavour and atmosphere. The Senate before declaring war submitted such a resolution to the Comitia Centuriata. Here the impression given of the assembly is of a rubber stamp, but such resolutions were not always a formality; for example, in 200 the senatorial proposal for war against Macedon was rejected (XXXI.6.3-4). Once the decision was made, legates (replacing the original fetials) were dispatched to the enemy capital seeking restitution with the alternative of a declaration of war.

indici: For the distinction between the infinitive and *ut* with the subjunctive after *iubeo*, see Woodcock, § 141 (ii); Nisbet on Cic. *De domo*, 44. The *ut* construction is used when *iubeo* is used in the statutory sense of "ordain" as at *Verr.* 2.161; the infinitive is a more literary construction. See Ogilvie on I.46.1.

supplicatio ... adorati di: The *supplicatio* was an occasion of public prayer to invoke divine aid at a crisis or to offer thanksgiving for success. A procession led by the priestly colleges began from the temple of Apollo on the Campus Martius and proceeded to each of the major temples, where all prostrated themselves *(adorati di)* before the statues of the gods.

5. naves longae clx: So also Pol. III.41.2.

6. Sempronius: Livy here leaves the impression that Sempronius left for his province before war was declared. This is clearly improbable, and Polybius (III.41.2) who makes both consuls set out ὑπὸ τὴν ὡραίαν, at the beginning of summer, is to be followed.

ita: Going closely as at 13.5 with the *si* which follows; "only if"—a regular Ciceronian usage (Kühner-Stegmann, 2.387).

in Africam: According to Coelius (fr. 12 P.), Sempronius actually sent a swift vessel to reconnoitre suitable landing-places.

transmissurus: The unaccompanied future participle (rare in earlier prose; 1.4 n.) is frequently found in Livy in this type of conditional expression. Cf. VIII.17.10, IX.29.4; Riemann, 305.

7. L. Manlius praetor: This is L. Manlius Vulso, probably *praetor peregrinus* (Broughton, 1.240) who unsuccessfully contested the consulship for 216 (XXII.35.1). After the acquisition of Sardinia and probably in 227 the number of praetors had been raised from two to four. Two continued to exercise the judicial powers traditional to the office since its inauguration in 366; the other two were given provinces outside Rome.
et ipse: "Likewise with no mean force"—an expression rare in Cicero/Caesar (but cf. *B.G.* VII.66.6) but common in Livy. Riemann, 277.
in Galliam: As in § 9 below, this is Cisalpine Gaul, which Manlius had been allotted as his province; cf. Pol. III.40.11.

8. maxime ... deminutus: *Maxime* goes closely with *navium*, not with *Cornelio*. *deminutus* is a word often used by Caesar (*B.C.* III.2.3, etc.).
lx quinqueremes: So also Pol. III.41.2. This was sufficient to outnumber the Punic fleet in Spain which consisted of 57 vessels (Pol. III.33.14, the figure taken from the tablet at Lacinium). Roman intelligence on the Punic naval strength was obviously well-informed, presumably through Massilia; see Livy's parenthetical comment.
iusto equitatu: The "due complement" of cavalry for each legion was 300, since 1800 had been enrolled for the six legions.

9. duas legiones, etc. This is the force entrusted to Manlius Vulso; they were in Cisalpine Gaul not because the Romans envisaged it as a possible battlefield against the Carthaginians but to secure their northern frontier against the Gallic danger. See Pol. III.40.3 ff.

Chapter 18.

1. ut omnia iusta fierent: "so that protocol should be duly observed". In dealing with the overseas enemy Rome had to adjust the mechanism for the declaration of war. It has been argued that after the Senate's recommendation and the Assembly's approval, a conditional declaration of war was made; if the legates' reply was unsatisfactory, this declaration was then ratified. This was certainly the case in the second century (cf. Walbank on Pol. III.20.6; Sumner *PACA*, 1966, 17 is more doubtful).
legatos ... mittunt: The date is disputed; estimates vary between March and June, and no definite time can be established. See Walbank on Pol. III.41.2; Sumner (*PACA*, 1966, 21) persuasively argues for March, before the Comitia declared war. The number of legates was usually three, but on occasion was two, four, five, or ten (Walbank on Pol. VI.13.6).
Q. Fabium (*Cunctator*). Livy has probably erred here; it is more likely to have been M. Fabius Buteo, consul in 245 and censor 241. See Scullard, *Roman Politics,* 42.

M. Livium: This is Livius Salinator, who was to be one of the heroes at the Metaurus in 207 and censor in 204. He had been consul in 219, and in company with L. Aemilius Paullus he had an impeachment overhanging him for unfair apportionment of the booty accruing to him from the Illyrian campaign of 219. It must have been later in the year that he retired into exile.

L. Aemilium: Also consul in 219, he was acquitted on the charge on which Livius was condemned. Consul again in 216 (XXII.49), he was killed at Cannae.

C. Licinium: Probably Licinius Varus, consul in 236.

Q. Baebium: Baebius Tampilus, the only non-consular, selected since he had been on the previous embassy of 220-19 (6.8 n.). So at Sall. *Jug.* 21.4 the Romans first sent less imposing ambassadors to Africa before later bringing in more venerable figures (25.4).

3. ex Carthaginiensibus unus: Likewise anonymous at Pol. III.20.10: τὸν ἐπιτηδειότατον ἐξ αὐτῶν.

4. Praeceps vestra, etc. The central motif in this speech is the *iustum*, as is apposite. Hence after the *exordium* (*principium ab adversariis*, §§ 4-5), the *tractatio* concentrates on the injustice of Rome's demand (§§ 6-12), and the *conclusio* denounces the Roman attempt to put a fair face on their hidden motives.

praeceps: "importunate".

adhuc: "up to this point".

5. insimulabatur: The word is used because of its connotation of "charge falsely", as at IV.56.3, etc.

6. censeam: This subjunctive of "polite assertion" is in origin potential. See Woodcock, §§ 118-9; Handford, § 119, who stresses that the perfect subjunctive is much commoner than the present.

7. haec ... animadversio: Since *haec* points forward to the *quid* clause ("the investigation of what he has done"), *animadversio* probably means inquiry rather than chastisement. Such *congeries verborum* ("*quaestio atque animadversio*") is characteristic of the Livian speech; see my *Livy*, 236, and 10.1 above.

8. itaque: introduces the whole of the Carthaginian argument, the sense being: "We have only one subject for dispute; therefore let us examine it."

foedus a C. Lutatio ictum: In his account of this treaty negotiated by the plebeian Lutatius (consul in 242) in 241, Polybius (I.62.8 ff.) refers to no other ally except Hiero; though elsewhere (III.21.4, III.27.2 ff.) he does make the general statement that the allies of each side were to enjoy security.

necdum enim erant: As is mentioned at 2.7 n., the date of the Roman alliance made with Saguntum is unknown, but it probably preceded the Ebro treaty, and it may have been concluded by the Roman embassy of 231. The Carthaginian spokesman is here stressing that in 241 the Saguntines were not allies of Rome and could not have been cited in the treaty.

9. at enim: The stock rhetorical technique for anticipating the argument of an opponent (cf. *at, at hercle*), which lends the speaker an air of reasonableness. For a discussion of this *praesumptio* ($\pi\rho\delta\lambda\eta\psi\iota s$), see Quint. IX.2.16 ff.

quod cum Hasdrubale ictum est: The Ebro treaty; 2.7 n.

Saguntini excipiuntur: Livy's attribution of this admission to the Carthaginian spokesman reflects gullibility rather than dishonesty; 2.7 n.

10. icit: Scribes regularly write *iecit* in mistake for *icit*; see Madvig, *E.L.* 213 for examples. Alschefski's *fecit* is misguided.

negastis vos eo teneri: When Lutatius' proposed terms were heard at Rome, the Roman assembly sent ten commissioners who imposed more severe penalties (Pol. I.63.1-3). In this sense there was *"aliud de integro foedus"*.

11. nobis insciis: It is sufficiently attested that the Carthaginians never ratified the Ebro treaty (Pol. III.21.1).

13. utrum placet: *utrum* is used also in Cicero as an indefinite relative; cf. *Sest.* 92.

succlamatum est ... omnes responderunt: A more dramatic and incriminating version than that of Polybius, who states that the Carthaginian suffete told Fabius to shake from his toga whichever he wished, and that the majority ($\pi\lambda\epsilon\acute{\iota}ovs$) accepted war; nor does the last clause (*et ... gesturos*) appear in Polybius.

14. iterum sinu effuso: "loosening the fold to its former shape".

Chapter 19.

1. Haec derecta, etc. 19.1-5, a general comment on the illegality of the Carthaginian attack on Saguntum, is strikingly close to Pol. III.29. 6ff., which may well have inspired this footnote.

dignitate populi Romani: *dignitas* is the quality by which individual Romans, and the state as symbolised by its representatives, refuse to demean themselves either in contentious dispute, as here, or in public joking. See my *Livy*, 78.

cum ante: Presumably in the speech mentioned at 10.1.

Sagunto excisa: The feminine form Saguntus is not found elsewhere in Livy, and this is perhaps a strong argument that Polybius is the source here, for the town is feminine in Greek (Pol. III.30.3, etc.). This feminine is later frequent in the poets and appears also in Florus. See Neue, 1.947.

2. disceptationis: The genitive is descriptive.

si res esset ... comparandum erat: The imperfect subjunctive in past unreal conditions remains common up to the time of Livy, but is rarer thereafter; Woodcock, § 199. The indicative with a gerund in the apodosis of such conditions is of course regular; Woodcock, § 200.

3. diserte: "explicitly" as at XXXIV.59.2, but not earlier in prose; Kühnast, 349. Polybius uses ῥητῶς in the same sense (III.21.4, etc.).

ita ... si: "only if"; 17.6 n. Cf. Pol. III.29.3.

censuisset: In the technical language of Roman political procedure, this word is used for senatorial recommendations and *iubere* for the decree of the people, but Livy is using it non-technically here.

tot annorum: Actually only four or five; 226/5-221.

vivo eo: Often as ablative absolute; cf. Caes. *B.G.* VII.33.3.

4. priore: i.e., *foedere Lutati.*

exceptis: "were specifically excepted", *i.e.* from hostile operations. Cf. Pol. III.21.4.

nam neque additum erat: It will be seen that this is the crux of the whole argument. Thus the dispute centring on Saguntum arose over differing interpretations of the treaty of 241, the Carthaginians believing that the inscribed list of allies was exclusive, and the Romans considering that all allies present and future were inclusively inviolate. See Walbank on Pol. III.30.4. Livy's argument in § 5 is certainly a reasonable one.

5. ob nulla ... recipi: The sense is: "Who could have considered it fair that no people, however great their deserts, should be befriended ..."

amicitiam ... fidem: At Rome, in both private and public relationships, the stability of *amicitia* was ensured by the obligations of *fides. Recipere aliquem in fidem* is the guarantee of all the protection and help which the Roman state can afford, and it was precisely the failure to afford such protection which gave Romans a bad conscience about the failure to aid Saguntum. On the concepts, see Earl, *The Political Thought of Sallust,* 12 ff., 109 f.

tantum ne: "always provided that", a usage not found in prose before

Book XXI

Livy. Cicero writes *tantummodo ne* (*Att.* IX.10.4); *tantum ne* appears in Propertius and Ovid. Kühner-Stegmann, 2.448; Mikkola, 114 n. 2.

aut sollicitarentur . . . : So also Pol. III.29.9.

19.6-22.9. *Roman legates in Spain and Gaul; Hannibal prepares his Italian invasion*

6. legati Romani . . . : Polybius has no record of this tour of Spain and Gaul; his account (III.40.2) implies that the legates returned to Rome directly. The probable explanation is that they returned via Tarraco and Massilia, holding brief consultations with Spaniards and Gauls en route.

traiecerunt: This intransitive use is very rare in earlier prose, though Cicero, *Fin.* 4.22, has the accusative of the thing crossed. It is frequently used without an object in Livy; see 27.1, 7, 8, etc.

7. Bargusios: The sense of this vague comment appears to be that because the Bargusii who dwelt north of the Ebro (cf. 23.2 and Pol. III.35.2) received the Roman legates, other tribes south of the river were encouraged to revolt from Carthaginian dominion—perhaps through the influence of Bargusian infiltrators. The alternative explanation is that Livy has assigned the Bargusii to the area south of the Ebro, and that he envisages the Roman legates operating in enemy territory. Such a mistaken reading of the situation—the legates will have put in to Tarraco, and visited tribes in that area to incite resistance to possible invasion by the Carthaginians—is perhaps indicated by the *quia taedebat* clause, which goes more naturally with *benigne excepti* than with *erexerunt*.

novae fortunae: "condition" as at 13.8, 41.17, 45.6, but the phrase is almost equivalent to *novarum rerum*, revolution.

8. Volcianos: mentioned only here, but presumably dwelling north of the Ebro.

9. quae verecundia est, etc. This is an excellent illustration of the tendency of Roman historians to admit to their pages criticism of Roman policies, but to attribute such criticism to foreign spokesmen. So in Sallust the letter of Mithridates (at *Hist.* IV, fr. 69 M) is a bitter attack on Roman *perfidia* composed by Sallust himself; see F. Bikerman, *REG* (1946), 131 ff. In Livy we can compare the condemnation by the Samnites at X.16.4 ff., and by the Capuan Vibius Virrius at XXVI.13.4 ff.

[Saguntini]: Madvig (*EL* 212) quotes a similar example from Cic. *Verr.* 1.53 in support of the exclusion of this word as an interpolation.

perdidit: All the manuscripts read *prodidit*, but confusion between *pro* and *per* is the most regular cause of corrupt readings; see Conway's

NOTES

Praefatio to the *O.C.T* of XXI-XXV, § 78.   For the *adnominatio, perdidit/prodideritis,* see 4.3 and 24.4.

10 quaeratis: The paratactic jussive (cf. Handford, § 49) is especially common after *censeo*; examples in Kühner-Stegmann, 2.228.

sicut ... ita: "as conspicuous as it is mournful".

documentum ... ne: For the construction, "a warning not to ..." compare VII.6.11; Plautus, *Captivi* 752 f.

11. in Galliam transeunt: Dio fr. 56 specifies the Narbonenses, but Conway's suggestion to add *Narbonensesque adeunt* to Livy's text hardly makes the legates' movements clearer.

Chapter 20.

1. armati: Caesar describes (*B.G.* V.56) how a Gallic war-council meets in arms; so also the Germans, according to Tac. *Germ.* 11.

2. cum verbis extollentes: The shift in subject to the Roman legates would have been indicated by *illi* in Caesar/Cicero.

3. sedaretur: Regularly with an abstract object in Cicero; *iuventutem sedare* for *animos iuventutis sedare* is a natural development of language through colloquialism.

4. adeo: 11.1 n.

censere: The infinitive is here substantival, and the complement after *visa est.* The use of the infinitives *avertere* and *obicere* is not so common as the gerundival expression *id avertendum esse* after *censere,* but such simple infinitives are found, as at Cic. *Phil.* V.10, Livy XXVI.32.2, etc.

5. neque ... in se meritum: "Had shown no deserving kindness towards them"; *se* is accusative.

sumant: 8.8 n.   "Conway's Law" (10.3 n.) is not observed here.

6. contra ea: "On the contrary".   This adverbial phrase is a common variation for the simple *contra* in Livy; cf. II.60.1, III.57.1, XLI.24.8.

agro finibusque pelli: See Pol. II.25-35, III.40.   The reference is to the Roman colonisation of Placentia and Cremona (below, 25.2) planned in 219 (*epit.* 20) and carried out in 218 (Asconius, *In Pis.*).

stipendiumque pendere: A phrase common in Caesar.   The *stipendium* was payment in money as distinct from *vectigal,* payment in kind; the first was more humiliating.

cetera indigna: The requisitioning of manpower and supplies is doubtless meant.

7. pacatumve: "nor friendly word"; as at VIII.34.9 the contrast is with *hosticum.*   Cf. 26.6; Sen. *N.Q.*VI.7.1.

Book XXI

Massiliam: On its foundation and reinforcement about 600 and 540 from Phocaea, see the references in Ogilvie on Livy V.34.8.

8. ab sociis: The Roman alliance with Massilia, like that with Carthage, was of great antiquity, and was believed by the ancients to go back to the regal period; cf. Strabo IV.179 f.; Iustin. XLIII.3.4.

cum cura ac fide: to be taken with the preceding participle, not with *cognita*.

praeoccupatos iam ante: (For the pleonasm compare 32.7, *prius . . . praecepta*). Pol. III.34.4-6 states that Hannibal had sent messengers to the Celtic chiefs, and that they returned with promises of help.

ferocia: The Gauls are regularly characterised in Livy as *"gens efferata"*. See V.44.6, VIII.14.9, X.10.12, etc.

subinde: "From time to time". Even in its primary sense of "immediately after", *subinde* is not found in earlier prose (Kühnast, 357). It is frequently found in Livy in this secondary sense, as at VII.10.10, XXXV.21.9.

auro: Cf. Hannibal's promise at Pol. III.34.4: πᾶν ὑπισχνεῖτο . . .

concilientur: 10.3 n.

9. haud ita multo post quam: In Polybius' version (III.40.2) the embassy returns direct from Carthage and arrives before the departure of the consuls. Livy may have assumed that the tour of Spain and Gaul, the scope of which he exaggerates (19.6-7 nn.), would make such an early return impossible. He believes that the embassy had not left Rome till after the declaration of war, and he has already implied (17.6) that Sempronius left for his command earlier. The whole chronology is of course hopelessly entangled, and Livy's clear annalistic order covers a multitude of difficulties; see Introduction, p. 32.

in exspectationem: The reading of MDA is *in exspectatione*. Heerwagen's *exspectatione* is probably the correct reading, since the phrase *exspectatione erigi* is found at II.54.8, III.47.1, XXXVII.1.9.

satis constante fama: Note that Livy does not say that the legates brought back the news that Hannibal had crossed the Ebro. This would have dated their return to late May at the earliest. Since Pol. III.40.2 implicitly suggests (*pace* Walbank) that they made their report from Carthage before the news of the crossing of the Ebro, one may legitimately be sceptical of this suggestion that Rome was already buzzing with the news when they returned.

Chapter 21.

1. Hannibal: Livy now returns to the description of Hannibal's operations. Klotz suggests that Coelius is the source throughout the previous section and in the next four chapters, and that Coelius draws his information earlier from Fabius Pictor but henceforward from Silenus. I incline to the view that 19.6-20.9 has been taken from Antias, and that here Livy reverts to Coelius. At any rate, in these four chapters (21-24) we have a detailed description from the Carthaginian viewpoint, ultimately stemming from the account of Silenus.

in hiberna concesserat: The date is January 218, and Livy now tacitly assumes that the Polybian chronology (see 15.3 and 6) is correct; if Coelius is indeed the source here, we may assume that he too had the correct chronology, and that Livy has earlier been misled by Valerius Antias. This is preferable to Klotz's inference that Coelius included first the tendentious chronology of Fabius Pictor and then the correct version of Silenus.

auditis quae Romae acta decretaque forent: This is not in Pol. III.34.6, but is not impossible, since Carthaginian traders still had free access to Rome.

2. partitis divenditisque: "having divided out or sold piecemeal . . ." *partitus* in its passive sense is frequent in Caesar; *divendere*, used to establish the precise sense of small-scale selling, is rare but Ciceronian (*Agr.* 1.7).

reliquiis praedae: See 15.1-2.

nihil: i.e., *haud*; 8.7 n.

3. credo ego vos: For the exordium-formula, cf. Cicero, *Pro Sex. Roscio.*

pacatis: "made friendly", "won over"; 20.7 n. The statement is an exaggeration, as is proved by the rapidity with which Spain changes hands later in the war.

4. ita: 17.6 n.

5. ab domo: The Ciceronian usage, no motion being implied (Riemann, 274, n. 3).

instet: "is at hand", as often in Cicero (*Pis.* 65, etc.)

invisere: The frequency of this verb in Comedy and in Cicero's letters points to a colloquial flavour; "take a trip to . . .".

commeatum: "leave", *i.e.*, military furlough. *"commeare, ultro citro ire; unde commeatus dari dicitur, id est tempus quo ire redire quis posset."* (Festus).

6. dis bene iuvantibus: 4.9 n.

incipiamus: The verb is often found with an accusative in Livy (VII.34.13, XXVI.37.9, etc.), but only once in Cicero (*Planc.* 48, where *facere* can be supplied) and once passively in Caesar (*B.G.* VII.17.6; *inceptam oppugnationem*).

Book XXI

8. exhaustos ... aut mox exhauriendos: In Cicero the verb means "to drain out" and, thus, "to bring to an end"; the sense of "endure" is Augustan, being used by Virgil with *poenas, pericula, bella* (*Aen.* IV.14, IX.356, X.57). *Laborem exhaurire* is a favourite phrase of Livy's; cf. 30.9 below, XXV.31.7, XXVI.31.7. The gerundive is of course used in the absence of a future participle passive in Latin.

9. Hannibal: For what follows, compare Pol. III.33.5 ff.

Gades: In ancient times Cadiz lay at the north end of a narrow island which has since become joined to the mainland. It was the earliest Phoenician foundation in the west, being colonised from Tyre allegedly in the twelfth century. But no archaeological evidence antedating the seventh century has been found because the site has been occupied continuously since ancient times. Archaeologists doubt whether the foundation can be earlier than the ninth century (cf. Harden, *The Phoenicians*, 64; Warmington, *Carthage*, 25 ff.). Strabo III.5.3 ff. describes the ancient site.

Herculi vota exsolvit: With the Phoenicians' tendency towards syncretism their deity Melqart ("Ruler of the city") was equated with Herakles. Silius Italicus, a Spaniard, describes (3.17 ff.) how the cult was still observed at Gades in the first century A.D. The temple was at the southern end of the island on which Gades then stood; now the site of the temple has been cut off by the sea, and is known as the Isla de sancti Petri (Harden, 42).

Polybius has no mention of this visit to Gades, but we may assume that Livy's evidence goes back to Silenus and is further evidence of that religious attitude of Hannibal mentioned at 4.9 n.

prospera: Madvig's *prospere* should have been adopted. Note that the reading of M is *prospere venissent*. At XXIII.27.12 we find *cui si omnia prospere evenirent*. Cf. V.51.5, where all the manuscripts read *prospere*: XXII.28.13: XXIX.30.7: XLII.49.7. There is no certain use of *prospera* in any such Livian context.

10. partiens curas: Polybius praises Hannibal's strategy here; III.33.8: πανὺ δ' ἐμπείρως καὶ φρονίμως ἐκλογιζόμενος ...

11. pro eo: "As a substitute for this force".

iaculatorum levium armis: It is tempting to posit *levium armis* as a gloss, but the word *iaculator* does not appear before Horace (*Carm.* III.4.56); Caesar uses *funditores* and *sagittarii*. Thus Livy may have felt the necessity for an explanatory phrase. This general description of the troops brought to Spain from Africa is made more specific in the next chapter (22.2-3).

velut mutuis pigneribus obligati: So Pol. III.33.8: ἐκδεσμεύων τὴν ἑκατέρων πίστιν εἰς ἀλλήλους ...

12. **Tredecim milia,** etc. These figures all echo Pol. III.33.10 ff., where there is additional detail of the provenance of these Spanish troops.

caetratos: Since the *caetra*, the light shield, was believed to be of Spanish origin (cf. Lucan VII.232: *illic pugnaces commovit Iberia caetras*, and Caesar, *B.C.* I.39.1, 48.7) Livy is here using the expression for Spanish targeteers.

funditores Baleares: from the Balearic islands, the modern Ibiza, Mallorca, and Minorca. As Polybius explains (see III.33.11 with Walbank's note) Baleares in Iberian meant "slingers", and was extended to the people of these islands as a proper name. It is not derived from βάλλω as Diodorus 5.17.1 suggests.

equites mixtos ex multis gentibus: Livy or Coelius has in all probability misread the source here. It is not just the cavalry but also the infantry which is drawn from many races (see Pol. III.33.9 f.).

13. **partim distribui per Africam:** Livy's vague phrase (cf. Pol.'s εἰς τὰ Μεταγώνια τῆς Λιβύης) conceals the difficulty of identifying Metagonia, which probably comprised the towns around Cape Bougaroun rather than those around the Moulouya much further west. The Cape Bougaroun area would naturally have more to fear from a Sicilian invasion than would the area further west.

conquisitoribus in civitates missis: Livy should have made it clearer that he means African townships; they were in fact the Metagonian towns mentioned in the note above (cf. Pol. III.33.13).

delectae iuventutis: Not in Polybius, who does however record that they were to be *praesidium . . . et obsides*, and perhaps Livy has inferred that they were *delecta* because they were chosen as *obsides*.

Chapter 22.

1. **atque id:** The phrase is found in Cicero (cf. *Att.* V.12.1) but the commoner formula is *et id quidem* (cf. *N.D.* 2.18, *Cato M.* 75).

circumitam ab Romanis: Cf. 19.6 ff. with notes.

2. **viro impigro:** Note this characterising addition for the first mention of the brother of Hannibal; the phrase is not in Polybius.

firmatque eum: Walters explains *eum* with "i.e., *auctoritatem eius*", but the fact remains that *firmare* never has a personal object in Livy. *cum* is impossible for the reason that he always renders the thing supplied in the simple ablative. The alternatives are to exclude *eum* with Wölfflin, or to read *eam* with CM², which I prefer.

peditum Afrorum, etc. The numbers which follow are identical in the Livian manuscripts with Polybius' version except in three respects. 1.

quingentis has to be supplied with *Baliaribus*; a number has clearly dropped out and D has been presumably lost because of the following *ad*. 2. *quinquaginta* has to be inserted after *quadringenti* (L may have fallen out before *et*), and Livy has simplified Polybius' description of "Libyo-Phoenician and Libyan" cavalry by omitting the Libyan; this is an unfortunate simplification, because the distinction is between those cavalry raised in or near Carthaginian territory, and those from Numidian tribes further west. 3. In Livy the band of Ilergetes is 200 strong, in Polybius 300. It is quite feasible that Livy has turned to Polybius for these numbers; no less than 28 items are identical. I agree with E. Von Stern, *Das Hannibalische Truppenverzeichnis bei Livius* (Berlin, 1891), that *trecenti* should be read here. It is certainly illogical to emend *quadringenti* to *quadringenti quinquaginta* in 2 above, and not to emend also here.

Liguribus: Rome had attempted to crush the Ligures in north-west Italy between 238 and 230, but they were not finally reduced till 150 B.C. Ligurian mercenaries had fought for Carthage as early as the first Punic War. See Pol. I.17.4, 67.7.

3. Numidae Maurique accolae Oceani: A simpler version than the Polybian account, which gives four different tribes; Livy uses the conventional expression Numidae for the peoples between Carthaginian territory and the river Moulouya. The "Moors bordering on the Atlantic" inhabited the modern Morocco. It is perhaps significant that Coelius (*HRR* 55) calls them Maurusii; Livy's Mauri may indicate that he follows Polybius in this section.

ad: Adverbial; 8.3 n.

parva Ilergetum manus: Livy's account is much tidier than Polybius', which places this Spanish force in the middle of the African contingents. The Ilergetes are located in the Saragossa-Lerida area, east of the Ebro.

4. vicerant: Cicero and Caesar would have written *vicissent*, since the clause is in *oratio obliqua*. There are many examples of indicatives in such subordinate clauses in Livy (cf. II.15.3, III.2.3, etc.), this being one of the decisive shifts from the canons of Ciceronian syntax. The evolution is natural with such phrases as *credi poterat*, which amount to little more than *fortasse* or *sine dubio*.

aptae: For the more frequent *aptatae*; cf. XXX.10.3.

5. ab Gadibus: (For *ab*, 5.7 n.). Livy leads us to assume that the complex administrative decisions just recounted were taken at Gades, which is nonsense. Hannibal must have returned to New Carthage to make these arrangements, and *redierat* here would have expressed the chronological sequence better.

NOTES

Onussam: The site is uncertain, but the town is clearly on the coast (*maritima ora*), probably in the vicinity of Valencia. Cf. XXII.20.4.

6. ibi fama est: This account of Hannibal's famous dream has survived also in Cicero, who recounts the version of Silenus as tendered by Coelius (*Div.* 1.49). It is possible therefore to examine Livy's handling of the passage against the source which he followed. Here is Cicero's reproduction of Coelius: *Hannibalem ... visum esse in somnis a Iove in deorum concilium vocari; quo cum venisset, Iovem imperavisse ut Italiae bellum inferret, ducemque ei unum e concilio datum, quo illum utentem cum exercitu progredi coepisse: tum ei ducem illum praecepisse ne respiceret: illum autem id diutius facere non potuisse elatumque cupiditate respexisse: tum visam beluam vastam et immanem circumplicatam serpentibus quacumque incederet omnia arbusta virgulta tecta pervertere; et cum admiratum quaesisse de deo quodnam illud esset tale monstrum, et deum respondisse vastitatem esse Italiae, praecepisseque ut pergeret protinus, quid retro atque a tergo fieret ne laboraret.*

It is instructive to examine Livy's artistic simplification of this dream. In his version Hannibal is not invited to the gods' council, nor does Jupiter bid him invade Italy; instead a *iuvenis divina specie* appears *claiming* to be Jupiter's envoy. Thus the religious justification for Hannibal's departure is undercut. The psychological facet is next emphasised in Livy's typical manner—"*pavidum primo ... deinde cura ingenii humani ...*". When Hannibal looks round he sees not "a monstrous beast girt by snakes" but "*serpentem mira magnitudine*", and it destroys only bushes and shrubs, since "*tecta*" are an anomaly in such a scene. The dramatic effect is intensified by the attendance of a storm-cloud (*cum fragore caeli nimbum*). And the final words of the divine guide's reply, "*sineretque fata in occulto esse*", were not in the source; Livy has introduced here a note of dramatic irony.

Based on Livy's account are Val. Max. I.7: Sil. Ital. III.168-214. Cf. Zon. 8.22 (not from Livy). See Meyer, *Kl. Schrift.* 2.368; Peter, *HRR* 1.160.

ab Iove: For the syncretism (Jupiter is Baal Hammon) see 21.9 n.

diceret ducem: Livy favours the alliterative order in such artistically modulated passages as this (cf. *pavidum primo ... post sese serpentem mira magnitudine ... pergeret porro*) and ch. 1: *professi plerique ... primo Punico ... victoribus victi*, etc.

7. cura: "curiosity" as at XLII.39.3: *cura insita mortalibus videndi nobilem regem*. Note that in the Ciceronian version *cupiditas* is used; Cicero elsewhere uses *curiositas* (*Att.* II.12.2).

temperare oculis: Cicero/Caesar have only the reflexive as dative after this verb (Kühner-Stegmann, l. 340). Plautus has *temperare linguae*, and Livy uses the dative frequently of parts of the body (examples in Kühner-Stegmann).

9. moles: "massive bulk", a poetic use in Latin before Livy; cf. VII.10.9: *Gallus velut moles superne imminens . . .*

quidve prodigii: "What by way of portent?" Cf. *quid negotii, quid praemii*, etc., and Woodcock, § 77.

pergeret ire: A Ciceronian phrase; cf. *Ac.* 1.1, etc.

fata: "The divine will", *i.e.* the utterances of the gods made through oracles, dreams, prodigies; see Otto, *RE* 6.2048.

23.1-24.5. Hannibal crosses the Ebro and Pyrenees

Chapter 23.

1. visu: "apparition"; cf. VIII.9.10, etc.

tripertito: 7.4 n.

Hiberum copias traiecit: So also with two accusatives often in Caesar (*B.C.* I.55.1, 83.5, etc.); likewise the use of *traducere* with two accusatives in the next sentence (*B.G.* I.12.2).

praemissis qui ... conciliarent: Livy appears to have forgotten that at 20.8 he has already mentioned Hannibal's conciliation of the Gallic tribes in the previous year (cf. Pol. III.34). It is highly unlikely that he would have left these strategic details to the last moment, but this passage may refer to a second and confirmatory reconnaissance.

transitus: The concrete sense of "passes" is not found earlier in prose (Riemann, 70).

nonaginta milia, etc. These numbers, consistent with Polybius' figures (III.35.10), are certainly exaggerated. 10,000 infantry and 1,000 cavalry are entrusted to Hanno, and 10,000 desert or are sent home. Polybius says that 50,000 infantry and 9,000 horse reached the Pyrenees; this would mean that 20,000 infantry and 2,000 cavalry were lost in these preliminary Spanish operations. This is so incredible a figure that Livy does not set down the Polybian assessment of the numbers who crossed the Pyrenees.

2. Ilergetes inde: This list differs from Polybius', revealing Livy's use of a different source (Coelius). Both historians mention Ilergetes and Bargusii, but Polybius then adds: ἔτι δὲ τοὺς Αἰρηνοσίους καὶ τοὺς Ἀνδοσίνους μέχρι τῆς προσαγορευομένης Πυρήνης.

NOTES

These two tribes are virtually unknown (see Walbank's note), whereas the Ausetani mentioned by Livy are known to have lived in the vicinity of Vich (*vicus Ausetanorum, CIL* 2.1181). The Ausetani are combined with the Lacetani again at 61.8; Livy's claim that Lacetania is at the foot of the Pyrenees suggests a site north of Saragossa (so Weissenborn-Müller), but at 61.8 the two tribes are located *"prope Hiberum"*.

oraeque huic omni: The eastern strip between the Ebro and the Pyrenees. Pol. III.35.4 adds that the Bargusii, being friendly to Rome, were Hannibal's chief source of anxiety.

Hannonem: He is captured later in the year by Gnaeus Scipio (see 60.7 and Pol III.76.6); nothing further is known of him.

3. decem milia peditum ... mille equites: So also Pol. III.35.5, who adds that Hannibal also left with Hanno τὰς ἀποσκευάς—a generous Hellenistic term embracing wives, concubines, slaves, and other possessions (Holleaux, *REG*, 1926, 355 ff.).

obtinendae regionis: This gerundival genitive of purpose (cf. XXXVI. 27.2: *pacis petendae oratores miserunt*) is especially common in Sallust and Tacitus, and may reflect the influence of τοῦ with the infinitive, so common in Thucydides. See Woodcock, § 207.4 n. 2; Kühner-Stegmann, 1.740.

4. per Pyrenaeum saltum: Neither Polybius nor Livy indicates the route, both apparently assuming that the pass was that over which the Roman road went by Junicaria (Junquera). Mela (2.89) speaks of the *scalae Hannibalis* in connection with this route.

tria milia ... Carpetanorum: This detail of the defection of 3,000 Spanish troops is not found in Polybius, who merely says that Hannibal sent 10,000 troops home to win benevolence and the expectation of the safe return of the others (35.6). Livy's statement rings much truer, that 3,000 deserted and that 7,000 others chafing under military discipline were sent home, so that Hannibal could pretend to have authorised the departure of all of them. Again a source other than Polybius is indicated.

5. anceps: "hazardous"; this secondary sense, a natural extension of the word's meaning, is not found before Ovid and Livy.

6. et ipse: *ipse* has good manuscript support, but Walters' explanation ("Hannibal himself, as well as those he sent away") does not convince. Mureius' *ipsos* ("as well as the Carpetani") makes good sense but is palaeographically improbable; Unger's *ipsa* is the probable reading—the 7,000 were oppressed not only by the prospect of the journey but also by army-life itself.

Book XXI

Chapter 24.

1. Pyrenaeum: The singular form appears again in § 2 and XXIII.45. 3; cf. Pliny *N.H.* III.34.18. Perhaps *saltum* is to be understood; cf. 23.4.

Iliberrim: Note that Polybius has no mention of the town; Livy's account is fuller here. The site is that of the modern Elne. Though the manuscripts favour *Iliberri*, claimed by Weissenborn-Müller to be indeclinable here, the accusative form *Iliberrim* is the more probable reading because it is found in § 3 and §5 below.

2. consternati: 11.13 n.

Ruscinonem: Tour de Rousillon, close to the modern Perpignan, is about ten miles north of Elne and can reasonably be regarded as the site of Ruscino.

3. et vel illi: Walters' suggestion that *et* has the sense of *et orabat* can hardly be taken seriously. Madvig (*E.L.* 213) proposes that the oratio recta would be *colloqui vobiscum volo; vel vos propius accedite vel ego procedam* or perhaps . . . *itaque vel vos*, etc. There is a strong case for reading *ita vel illi* . . . in view of the following *ut*.

4. hospitem non hostem: 4.3 n.

liceat . . . venisset: The tenses again, as at 20.5, fail to adhere to "Conway's Law", according to which we should expect *venerit*.

5. cum bona pace: "unmolested", a favourite Livian phrase (cf. 32.6 below) also found in comedy (Plaut. *Persa* 189).

25.1-26.2.   *Revolt of the Boii and Insubres*

Chapter 25.

1. In Italiam, etc. Livy now shifts the focus to Italy. Klotz believes that the source continues to be Coelius. But the confusion between the *triumviri* (§ 3) and *legati* (§ 7) suggests that he has turned from Coelius to Antias from 25.6 onwards.

a Massiliensium legatis: The long-standing allies of Rome (20.7 n.), perhaps afraid for their own safety.

2. Boii sollicitatis Insubribus defecerunt: For the previous history of Rome's relationships with them, see 16.4 n.

nuper: *i.e.* in late May 218 (Asconius *In Pis.* p. 3, Clark). The Latin colonies, consisting of 6,000 settlers each, were probably founded on existing settlements (see Walbank on Pol. III.40.5). Placentia (Piacenza) lies on the south bank of the Po some 40 miles south-east of Milan; Cremona on the north bank some 20 miles east of Piacenza. For the strategic positions of the two colonies, see Chilver, *Cisalpine Gaul*, 33 f.

3. tantum terroris ac tumultus: An alliterative cliché; cf. XXV.25.9, XXXII.21.17. *Trepidatio* and *tumultus*, *turba* and *tumultus* are similarly combined, *e.g.* XXV.13.10, XXV.4.10.

agrestis . . . multitudo: The 6,000 settlers, now working the land.

ipsi triumviri: The commissioners who founded a settlement were elected by the people of Rome and subsequently acted as *patroni* of the colony.

Mutinam: The modern Modena, 70 miles south-east of Placentia. Polybius (III.40.8) describes it as a Roman colony, but this is the case only after 183 B.C. (Livy XXXIX.55.6); at this time it is an Etruscan city in alliance with Rome, and defended by a Roman garrison (*praesidium* § 8).

C. Lutatius, C. Servilius, M. Annius: This is presumably Coelius' list, the variant versions in § 4 being those offered by Valerius Antias and Claudius Quadrigarius. The only name cited by Polybius is Lutatius; he adds that the others were of praetorian rank (III.40.9). The claim of Servilius is however confirmed at XXVII.21.10 and XXX.19.7; it seems probable therefore that Coelius' list (from Fabius Pictor?) is accurate, and that the others' refer to embassies dispatched about this time. The final pair cited, Cornelius Asina (consul in 221) and Papirius Maso (consul in 231), are disqualified as triumvirs on Polybius' statement that the two triumvirs were only of praetorian rank.

This passage is a clear example of how Livy constantly consults other accounts to confirm the testimony of the main source currently followed.

5. dubium est legati ... [incertum] an ...: "It is also uncertain whether they were attacked in the role of ambassadors . . ." The exclusion of *incertum*, adopted by both Weissenborn-Müller and the Oxford editors, is the easiest solution to the textual difficulty, the assumption being that *incertum* was added by a scribe who did not observe the double question and who punctuated after *sint*. For *dubium est* followed by a double question without *utrum* or *-ne*, cf. Cic. *Caecin.* 31: *an dubium vobis fuit inesse vis aliqua videretur necne?*

Polybius has no mention of an embassy, stating that the triumvirs came to assign the lands of the colony. If there were an embassy as well as a land-commission, this might account for the variant names offered by other authorities. Alternatively, the existence of *legati* may have been invented by Livy's sources to make the crime of the Gauls more heinous in international law.

BOOK XXI

6. gens ... rudis, pigerrima ... segnis: Livy frequently characterises the Gauls not only as *feroces* (20.8 n.) but also as lacking staying power
(V.48.1-3: X.28.3: XXII.2.4: XXVII.48.16: XXXVIII.17).

rudis ad: Cicero uses *rudis* with genitive or with *in* and the ablative;
rudis ad does not appear in extant prose before Livy, who uses it frequently;
XXIV.48.5, XXVIII.25.8, etc.

adsideret: This variation for the preceding *obsidere* is not found in this
sense in Cicero or Caesar.

7. evocati ... legati: Having begun by assuming that the triumvirs
were a land-commission (§ 3), Livy seems now to be describing them as
legati, unless this word is used merely to describe ad hoc ambassadors from
Mutina. The whole section, however, reeks of the influence of Valerius
Antias with its emphasis on Gallic duplicity; hence *legati* will mean "the
Roman ambassadors" who in § 5 above have been sent *ad expostulandum*.
The whole chapter is a good example of Livy's muddled handling of
sources in conflict.

non contra ius modo gentium: 10.6n.; cf. Pol. III.40.10:
παρασπονδήσαντες συνέλαβον αὐτούς ... Livy's more violent emphasis (*violata
etiam ... fide*) reflects both the bias of his source and his own central
preoccupation with moral criteria. For his eager assertion of the importance of *fides* in international relations, see my *Livy*, 67 ff.

obsides: Taken in the operations of 221 B.C. (*Per.* 20).

8. L. Manlius praetor: Though Livy does not make it clear here,
Manlius was already in the Cisalpine Gaul area, προκαθήμενος ἐπὶ τῶν τόπων
μετὰ δυνάμεως. According to Livy (17.9) Manlius had two legions, which
were later reinforced by a third (26.2 f.); according to Polybius, only one
initially but later two more. For modern discussions, see Walbank, 375 ff.

ira accensus ... effusum agmen: Again Livy teaches the moral lesson.
Manlius, blinded by anger, shows a lack of *prudentia* and *disciplina* (cf. § 9:
inexplorato profectus), the essential attributes of a commander like Fabius
Cunctator (cf. XXII.12.2 ff., XXII.25.14). Like Manlius, Ti. Sempronius
Longus and M. Minucius Rufus are condemned for *temeritas* or *ferocitas*
(XXI.53.1 ff.; XXII.29). It is worth noting that no such moral con-
demnation of Manlius' lack of discipline appears in Pol. III.40.

ad Mutinam: "towards Mutina".

9. plerisque incultis: "Since the area was largely uncultivated".
Livy is fond of *pleraque* in such expressions; see Riemann, 91.

inexplorato: Not found before Livy, who uses it frequently; XXII.4.4,
XXVII.26.6, etc.

NOTES

praecipitat: The manuscripts have *praecipitatus*, but a verb is clearly required, and the active rather than the passive. Madvig, *E.L.* 143, rightly remarks that the active and intransitive form is regularly used in the sense of "falling into ambush" and the like; II.51.5, V.18.7, VI.30.4, XXV.11.6, etc.

10. quamquam ad ⟨quingentos⟩ cecidisse: Polybius' phrase, πολλοὺς ἀπέκτειναν τῶν ‘Ρωμαίων, is too vague to be of assistance in supplying the missing number. Gron.'s *ad D* and Stroth's *ad DC* are of equal merit palaeographically.

11. iter deinde coeptum: A more dignified version than Polybius' ὥστε μόλις εὐσχήμονα ποιήσασθαι τὴν ἀποχώρησιν (40.13). As Wölfflin remarks, §§ 12-13 curiously repeats the pattern of §§ 9-11; but the attack now comes from the rear, and this second reverse is further distinguished by the loss of military standards.

apparuit: The manuscripts have *cum apparuit*; Walters' explanation of the corruption (*nec dum* mistakenly regarded as a single word) is acute. Drak.'s *comparuit* is vitiated by the fact that the verb in this sense appears always to have a neuter subject in Livy.

12. septingentos ... occiderunt, sex signa: There is again more circumstantial detail here than in Polybius. Antias is fond of recording the loss of standards (see my *Livy*, 134, with bibliography there), a useful indication of the probable source here. If the *signa* are manipular standards, the total complement of six maniples would be 840 *hastati* and *principes*, 480 *triarii*; the losses cited in the two engagements (1200/1300 men) come close to this.

13. invio atque impedito: The alliterative combination of an adjective not found before the Augustan period and a regular Caesarean word.

vicum propinquum Pado: Tannetum (modern Taneto) is in fact 50 miles south of the river (*Itin. Ant.* 287.8). Klotz blames Coelius for the error, but Antias is more probably the source here; in any case this may be a geographical clarification (!) in the manner of Livy himself.

contendere: Perfect, like *evasere* in the previous sentence.

14. munimento ad tempus: Cf. XXVIII.42.5, *dux ad tempus lectus*, but elsewhere frequently without a supporting participle. So Cic. *De amic.* 53; Livy III.64.4.

commeatibus fluminis: "Supplies afforded by the river". This phrase in the source may have led Livy to make the error about the position of Tannetum. The river is not the Po, but its tributary the Enso.

Brixianorum Gallorum: Livy here refers to the Cenomani, whose capital was at Brixia (Brescia). This Celtic tribe, hostile to the Insubres, had for this reason become firmly allied to the Romans (Pol. II.23.2). Polybius has no mention of such help, and their usefulness to the Romans at Tannetum so far to the south seems problematic.

Chapter 26.

1. insuper: "in addition", apparently a colloquialism before the Augustan period.

2. C. Atilium praetorem: Atilius Serranus, presumably the *praetor peregrinus*, because the *praetor urbanus* was not permitted to be absent from Rome for more than ten days; but cf. Broughton, I.240 n. 3.

cum una legione ... et quinque milibus sociorum: 25.8 n. Pol. III.40.14 says that the legions (στρατόπεδα) projected for Scipio's command were sent under the command of a praetor. Livy's documentary detail (one legion plus an allied contingent) is probably to be preferred.

a consule: P. Cornelius Scipio (15.4 n.), Sempronius having left for Sicily (17.5). See Sumner, *PACA* (1966), 26.

26.3–29.4. First encounter between Romans and Carthaginians; the Rhône crossing

3. Et P. Cornelius, etc. Livy now reverts to Coelius as source; whilst his account is similar to Polybius' (*e.g.* Pol. III.41.8-9 and Livy 26.5), there are details in Livy not appearing in Polybius (26.6 n.).

profectus ab urbe: Scholars are generally agreed that the date is August 218. If, as Polybius claims, he had left Rome ὑπὸ τὴν ὡραίαν (III.41.2), he had been recalled to cope with the Gallic crisis.

sexaginta longis navibus: To confront Hasdrubal's 57; see Thiel, *Roman Sea-power*, 35. n. 11.

Saluum montes: On the orthography, see the reading of the manuscripts at V.34.7. The Salyes or Salluvii are described by Pliny (*N.H.* III.47) as a Ligurian people, by Strabo (IV.6.3) as "Celtoligurian". Livy himself vacillates between the Gallic and the Ligurian labels (*Per.* 47 and 60). They inhabited the region between the Maritime Alps and the Rhône.

4. ad proximum ostium: *i.e.* the "Massaliotic" mouth, the modern Port St Louis. See Pol. III.41.5.

pluribus enim divisus amnis: "The river is divided and runs into the sea in several channels". In fact, as Polybius states, the Rhône has only two mouths. This is a characteristic Livian insertion for geographical

Notes

"clarification", and follows the tradition reflected in Timaeus' claim that there were five mouths (Diod. V.25.4).

castra locat: Perhaps anticipating an attack on Massilia.

5. auxiliaribus Gallis: So Pol. III.41.9, καθηγεμόνας ... Κελτούς, presumably from the area of Massilia.

6. in Volcarum agrum: The Carthaginians had proceeded along the coast (Pol. III.41.7) until they reached the territory of the Volcae. Polybius does not give the name of the tribe, which had two branches, the Volcae Arecomici (Caesar, *B.G.* VII.7 and 64) and the Volcae Tectosages (*B.G.* VI.24). The capitals were at Nemausus (Nîmes) and Tolosa (Toulouse) respectively. It appears that the Tectosages had put up no resistance.

citeriore agro: That is, from the standpoint of Hannibal; their territory west of the Rhône.

7. eorum ipsorum: *i.e.* the Volcae who had not crossed to the east bank.

8. temere: "carelessly"; cf. VII.2.7.

vicinalem usum: (*vicinalis* is not found before Livy; Kühnast, 388). For the considerable river-traffic on the Rhône, cf. Pol. III.42.2.

novasque alias . . .: A contrast is indicated here between the practised efforts of the natives and the rough imitations of the Carthaginians.

primum . . . incohantes: For the pleonasm, cf. III.54.9.

9. dummodo: For the sense (= *nisi ut*) cf. XXIV.6.9, XXIV.29.10, etc.; Mikkola, 114 n.l.

Chapter 27.

1. ad traiciendum: Characteristically Livy gives no indication of the site of the crossing, beyond the name of the tribe. Polybius clearly believes that the crossing took place at the regular ford (see III.39.8, 41.7) which was at Tarascon (Strabo IV.178 f.; Jullian, I. 464 n. 4 and *REA*, 1907, 14) or at Arles (cf. the Antonine Itinerary). He further states that it was "about four days' march from the sea", and implies that it was just north of the fork in the river (cf. III.42.1). "Four days' march" is a vague phrase which might mean anything from 320 stades (cf. Pol. III.50.1) to 600 stades (Pol. III.39.9, III.50.1, III.49.5). On the higher computation, four days' marching from the sea at Aigues Mortes could establish the crossing as far north as Pont St Esprit. But it is more prudent to accept Polybius' own view that Tarascon or Arles was the crossing-point. The argument advanced against these and other sites south of the Durance junction, that by crossing south of that river Hannibal would have exposed himself to Scipio's attack, is met by the fact that Hannibal was at the time unaware of Scipio's presence (Pol. III.44.3). For bibliography, cf. Jullian and Walbank.

virique: As *variatio* for *pedites*; cf. V.37.5.

2. Hannonem Bomilcaris filium: So specified to distinguish him from the Hanno left in command north of the Ebro (23.2). Polybius (III.42.6) calls the father Bomilcar Basileus, which suggests that he was suffete. See Lenschau, *RE* Hanno (16).

vigilia prima noctis: Livy omits to tell us that this was on the third night after arriving at the Rhône (Pol. III.42.3 and 6).

maxime Hispanis: With this detail, together with the Spaniards' method of crossing and the mention of horses on the diversionary operation (see § 5), Livy shows that he is following a fuller source than Polybius, namely Coelius.

3. adverso flumine: "upstream", a Caesarean phrase (cf. *B.G.* VII.60.3) as its opposite also is, *secundo flumine* (*B.G.* VII.58.5), for which Livy writes *secunda aqua* at 28.7.

facto: The neuter ablative of the perfect participle after *opus esse* is especially common in comedy (for *facto*, cf. Plaut. *Merc.* 565 f., *Amph.* 505, etc.) and this betrays its colloquial origin; cf. the English "this needs done". Cicero writes only *quaesito* and *properato* in this construction, but *facto* appears in Caesar (*B.G.* I.42.5) as well as Sallust.

4. latiore: This emendation of the manuscripts' reading *latiorem* is clearly right, as is shown by *eoque* (which is found first in Augustan writers; cf. Kühner-Stegmann, 2.146).

alveo: Not found in this sense before the Augustan period.

5. fabricatae: This passive form is not found in prose before Livy.

alia onera ... alius exercitus: For this usage, 11.3 n.

6. operis: "construction-work", referring to the raft-building.

7. dat signum: It was dawn on the sixth day after arrival. It is most instructive to note how Livy is much more indifferent to chronological precision than is Polybius.

8. eques fere propter equos nantes: Clearly there is either a corruption or a lacuna here, and Pol. III.43.2 indicates the general sense required. The light infantry had canoes, the light cavalry small boats (τοὺς μὲν λέμβους πεπληρωκὼς τῶν πελτοφόρων ἱππέων). Livy (or Coelius) does not trouble to specify *light* infantry or *light* cavalry. The easiest solution is to read *naves* for *nantes*, as Heerwagen does; but as Walters says, this leaves *fere* without point, for all the cavalry cross on boats. Walters' own suggestion that two lines have fallen out (*eques fere propter equos nantes ⟨navibus latiore puppi vehendus erat⟩*) is a possible but rather desperate solution. Much simpler would be to read ... *habebat pedes lintres, ⟨lembos⟩ eques fere propter equos nantes.* "Almost all the cavalry had cutters for their horses to swim behind." The point of *fere* is then clear; a few horses were put aboard larger vessels to be ready for operations on landing (see § 9 below).

ad excipiendum impetum: So also Pol. III.43.3.

   9. instratos frenatosque: "saddled and bridled". *Insternere* in this sense appears earlier only in Lucretius and Virgil.

Chapter 28.

   1. Galli: There is no trace in Polybius of this lively description of the noise and gestures of the Gauls. It may well have been inspired by Caesar, *B.G.* V.37.3: *suo more ... ululatum tollunt.* For a similar insertion by Livy, contrast XXXVIII.18.9 with Pol. XXI.37.5.

   2. et ex adverso: "Yet the scene confronting them was also terrifying ..." The function of *et* is to stress that whilst the Gauls presented a fearful sight and sound to the Carthaginians, the massive invasion and accompanying din was likewise formidable to the Gauls. See the fine description of Polybius III.43.7-8. Walters' explanation of *et* is erroneous.

cum ingenti sono: The great roar of the river is not in itself terrifying, but it contributes to the cumulative din. The scene as a whole, with the shouting from both banks, is reminiscent of the famous description of Thucydides VII.71. The connection is made closer by the description of the men afloat as "nautarum".

   3. iam satis paventes: Notable as a staple technique in Livy's battle-accounts is the way in which he introduces Hanno's force in the rear as a *deus ex machina*, the capture of the Gallic camp being presented as a *fait accompli* which he does not stop to describe; contrast the account of Polybius III.43.9. The theatrical effect is enhanced by the lively Latin, in which the alliterative effects are especially notable.

   4. utroque vim facere: "To carry the fight in both directions". *vim facere* probably originated as a colloquialism (cf. Ter. *Eun.* 807) and is common in Livy; III.5.5, XXXVIII.24.4, etc.

   5. varia consilia: not "devices" (Church and Brodribb) but "suggestions".

variata: The adjectival form does not appear elsewhere before Apuleius. Mehler's *variat* is attractive; cf. XXVII.27.12.

quidam ... ceterum magis constat: Polybius has the second version
(III.45.6 ff.) and Livy probably found the same account in Coelius, who
like Polybius followed Silenus. The first version will accordingly be
Antias'; it is also found in Frontinus, *Strat.* I.7.2, with the additional detail
that the elephant was goaded by being poked in the ear. As often elsewhere, Livy rejects the version of Antias.

refugientem in aquam nantem: Madvig's exclusion of *nantem* as a gloss
is the best solution here. Walters' appeal to the insecure reading at
I.14.7 (see Ogilvie's n.) is hardly sufficient to justify the retention of the
participle.

ut ... destitueret vadum: A simple temporal clause in *oratio obliqua*,
following after *impetu ipso ... rapiente.*

6. foret: The subjunctive expresses hypothesis; "This would have
been the safer plan ..."

ad fidem pronius: "More credible". The phrase does not appear in
prose before Livy; Kühnast, 381.

7. ratem unam: Livy's technique of simplifying technical detail for
his audience (cf. my *Livy,* 158) emerges here from a comparison with Pol.
III.46. There was not one raft, but a series of them set two by two with
a combined width of 50 ft and a length of 200 ft, lashed together to form a
unit. See the note on § 10.

secunda aqua: 27.3 n.

retinaculis: A word favoured by agricultural writers (Cato and Columella)
and not in Cicero or Caesar, who prefers *funis.*

parte superiore ripae religatam: "Fastened at a point higher upstream." Caesar writes *religare ad terram (B.C.* III.15.2); the ablative of
separation is found in Ovid and Horace.

8. longa pedes centum: A detail not in Polybius, who again says
that there were two rafts roped together.

tres tum: Walters (*ut cum* codd.; *sex tum* Harant; *tum* Madvig). The
change from *ut* to III or VI is easy. Which is it to be? Since they jostle
each other (§ 11) with some on the outside, the larger number seems more
probable.

praegredientibus feminis: Two in number (Pol. III.46.7).

9. ab actuariis aliquot navibus pertrahitur: "Towed by several
light vessels." *pertrahere* is not found before Livy.

alii deinde repetiti: Several journeys were required for the 37 beasts
(Pol. III.42.11).

10. agerentur: *donec* in the sense of "while" is not found before the

Augustan period (Kühner-Stegmann, 2.373) and takes the indicative. The sole reason for the subjunctive here is the frequentative nature of the sense ("while on each occasion they were being driven . . .").

ab ceteris: Charitable editors like Weissenborn-Müller and Dimsdale take *ceteris* as neuter here. But it clearly means "from the other rafts". Livy has forgotten his simplification at 28.7.

11. donec . . . fecisset: From Livy onwards the subjunctive after *donec* meaning "until" is frequent even where no element of anticipation or intention is present. But the tenses employed are perfect and imperfect. Here the pluperfect is used to denote the same frequentative action as in § 10. Cf. I.32.14 and Woodcock, § 224 n. 1.

12. quidam: here in the sense of *nonnulli* (5.15 n.).

deiectis rectoribus: Polybius says they were drowned (III.46.11).

pedetemptim: "By treading water", a mild academic joke. The literal meaning is found only in Plautus and Pacuvius.

Chapter 29.

1. Interim: One notices here, by comparison with Polybius, Livy's superiority as a narrator. He has described the crossing as a unified scene (chs. 27-28); he next turns to the skirmish between Numidians and Romans, using the pluperfect (*miserat*) so as not to misrepresent the chronology; and he finally recounts the speech of Hannibal immediately before the resumption of the march, the task to which the speech is addressed. In Polybius, the description follows the chronology; the main crossing, the despatch of the Numidian reconnoitring force, the speech of Hannibal, the return of the Numidians, the crossing of the elephants (III.43-6).

ubi et quantae copiae . . . et quid pararent: So also Pol. III.44.3: ποῦ καὶ πόσοι . . . καὶ τί πράττουσιν οἱ πολέμιοι, revealing Livy's close adhesion to the detail of his source.

2. ut ante dictum est: cf. 26.5.

quam pro numero: Caesar uses *pro* after a positive adjective to express this sense of "considering the number" (cf. *B.G.* I.2.5). The comparative followed by *quam pro* (cf. the Greek ἢ κατά) appears first in Livy; see Riemann, 275.

editur: *proelium edere*, a favourite expression of Livy's, does not appear earlier in prose; Kühnast, 380.

3. centum sexaginta: This reading of all the manuscripts diverges from the testimony of Polybius, who says that the number was 140; since the two accounts are in general close, there is a strong case for adopting Gron.'s *centum quadraginta*.

nec omnes . . . amplius ducenti: All as in Pol. III.45.2.

4. **hoc principium:** A comment of Livy's own, recalling the phrases of his Introduction in 1.2.

29.5–32.5. *Preliminaries to the crossing of the Alps*

5. **nec Scipioni stare sententia:** "Scipio could not adhere to his plan . . ." *stat sententia* occurs also at Ter. *Eun.* 224; Ovid, *Met.* VIII.67.

6. **Boiorum legatorum regulique Magali:** Polybius (III.44.5) calls them chieftains from the Po plain and their leader Μάγιλος; there is nowhere in his account the suggestion that they induced Hannibal to disengage. The decision was in fact taken by him (on good strategic grounds which Livy perhaps fails to appreciate) before the cavalry engagement just reported (Pol. III.44.10 ff.).

integro bello, nusquam ante libatis viribus: "before commencing hostilities, without impairing his strength anywhere beforehand."

libare: is earlier a highly poetic expression; see Lucr. V.260 and 568; Ovid, *Her.* II.115.

7. **utique:** Perhaps a colloquialism before the Augustan period in this sense ("especially for men without experience of it . . ."), or at any rate common only in epistolary Latin. But cf. Cic. *Div.* 2.119; Nep. *Epam.* 2.3.

Chapter 30.

1. **ipsi:** In contrast to the fearful *multitudo* at 29.7.

pergere ire: 22.9 n.

castigando: There is no trace of this in the Polybian speech.

2. **Mirari . . . :** Detailed comparison with Polybius' version of the speech (III.44.10 ff.) is instructive because Polybius seeks to record what really was said.   In his version, Hannibal

   (i) reminds his army of its past achievements (§ 10);
   (ii) claims that the worst part of the journey is behind (§ 11);
   (iii) urges obedience and trust in him for the future (§ 12).

Livy has recast his speech according to his usual practice.   It is constructed as follows:—

   Exordium: *Principium ab auditoribus:* why are you fearful? (30.2).

   Tractatio: Your invasion is justified (*iustum*) (30.3 f.).
               your journey easy (*facile*) (§§ 5-9).
               your target splendid (*gloriosum*) (§ 10).

   Conclusio: Prove yourselves superior to the Gauls (§ 11).

quinam repens terror: In direct contradiction to "the eagerness and enthusiasm" of the Carthaginians recorded by Polybius (III.44.13), this imaginative emphasis on the fear of armies and individuals under stress is characteristic of Livy's approach. (See my *Livy*, 163 n. 1).

invaserit: 10.3 n. (but the introductory verb here is historic present, which in Cicero can be followed by primary or secondary tenses of the subjunctive).

facere: "Their record of campaigning all these years was one of victory." The present infinitive is necessary to emphasise that the run of victories continues into the present, and the present tense is regular in such circumstances; cf. II.7.2 and Kühner-Stegmann, 1.117 ff.

omnes gentesque et terrae: (... *que* ... *et* is not found in Cicero and Caesar, but is common in comedy, in Sallust and in Livy; Kühner-Stegmann, 2.37). The claim is of course an exaggeration residing on Livy's misunderstanding of the nature of the Carthaginian conquest, the aim of which was control of the coastal plains and guaranteed access to mineral deposits.

amplectantur ... essent: The tenses reflect those of the *oratio recta* (*amplectuntur ... erant*).

3. quicumque Saguntum obsedissent: At Pol. III.20.8 the Roman ambassadors demand that the Carthaginian government surrender Hannibal and his military advisers (τοὺς μετ' αὐτοῦ συνέδρους). The suggestion here that all who fought at Saguntum are demanded (repeated at 44.4) is rhetorical exaggeration attributed to Hannibal by Livy, and not in Polybius' version of the speech.

dedi: After both *postulare* and *imperare* it is not uncommon to have accusative and passive infinitive (Cic. *Verr. II.* 3.138, *Quinct.* 56, etc.), but the active infinitive is rare. See Kühner-Stegmann, 2.231.

orbem terrarum: As Weissenborn-Müller notes, an anachronism, for Rome's overseas conquests were restricted to Sicily, Corsica, and Sardinia.

4. ad exortus: The plural of the less common word (also in Varro, *R.R.* I.12.1) perhaps for euphonious balance after *ab occasu;* but see § 6 below.

5. emensam: The passive sense of the deponent verb is also found at XLIII.21.9. For a full list of such deponents used passively, see Kühnast, 270 ff.

cernant ... habeant ... sit: 10.3 n.

6. quid Alpes aliud esse credentes: This appendage of a participle, here agreeing with *fatigatos*, with a question depending on it is an awkward

Book XXI

but frequent construction. Cic. *Tusc.* 1.31: *... quid spectans nisi etiam postera saecula ad se pertinere?* Since the question is rhetorical (= *nihil aliud esse credentes*) the accusative and infinitive is normal; Woodcock, § 267 ff.

altitudines: Livy is fond of such plurals of abstracts; cf. XXVII.18.9 and Riemann, 65. Cicero almost always uses the singular of this word.

7. Fingerent: The word denotes a *mental* picture; they are still at the Rhône, and only at 32.7 do they appreciate the reality. The *oratio recta* would be *fingite*, "Picture them, if you like . . .".

Pyrenaei: 24.1 n.

nullas ... nec insuperabiles: (*insuperabilis* is a favourite Livian word (see § 9 below) very rare elsewhere). Livy here imagines Hannibal encouraging his troops by softening the realities as described at V.34.7: *per iuncta caelo iuga . . .*

gignere atque alere: reinforcing *habitari* and *coli* respectively; cf. Pol. III.48.7.

pervias paucis esse, esse et exercitibus: The manuscripts have *pervias paucis esse exercitibus*. Heerwagen's attractive *fauces* for *paucis* should be resisted in spite of 23.2; the word is not apposite to the longer journey through the Alps. But the clinching argument against it lies in the following sentences, which demonstrate Hannibal's point that the Alps have been crossed both by small groups (*paucis*) and by armies (*exercitibus*). Hence Madvig's reading adopted by the Oxford editors is on the right lines, though a second *esse* seems hardly necessary; *pervias paucis esse ⟨et⟩ exercitibus* would be sufficient.

8. cernant: see § 5 n.

pinnis sublime elatos: Cf. Virg. *G.* III.108, *iamque elati sublime videntur.* Cicero has *sublime ferri* (*Tusc.* 1.40. etc.).

ne maiores quidem: Livy describes the Gallic migration at V.34 f. See Ogilvie's notes there.

advenas: Regularly used adjectivally in poetry (in Virgil, Horace, Ovid), and Livy elsewhere has *advenae reges* (IV.3.13).

liberis ac coniugibus: The order (contrast Cic. *Att.* VIII.2.3) perhaps emphasises the ease of the journey, but cf. XL.38.3.

migrantium modo: "as immigrants". Cf. XXXIX.26.8, *servorum modo*, for which Cicero writes *servilem in modum* (*Verr.* 1.13).

9. instrumenta: This Caesarean term (*B.G.* VI.30.2) embraces not only weapons but camping and cooking equipment; but the Gallic immigrants would be more heavily laden with household furniture.

quid ... esse?: See § 6 n. above. The string of rhetorical questions brings the speech to the desired emotional climax.

per octo menses: Again tacitly accepting the Polybian chronology; 15.3 n.

    10. caput orbis terrarum: § 3 n.

asperum atque arduum: An alliterative cliché; see Cic. *Sest.* 100; Livy XLIV.3.3.

    11. cepisse quondam Gallos: For the probable date of 387/6, see Pol. I.6.1 with Walbank's note; Ogilvie, 629.

Gallos ... Poenus: 8.3 n.

aut cederent ... aut ... sperent: The examples cited by Weissenborn-Müller of such variation of tenses (XXII.18.8, XXXIV.49.8, etc.) all have the imperfect and present subjunctives in successive sentences, and such a change is not uncommon in Livy. See 10.3 n. But the combination of the two in the same sentence is disconcerting, unless as at IV.15.1 the clauses are of different kinds. Accordingly the variation may here conceivably reflect an implied distinction between *cederent* (oratio recta *cedite*, "yield now") and *sperent* (oratio recta *sperabitis*, "you must expect in the future", a more polite formulation). Livy's deployment of tenses in such *oratio obliqua* is much more subtle than is commonly realised.

interiacentem Tiberi ac moenibus: At VII.29.6, XXVII.41.4 the verb takes accusatives; here and at XL.22.1 (*solitudines interiacentes Maedicae atque Haemo*) datives which indicate the areas affected. Cf. *intervenire proelio* (XXIII.18.6), *interesse* with the dative (XXIII.9.1).

Chapter 31.

    2. adversa ripa Rhodani: "upstream". For *ripa*, 5.13 n.

mediterranea Galliae petit: (The neuter plural of the adjective with a partitive genitive is occasionally found in Cicero/Caesar, and is very frequent in Sallust, Livy, and Augustan poetry; see Riemann, 102 ff.). Polybius III.47.1 says Hannibal advanced along the river eastward (ὡς ἐπὶ τὴν ἕω) "into the centre of Europe", an error attributable probably to his ignorance of the course of the Rhône (see Walbank, 381).

quantum ... minus: A linguistic simplification of the fuller *eo/tanto minus*; cf. XL.22.2, etc.

recessisset ... ventum foret: Representing future perfect indicatives in the *oratio recta*.

    3. manus conserere: Livy uses *manum* (cf. 41.4, XXV.11.3) but more commonly *manus* (cf. 39.3) with this verb; Cicero prefers the singular.

Book XXI

4. quartis castris: Livy adopts this military terminology (*castra* = day's march) perhaps from Caesar (e.g. *B.G.* VII.36.1) and employs it frequently (XXVIII.19.4, XXXVIII.13.11, etc.).

ad Insulam: Pol. III.49.5 writes: ἐπὶ τέτταρας ἡμέρας ... ἧκε πρὸς τὴν καλουμένην Νῆσον. If we compare Pol. III.39.9 with III.50.1, the four days' march comprises 600 stades, some 70 miles. Of the two sites usually proposed, the junction at the Aygues is less than 40 miles north. That at the Isère is 100 miles away, a formidable march for an army in four days but possible in an emergency. See the next note and §5 n.

†Sarar†: Polybius has ἡ δὲ Σκαρας which is usually emended to ἡ δ' Ἰσάρα, just as Sarar in Livy is frequently emended to Isara. We cannot of course know what Silenus, the source of Polybius and Coelius, wrote, and so it is impossible to establish the reading here. De Beer and Proctor both claim that the Sarar/Skaras are close to medieval names of the Aygues, but the arguments are not cogent. Hence "there seems about a 90 per cent. chance that they (sc. the emendations to Ἰσάρας and Isara) are right; whereas de Beer's attempt to identify the river in question as the Aygues ... is manifestly wrong". (Walbank, *JRS*, 1956, 42.)

diversis ex Alpibus: The Rhône rises in the Lepontian Alps, the Isère in the Graian.

agri aliquantum amplexi: Pol. III.49.7 says it is like the Nile Delta in size (!) and shape, except that the third side is bounded by almost inaccessible mountains (the Grande-Chartreuse; Walbank, 388).

inditum: This archaic word, avoided by Cicero, is a favourite of the historians Sallust and Tacitus, and even more of Livy.

5. Incolunt prope Allobroges: This is a further indication of the site of the Island; cf. Pol. III.49.13. They occupied the area north of the Isère in what is now the diocese of Vienne. See the references in the note below.

iam inde: "since then", as often in Cicero (*N.D.* 2.124, *Prov. Cons.* 33) and Livy (IV.36.5, etc.).

opibus aut fama: Livy looks back on the century since Q. Fabius Maximus Allobrogicus first conquered them in 121 B.C. (Caesar, *B.G.* I.45: Livy, *Perioch.* 61: Val. Max. IX.6.3: App. *Celt.* 1.12: Strabo IV.1.11: Pliny, *N.H.* VII.166: Florus 1.37: Oros. V.13). They achieved fame during the Catiline affair when their ambassadors at Rome revealed the plot to Cicero and were instrumental in the exposure of the conspiracy (Sall. *Cat.* 40 ff.). But their appeal for relief of debt was not heard, and they rebelled in 61, being subjugated only after the destruction of Valentia. Their position on the northern frontier of Transalpine Gaul made them strategically important in Caesar's campaigns (*B.G.* I.6 and 10 ff.; VII. 64).

6. regni certamine ambigebant: The verb is frequent in this sense of "dispute" in Cicero, who would however have written *de regno*. The ablative is here local, a regular Livian usage reflecting a linguistic simplification of the earlier *in* with the ablative.

Braneus: The name is not in Polybius, revealing once more Livy's use of a different source, Coelius.

pellebatur: Imperfect because the usurpation had not yet succeeded. Cf. Pol. III.49.8: μετὰ στρατοπέδων ἀντικαθημένους ἀλλήλοις.

7. disceptatio: "adjudication" as at XXXVIII.32.7, XLI.22.4: Quint. XI.1.43: *Digest* II.15.8. § 24. This sense, unprecedented before Livy, may have caused the corruption in M from *delecta esset* to *delectasset*. The choice is between the *delata esset* of D (cf. XXVII.30.9, XXVIII.27.14, etc.), *delegata esset* (Wölfflin; cf. V.20.9, IX.29.9), and *reiecta esset* (Weissenborn-Müller, taking into account *deiecta*, the reading of AN, and *delecta*, the reading of CM). The claims of *reiecta* are particularly strong; see the many parallels adduced by Weiss.-Müll. at V.22.1.

quod ea ... sententia: Again extra information not in Polybius.

8. copiaque rerum omnium: Arms and footwear, according to Pol. III.49.12, as well as clothing.

9. sedatis certaminibus: It is at this point that Livy switches sources. Up to this point his narrative is close to Polybius', and must stem from Coelius; it now diverges. Pol. III.50.1 states that Hannibal now made for the Alps with a march of 800 stades "along the river" (*i.e.* the Isère towards Grenoble). Livy's account seems to resume Hannibal's journey from the earlier Rhône crossing, probably drawing on Antias. So *non recta regione* (§ 9) echoes *non quia rectior ... via* in 31.2; *ad laevam* suggests northwards (so Kahrstedt and De Sanctis).

in Tricastinos: For their position, cf. Ptol. II.10.7 f.—north of the Vocontii, south of the Allobroges, and east of the Segallauni. One of their towns, Augusta Tricastinorum, is probably Aoust-en-Diois (see Pliny, *N.H.* III.36: Walbank, *JRS*, 1956, 39). Hence they inhabit the area east of the Rhône between the Drôme and the Isère.

Vocontiorum ... Trigorios: Strabo IV.185 states that "the Vocontii, Tricorii, Iconii and Medulli lie beyond (ὑπέρκεινται) the Cavari". The Cavari are assumed to live on the low ground east of the Rhône, and the Tricastini to be a sub-group of the Cavari. The others are further east, but one cannot say whether they are cited in west-east order or south-north (Walbank, *JRS*, 1956, 39 f.). Livy seems to envisage a march northward across the Aygues "in Tricastinos"; then eastward skirting the Vocontii on the north into the territory of the Tricorii. *Trigorios* is the reading of all the manuscripts, but in view of Τρικόριοι in Strabo, and *Tricorios* in Ammianus XV.10.11, there is a strong case for reading *Tricorios* here.

priusquam ad Druentiam flumen pervenit: This has not to be read solely in connection with the tribes just mentioned, but in the context of the whole journey from the Rhône to the Alps. The middle reaches of the Durance are probably meant, south-east of Gap and west of the confluence with the Guil. The river would have been highest here at the time of the crossing (cf. § 12; De Beer, 47 f.).

10. Alpinus amnis: Rising in the Cottian Alps.

difficillimus transitu: (*transitu*, the dative-ablative form of the supine, can be regarded either as dative of end contemplated "difficult for crossing" or locatival ablative "difficult in the crossing". Livy at XL.35.13 seems to regard it as ablative; Woodcock, § 153). For the tradition of the difficulties afforded by the river, see Sil. Ital. III.470: Amm. Marc. XV.10.11: Strabo IV.203.

11. pluribus simul neque iisdem alveis: De Beer notes that three branches of the river have become silted up since Livy's day, and that the present channel has widened. But this is in the lower reaches of the river, not in the middle reaches where he believes that Hannibal crossed.

nova semper ⟨per⟩ vada novosque gurgites: This is Walters' emendation (the 1470 Rome edition reads *per nova semper*) presumably to be taken with the preceding *fluens*: "flowing through shallows and whirling depths continually created . . .". But the structure of the sentence requires a participle here. The Durance does not tolerate ships because (*a*) *nullis coercitus ripis*, (*b*) *pluribus simul . . . fluens*, (*c*) *nova semper vada . . [?]*, (*d*) *ad hoc saxa volvens*, "it provides no firm or safe entry for anyone committing himself to it." My suggestion is: *nova semper vada novosque ⟨gignens⟩ gurgites* (*gignit*, Kiderlin).

12. tum forte imbribus auctus: The time is late August; it would be unusual to encounter a high river at that time. See de Beer's chart, p. 45.

super cetera: This usage of *super = praeter* (cf. 46.1), so frequent in Livy and subsequently, is not found in earlier prose; see Riemann, 275.

Chapter 32.

1. P. Cornelius: Resuming from 29.5; 29.1 n.

NOTES

triduo fere: (Strictly "within three days" as at Cic. *Mil.* 26). So Pol. III.49.1: ἡμέραις ὕστερον τρισί ...

movit: The verb is normally transitive in earlier prose, but the colloquial intransitive is already in evidence in Cicero (*Att.* IX.1.1) and this simplifying development in the language is frequent in Livy (cf. 39.4: XXV.9.8, etc.).

facturus ... occursurus ... defensurus: (§ 2 and § 5). See 1.4 n.

2. ubi videt ... rediit: The historic present in such clauses is common in historical writing, but only with verbs of perceiving. See Sall. *Jug.* 76.6; Woodcock, § 217. 3.

praegressos adsecuturum: The manuscripts have *progressos*, but cf. XXXVII.22.5 and Caes. *B.C.* III.77.3; Conway, *Praef.* XXI-XXV, § 78.

ad mare ac naves rediit: Livy makes no mention of the astonishment of Scipio recorded by Polybius at Hannibal's taking the overland route (III.49.1).

3. auxiliis: Cicero has the simple ablative after *nudus* in his letters but *a* plus ablative in his speeches (*Fam.* VII.13a.1; *Dom.* 58); likewise with *orbus* (*Fam.* IV.13.3: *Flacc.* 54). The more colloquial and simpler construction becomes the Augustan norm; Livy XXIX.4.7, I.26.9, etc.

quam provinciam: cf. 17.1.

Cn. Scipionem fratrem: Cn. Cornelius Scipio Calvus had already been consul in 222, with considerable military experience in the capture of Mediolanum and the subjugation of the Insubres (Pol. II.34, but cf. Scullard, *Roman World*, 172).

cum maxima parte: P. Scipio must have sent the great bulk of his two legions and allied contingent (see 17.8) on to Spain; he himself arrived in Italy μετ᾽ὀλίγων (Pol. III.56.5; see § 5 below). On the other hand, Cn. Scipio can man only 35 warships after arriving in Spain (Pol. III.95.5), and the Senate sends another 20 later (Pol. III.97.1), so that Scipio probably brought back 20 or 25 of his original complement of 60 warships.

4. veteres socios: Presumably the Massiliots as well as such cities as Emporiae (cf. XXXIV.9.10); *veteres* would hardly describe the Bargusii (19.7 n.).

sed etiam ad pellendum: But the strategy at this stage was surely defensive, to ensure that Hasdrubal did not reinforce Hannibal's expeditionary force. Hence Pol. III.56.5 says that Gnaeus was ordered πολεμεῖν ἐρρωμένως ᾽Ασδρούβᾳ, but expulsion of the Carthaginians from the firmly established cities in the south with so small a Roman force was hardly envisaged.

5. admodum: "quite"—a regular Ciceronian usage.

Genuam: Pol. III.56.5: κατέπλευσε ... εἰς Πίσας, but Genoa is en route, and

Livy names Pisa later as the port of disembarkation (39.3). This detail
does however suggest that Livy is not following Polybius.

exercitu: All manuscripts except M (reading doubtful) have *exercitus*,
which in view of such parallels as 29.6 ought to have been retained.

32.6-38.9.   The Crossing of the Alps

Livy's account divides dramatically into three parts.   First, the open
fighting—the stratagem against the *montani*, the capture of the fortified
stronghold, the subsequent advance (32.6-33.11); all this takes 5 or 6 days
(32.10, 2nd day; 33.1, 3rd day; 33.11, three more days).   Secondly,
fraus et insidiae from a second enemy (34.1-35.3), for a period of three more
days, for they arrive *nono die* at the summit.   Thirdly, the final stages
(35.4-37.6) lasting another nine days—two days' rest (35.5), advance on
day eleven, four days' delay at an impassable point (37.4), and three more
days for the easier part of the journey (37.6).   This is a total of 17 or 18 days,
as against the 15 days mentioned in 38.1, and there is an identical disparity
in Polybius' summary calculation at III.56.3 and the detail of the chronology
preceding it (Walbank, 391 f.).

32.6-33.11 is a good example of Livy's construction of a dramatic
episode.   After a prosaic introduction (32.6), Livy vividly paints the scene—
the hostility to the Carthaginians from nature and men (32.7-8).   Livy then
depicts Hannibal's preliminary activities in his usual economical manner—
the period-sentences in §§ 10-13 are his characteristic way of enclosing a
large number of prior activities in short compass.   The actual engagement
is recounted with the regular technique of alternation of standpoint; Livy
begins with Hannibal (33.1), then turns to the *montani* (§§ 2-3), then returns
to the Carthaginians (§§ 4 ff.).   The activities of both are recorded in
chronological sequence, with the psychology of the combatants preceding
the action (§§ 3-4; §§ 8-9).   The scene is concluded as prosaically as it
began with the bare mention of the capture of the fortified village (33.11).

6. campestri maxime itinere: This description hardly tallies with
any possible route from the middle reaches of the Durance.   Livy seems
to have reverted to his original source Coelius, and this *campestre iter*
describes the route along the Isère like ἐν τοῖς ἐπιπέδοις in Pol. III.50.1.
(De Beer transposes Livy's phrase to describe the terrain covered on the
fourth to the seventh days of the actual climb, which is clearly not what
Livy meant.)

ad Alpes: According to Livy's earlier interpretation, this would be near
Embrun; on the route described by Polybius, to which Livy seems now to

have returned, Hannibal would be beyond Grenoble, having journeyed 800 stades (Pol. III.50.1).

incolentium ... Gallorum: According to Polybius (III.50.2 ff.), these and the Gauls who next attack Hannibal are Allobroges. Livy may have dispensed with this detail because it does not harmonise with his earlier re-routing of Hannibal via the Durance.

7. Tum ...: There is no hint of the accession of Carthaginian terror in Polybius. But this psychological evocation by Livy of the reactions of the Africans in a frightening world, so magnificently described here, may owe something to Coelius, who likes to dwell on such dramatic moments (see my *Livy*, 132). Polybius is critical of such writing (III.47.6).

quamquam fama ... praecepta res: "Though the actuality had been anticipated by rumour, through which things unknown are often exaggerated." For *in maius*, cf. IV.1.5 and frequent parallels in Tacitus. For *maius vero*, cf. XXV.24.9, XXVII.44.10, *omnia maiora vero*. Hence Madvig's *in maius fere ecferri solent* (*E.L.* 217), is unnecessary.

immixtae: This verb is not found in prose before Livy.

pecora iumentaque: The distinction is between yoked animals (*iumenta* from *iungere*)—horses, mules, asses—and other beasts of pasture—cattle, sheep, goats.

torrida: "shrivelled"; Varro uses *torrere* of cold in his satire, *Eumenides* (fr. 161 Bücheler, *frigore torret*). Cf. 40.9, *membra torrida gelu*.

intonsi et inculti: "shaggy, shabby human figures".

animalia inanimaque: A distinction familar in Roman philosophy (*Tusc.* 1.54, etc.).

visu quam dictu: 31.10 n.

8. erigentibus ... agmen: *erigere aciem/agmen* is a favourite Livian expression, imitated by Tacitus and not found earlier. See Pol. III.50.3 for this sequence of events.

in primos ... clivos: On the Polybian itinerary at the foot of Mont du Chat.

imminentes tumulos insidentes: "occupying the overhanging hill-tops". The accusative after this verb, already found in early Latin and in Sallust, is very frequent in Livy (cf. 54.3) and subsequent prose.

si ... insedissent: The conditional is likewise in Polybius, revealing Livy's close use of his source.

fugam stragemque dedissent: Cicero uses *strages facere, edere*; *stragem dare* (cf. Virg. *Aen.* XII.454) does not occur in prose before Livy (Kühnast, 380). *repente* is of course to be taken with *coorti*.

Book XXI

9. Gallis: cf. Pol. III.50.6. These were the Boii, *duces itinerum* (29.6; Pol. III.44.5); the Allobrogian escort had now returned home (Pol. III.50.3).

ea: sc. *parte*, as at Cic. *Caecin.* 21, Livy V.43.2, etc.

inter confragosa omnia: For *omnia.* 11.6 n.; *confragosus*, perhaps an agricultural term, does not appear in Cicero or Caesar.

extentissima: The superlative of this participle does not appear before Livy.

10. cum . . . immiscuissent . . . edoctus. The economy of presentation here leads to a certain inelegance. The sense is that Hannibal's Gallic guides have affinities with the *montani*, so they can converse with them, as a result of which Hannibal gets information. The alternation of participle with temporal clause, the characteristic architecture of the period-sentence in Caesar and Livy, obfuscates this logical sequence.

interdiu: Invariably used in contrast with *noctu/nocte* in Caesar and Livy.

dilabi: expressive of "melting away"; the secondary military sense is earlier in Sallust.

ut . . . vim . . . facturus: In this sense of *tamquam si*, *ut* is found with ablative absolute in Cicero and Caesar (*B.C.* II.13.2, *B.G.* III.18.8, etc.), but its use with the future participle occurs first in the Augustan period. See Kühner-Stegmann, 1.790 f. For *vim facere*, 28.4 n.

11. die deinde: For the content, cf. Pol. III.50.9. This is a particularly good example of the complex of participles and subordinate clauses leading up to the main verb(s) which forms the typical period-sentence in *historia*:

die deinde . . . consumpto	ablative absolute
cum . . . castra communissent,	temporal clause
ubi primum . . . sensit	second temporal clause, with varied conjunction
pluribus ignibus factis,	
impedimentisque relictis	ablative absolutes
ipse . . . angustias evadit . . . consedit	main verbs

More frequently the participial phrase alternates with the subordinate clause in the juxtaposition of subordinate limbs preceding the main verb. See my *Livy*, 250 f. (and in more technical detail, Kühnast, 322 ff., Riemann, 309 f.).

cum . . . castra communissent: A Caesarean phrase (*B.G.* V.49.7, etc.).

12. degressos: The manuscripts, followed by Weiss.-Müll., read *digressos. Degredi* is the regular historian's word for leaving a hill-top (Sall. *Jug.* 49.4, 50.1, Livy VII.24.1, etc.) and if only one person were involved, *degressum* would be the correct reading (so at V.52.3 *degressus* is to be preferred against the *digressus* of the manuscripts). But *digressos* in the sense of "went their various ways" is of course perfectly defensible. Those who consider that Livy is stressing the descent of the *montani* from the hill-tops will prefer *degressos*, expecially as Pol. has ἀποκεχωρηκότων (50.9).

laxatas: not "thinned", as some editors, but "withdrawn", a common enough sense of the word. *All* the *montani* retired at night.

custodias: The plural invariably denotes a military watch.

pluribus quam pro numero: 29.2 n.

in speciem: "as a pretence"; Caesar writes *ad speciem*, *B.G.* I.51.1, *B.C.* II.35.6 (also Quint. Cic. *Pet. Cons.* 5.18), but Livy prefers *in speciem* (III.9.13, XXIV.1.8, etc.).

13. angustias evadit: The verb implies upward movement, "emerged at the top of the pass" (cf. Virg. *Aen.* IV.685, Livy II.65.3). The accusative is not found with it before Livy; Kühnast, 145.

iisque ipsis tumulis: For Livy's increased use of such locatival ablatives, found without attributive adjectives only rarely before Livy, see Kühner-Stegmann, 1.353; 8.7 n.

Chapter 33.
   1. incedere: "advance", a favourite word of Sallust (*Cat.* 60.1, *Jug.* 46.6).
   2. castellis: Properly "fortified villages" of smaller dimensions than a town, and set in isolated areas where the inhabitants gather for mutual protection. Cf. Sall. *Jug.* 54.6. The phrase here includes the main canton of the region and the surrounding villages (33.11).

repente: 9.2 n. The dramatic touch is notably absent from Polybius (III.51.1).

super caput: Singular, because the phrase has become adverbial, like the English 'overhead'; cf. XXXII.11.8. Sallust (*Cat.* 52.24), Cic. (*Q. Fratr.* I.2.6) and Livy elsewhere (IV.22.6) have *supra caput*, and Livy XLII.42.6 *supra capita*.

   3. utraque simul, etc. As often, Livy records dramatically the psychological reactions before the action; cf. II.10.7 (*parumper ... deinde*, as here), XXXIII.7.5, etc. Contrast the flat version of Pol. III.51.1: "The barbarians, noting what had happened, at first refrained from attacking ...". The chronological stages (cf. §8 below) marked by such adverbs as *primo ... deinde ... postremo* are also a regular technique; see my *Livy*, 197 ff.

Book XXI

defixit: A favourite Livian word in this psychological sense ("pinned them stock-still with astonishment"); cf. I.29.3, III.47.6, etc.

suoque ipsum tumultu: Livy is fond of appending the nominative or accusative of *ipse* to a noun, whereas a genitive (*suoque ipsius tumultu*) would be commoner earlier. Cf. 31.12, and Riemann, 156 f.

consternatis: Used of horses shying also by Sallust, *Hist.* 1.96; Livy XXXVII.41.10. Cf. Pol. III.51.5.

4. perversis rupibus iuxta invia ac devia adsueti decurrunt: Two problems arise here. (1) *adsueti* with the accusative (*iuxta invia ac devia*) is a poetic construction (Virg. *Aen.* VII.806, *femineas assueta manus*, etc.); but though there are no precise parallels in Livy, acceptance of this construction and the sense, "accustomed to areas impassable and untrodden alike", is much preferable to amending *invia* to *in vias* or *in viam* for more effective contrast with *devia*. (2) *rupibus* is clearly an ablative of separation after *decurrunt* (Pol. III.51.3: κατὰ πλείω μέρη προσπεσόντων τῶν βαρβάρων) but *perversis* is corrupt; the rendering of L & S, "craggy", is unsupported by any parallel. Walters' explanation, "throwing down rocks", is sadly astray; *rupes* cannot be thrown and *pervertere* cannot mean to roll down. The Polybian version suggests that the variant *diversis* may be right, and it is possible, as Mr Wright points out, that in an archetype with 18-letter lines, *diversis* lay below *perniciem* which caused the error.

5. ab iniquitate locorum: The *ab* is repeated for stylistic balance, with *iniquitate* personified; cf. Caes. *B.G.* V. 34.2, *ab duce et a fortuna deserebantur.*

6. clamoribus dissonis: An imaginative touch not in Polybius. The adjective, a favourite with Livy, is not found earlier.

repercussae: In earlier Latin, the participle is usually attached to "lumen", "clamor", etc. rather than to the agent of the refraction or echo.

7. deruptae: "sheer", only in Lucretius before Livy.

quosdam: As often in Livy, *quidam* has the sense of *nonnulli*—"several of them armed soldiers" (as distinct from camp-servants).

et ruinae maxime modo: "just like falling masonry".

8. visu: 31.10 n.

parumper . . . deinde: 33.3 n.

9. interrumpi: The tense should be carefully rendered.

ne exutum ... traduxisset: Cf. Pol. III.51.6. *exutum* represents the protasis of a condition; Hannibal's thought was "There is a danger that I have brought the column safely through in vain, if it is stripped of its baggage". When the fear is for the past, the pluperfect subjunctive after a historic introductory verb is regular; see Woodcock, § 188.

10. momento temporis: Polybius' version suggests a more protracted struggle (III.51.9).

11. castellum: 32.2 n. Livy summarises here; Pol. 51.10 ff. explains that it was virtually deserted since the inhabitants were on a plundering foray, and adds that Hannibal rested a day there.

Chapter 34.

1. Perventum: The second of the three stages of the crossing begins here, *fraus et insidiae*.

suis artibus: Cf. 4.9, *perfidia plus quam Punica*; XXII.16.5, XXVII.26.2, etc.

2. magno natu principes: In Polybius elders are not specified, and the natives carry olive-branches and wreaths. One wonders if Livy tacitly excises such detail as improbable in the Alpine region. Their message, and Hannibal's reaction, are pithily reported; contrast Polybius' rambling version in III.52.4 ff.

3. oboedienter: A favourite word of Livy's found virtually nowhere else in classical Latin.

commeatum: "food-supplies" here, not "passage"; cf. § 4 below. Polybius specifies them as cattle.

4. nec †asperandos† ⟨ratus⟩: Conway's suggestion that this is the correct reading, and that a line has fallen out, ⟨*ratus eorum animos*⟩ is unlikely; not only is the verb absent elsewhere in Livy, but *aspernari* is frequently contrasted with *credere* elsewhere, *e.g.* X.10.3: *nec aspernanda res visa neque incaute credenda*; XXXVII.10.6: *nec ut crederet nec ut aspernaretur dicta*. Since *aspernari* is regularly found with an object in Livy (cf. IX.41.3), *nec aspernandos ⟨ratus⟩* is to be preferred to *nec aspernandum*.

pacatos: 21.3 n.

5. primum agmen: Livy's compositional arrangement is again here much superior to Polybius', who recounts the attack (III.52.8) before describing the formation of the column. Polybius has no mention of elephants, but says the pack-animals were in front (cf. § 9 below).

6. in angustiorem viam: Probably beyond Briançon.

7. extrema agminis: On Livy's fondness for the neuter adjective with genitive, cf. § 8 below and Riemann, 104.

quin ... accipienda fuerit: Livy often uses the gerundive in the absence of a future participle passive in Latin (21.8 n., X.27.11); the active equivalent here would be *accepturi fuerint*.

8. Tunc quoque: "Even as it was"; cf. XXXVIII.41.12.

quia non: explaining not the main verb but Hannibal's hesitation.

Book XXI

9. occursantes per obliqua: The frequentative force is intended. For *per*, cf. *per viam* at XXIV.40.9, etc.

Hannibali: For other examples of the dative of the agent after a perfect passive, frequent in Cicero, cf. 39.1, 43.4.

Chapter 35.

1. intercursantibus: This frequentative does not appear in prose before Livy; cf. Lucr. III.262.

superatus: "topped".

2. latrocinii magis quam belli more: A cliché of military Latin; cf. Cic. *Cat.* I.27: Sall. *Jug.* 97.5; Livy XXIX.6.2.

concursabant: "skirmished"; cf. XXX.34.2 (*concursatio*), XXXI.35.6, XXVII.18.14 (*concursator*).

daret ... fecissent: Frequentative subjunctives; for the tenses, 4.4 n.

morative: For this use of *-ve* to express an alternative within an alternative, see I.29.2, XXV.1.12, and Ogilvie, 80.

3. per artas [praecipites] vias: The exclusion of *praecipites* is arbitrary, but its retention between *artas* and *vias* is a harsh asyndeton. I should prefer with Bauer to read: *sicut praecipites per artas vias.* ("Though great delays attended the attempts to drive the elephants headlong down the narrow paths ..."). *aliquem praecipitem agere* is of course a common expression; Cic. *Caecin.* 60, Livy VIII.7.8, etc.

inciderent: Frequentative; see § 2 above.

quia insuetis adeundi propius metus erat: The gerund is to be taken primarily with *metus* ("The enemy were afraid of getting too close because they were not used to it"), but the word-order also allows it to specify the sense of *insuetis*.

4. nono die: *i.e.* from the foot of the Alps; so also Pol. III.53.9.

per invia pleraque et errores: ("much of it by pathless detours"). Livy here indicates that the final stage of the crossing was a hit-or-miss affair, and this divergence from Polybius' version anticipates Livy's argument that Hannibal must have branched off southward from the Isère to Mt Cenis or Mt Genèvre. Polybius' criticism of historians who assume negligence in Hannibal's planning (III.48) is worth noting here.

esset: Frequentative; 4.4 n.

faciebant: Livy's fondness for using *facere* with an extraordinary range of abstract accusatives is exemplified earlier in the book at 5.16 (*fugam*), 12.2 (*proelia*). 14.4 (*finem*), 15.1 (*discrimen*), 18.12 (*mentionem*), 28.4 (*vim*), 28.11 (*quietem*), 30.2 (*stipendia*), 32.1 (*moram*), 33.6 (*stragem*), 34.3 (*imperata*), 35.2 (*occasionem*), and here with *errores*.

5. biduum in iugo: So also Pol. III.53.9.

6. occidente iam sidere Vergiliarum: For *sidus* as the correct term for a constellation, see Macrobius, *In somn. Scip.* 1.14. Vergiliae is the ancient Italian name (see Cic. *N.D.* 2.112 with Mayor's n.) for the Pleiades. De Beer, 100 ff., calculates that the Pleiades' morning setting in 218 was on Oct. 24, but it would have been invisible at sunrise; the first day on which it would have been visible was about Nov. 7. This date is far too late for the crossing. The setting of the Pleiades was the traditional expression for the onset of winter (cf. Hesiod, *WD* 383 ff., Columella XI.2.78, Virg. *Georg.* I.221); Polybius (III.54.1) and Livy may have had no precise date in mind. Snow begins to fall usually in late September, and Hannibal would have been criminally careless not to have made prior enquiry about this. We may assume with De Sanctis, III.2.79, Walbank (on Pol. III.54.1) and Sumner (*PACA*, 1966, 5 ff.) that the crossing was completed in late September.

ingentem terrorem: In Polybius they are δυσθύμως διακείμενα; Livy makes them panic-stricken southerners in a snowbound world.

7. omnia nive oppleta: 11.6 n.

segniter . . . pigritiaque: The words continue Livy's brilliantly evocative picture of the mood of the Carthaginians.

8. praegressus signa: *praegredi* is regularly followed by the accusative in Livy (XXVIII.1.6, XXXVI.31.7, etc.), but not earlier.

in promuntorio quodam: Though editors take this to mean "peak", it clearly connotes an overhanging ledge where the soldiers could assemble. The view from this site of the plains of Italy is one of the arguments favouring the Col de la Traversette (nearly 10,000 ft high) as the final stage of the crossing. It is doubtful, however, whether this speech of Hannibal is historically unimpeachable; note that Livy selects a more appropriate moment for it than does Polybius (III.54.2), where the speech is made the previous day during the rest-period. Weissenborn-Müller well compare Petronius, 122.153 ff., where Caesar is likewise made to look over the plains of Italy from the Graian Alps!

9. proclivia: In the double sense of "downhill" and "easy".

summum: "at most", invariably with expressions of number. Cf. Cic. *Mil.* 26, *triduo aut summum quadriduo*; Livy XXXIII.5.8, etc.

arcem et caput: "the main stronghold", cf. XXVIII.42.16, *ubi Hannibal sit, ibi caput atque arcem huius belli esse.*

in manu ac potestate: A legal expression, the distinction in law being that a woman is technically *in manu*, and both men and women are *in potestate*. See Gaius, *Inst.* 4.21.

Book XXI

10. ne hostibus quidem: The sense must be: "The column then began its advance, nor did the enemy now make any attacks ...". In other words, the Carthaginians were reassured, and moreover were no longer assailed. It is doubtful whether *ne ... quidem* can register this sense, and the correct reading may be *nec ... quidem*. Cf. XXXIII.40.4 and *CR* (1967), 54.

furta: "acts of stealth", cf. XXVI.39.11, *non vi ac virtute, sed proditione ac furto*. Cf. Pol. III.54.4.

ab Italia ... breviora ... arrectiora: A true assessment; cf. Franchi, *ad loc.*, in his edition of Book XXI.

12. titubassent: "staggered"; the word is much commoner in its metaphorical sense in classical prose.

adflicti: "once in difficulties". This reading of the 1495 Ven. edition is closer to the reading of the manuscripts *adflictis* (clearly corrupt) than is the attractive *adfixi* (cf. III.68.7, *haerete adfixi contionibus*, quoted in support by Weissenborn-Müller).

occiderent: "fell"; the sense is rare, but there is no need to emend to *succiderent* (Madvig) or to *inciderent*. Cf. XXIII.24.7.

Chapter 36.

1. ad multo angustiorem rupem: "a much narrower rocky descent", cf. Pol. III.54.7.

rectis: "perpendicular". The word is used regularly of a straight line, horizontal or vertical.

temptabundus: "feeling their way". Like Sisenna and Sallust earlier (Kühner-Stegmann, l. 260 n. 3), Livy uses adjectives in *-bundus* with a participial force, e.g. *vitabundus castra hostium* (XXV.13.4). Some appear in no other author, e.g. *deliberabundus*, *peregrinabundus*, *temptabundus* (Kühnast, 338 f.).

virgulta ac stirpes circa eminentes: "bushes and roots projecting all around", *circa* suggesting that they are a regular feature of the terrain.

2. natura locus, etc. Polybius' account (III.54.7) is significantly different here, and indicates that Livy (or Coelius) has misunderstood the topography. Polybius accounts for the narrowness of the path by stating that a section of the mountain extending laterally for one and a half stades (900 Greek feet) had fallen away in an earlier landslide, and that further falls coincided with the Carthaginians' arrival. In Livy, the landslide produces a thousand-foot chasm *in front of* the Carthaginians, so that they come *velut ad finem viae* (§ 3).

NOTES

admodum: "fully", a usage found with numbers also in Caesar (*B.G.* V.40.2), but much more frequent in Livy.

4. digressus: Hannibal is at the rear, and the narrowness of the track makes a detour impossible. *Degressus*, "he proceeded down" should surely be read here (cf. 32.12 n.). Dimsdale's explanation for *digressus*, "he started off", is untenable.

quamvis longo ambitu: The use of *quamvis* without a verb, common in Livy (XXII.8.3, etc., cf. Mikkola, 102) is occasionally found in Cicero, e.g. *Tusc.* 2.38, *quamvis levi ictu*.

circumduceret agmen: "He would have to lead the column round". In such *quin*-clauses dependent on *non dubitare* and the like, the present and imperfect subjunctives are frequently used with a sense of future compulsion. The usage develops from the original employment of *quin* in a repudiating question—*quin faciat?* "how shall he not do it?" Similarly here we have the subordinating of *quin circumducat agmen?* Cf. Cic. *Att.* VIII.11B.3, Livy IX.2.5; and Handford, § 168.

5. ea vero via: *i.e.* the detour; cf. Pol. III.54.8.

6. dilapsa est: "melted"; cf. Cic. *N.D.* 2.26.

7. [ut a lubrica]: Walters' excision of this phrase is a desperate remedy. In view of the ensuing *ut*, Heerwagen's *ita lubrica glacie* has much to commend it.

in prono: "on the slope"; so Pol. III.55.4, ἐπὶ πολὺ καταφερῶν ὄντων τῶν χωρίων.

adiuvissent: Frequentative; 4.4 n.

adminisculis: "supports", *i.e.* the hands or knee just mentioned.

8. prolapsa ... perfringebant: "As they fell, they struck out more strongly with their hooves in their struggle, and broke through the surface completely."

pedica: Instrumental ablative.

Chapter 37.

1. iugo: Polybius (III.55.6) makes it clear that Hannibal returned to the *rupes* inaccurately described at 36.3.

fodiendum atque egerendum: The two words, both with agricultural associations, are used to emphasise the laboriousness of the operation.

2. ad rupem muniendam: This usage, unexampled elsewhere (though cf. Tacitus, *Agr.* 31, *silvis ac paludibus emuniendis*), is an abbreviated way of saying *ad viam per rupem muniendam*, and is closely parallel to Polybius' τὸν κρημνὸν ἐξῳκοδόμει (but note that this means "built it up", "widened it"). Livy continues with his divergent interpretation (see 36.3 above), so that the path is constructed down the sheer face of the rock. It is doubtful if he had any clear picture of what he describes; see § 3 below.

detruncatis: The word does not appear before Livy.

ardentiaque saxa infuso aceto: This celebrated incident is not recorded by Polybius, who visualises the whole of this operation differently (36.2 above). The application of fire and vinegar has been made to appear more ridiculous through Juvenal's comically exaggerated picture (X.153, *diducit scopulos et montem rumpit aceto*). Livy merely suggests that the steep rock-face on the downward descent was softened by this means, and Pliny, *N.H.* XXXIII.71, shows that the technique of heating and splitting rock with vinegar or acidulated water was familiar from Spanish mining operations. No doubt the incident is "rhetorical elaboration" (Walbank), but it may have a modest basis in fact at some point of the crossing. Cf. Appian, *Hann.* 4; De Beer, *Alps and Elephants*, 73 f.

3. molliuntque anfractibus, etc. "They reduced the effect of the steepness of the slopes by short zigzag tracks". For *mollire* in a similar sense, cf. Caesar, *B.G.* VII.46.2, but referring to an uphill journey, as *mollis* often does. The description is wholly inconsistent with the detail at 36.2.

4. quadriduum ... absumptis: For the time-scale, compare Pol. III.55.7 f., but there the mules pass over on the first day, and it is the elephants who consume the other three days and are in bad shape from hunger.

5. inferiora vallis, apricos quosdam colles: As the text stands, *vallis* has to be taken as the first of four accusatives, and the comma is necessary to show its asyndetic connection with *colles*. But there is a strong case for reading *apricosque* with Weissenborn. For *quosdam* ("a number"), cf. Riemann, 188.

6. muniendo: with *fessis*.

triduo inde: So Pol. III.56.1.

locis ... ingeniis: Ablative absolute. The theme of the crossing has been *loca saevissima et accolarum ingenia*.

Chapter 38.

1. hoc maxime modo: A phrase suggesting Livy's mental reservations about some details. Cf. XXV.31.11, etc.

quinto mense: April/May–September 218; 15.3 n.

ut quidam auctores sunt: including Polybius (III.56.3) and presumably Coelius.

NOTES

quinto decimo die: See the preliminary note at 32.6, and Walbank, I 391.

2. Qui plurimum: Doubtless Valerius Antias. At 23.1, Hannibal is said to start out with 90,000 infantry and 12,000 cavalry, but 20,000 are left in Spain. Even on the basis of these inflated figures (23.1 n.) the round figures of 100,000 and 20,000 are absurd.

qui minimum: So Pol. III.56.4 (see Walbank on Pol. III.35.1). These are the figures which Polybius took from the column at Lacinium.

3. L. Cincius Alimentus: Praetor 210 in Sicily, where he remained in 209 as promagistrate (XXVI.28.11, XXVII.7.12). In 208 he blockaded Locri and was special envoy to the consul Crispinus in Bruttium (XXVII. 28.13, 29.4). Hence he was captured after 208, and must have composed his history in captivity. It covered the history of Rome from the foundation to his day, and was written in Greek, like that of Fabius Pictor. Seven fragments survive (cf. Peter, *HRR*[2], CI ff., 40 ff.). This is the sole citation from him in Livy (Cincius at VII.3.7 is probably the Augustan antiquary); hence it is likely that Livy took these figures from Coelius rather than directly.

4. adducta: "A tally of 80,000 was made up . . .".

5. triginta sex milia, etc. Polybius' estimate (III.60.5) is that Hannibal crossed the Rhône with 38,000 foot and 8,000 horse, and lost about half of these, arriving at the Po with 20,000 and 6,000 (III.56.4). Since Cincius' conversation with Hannibal took place after 208, the estimate of 36,000 lost may include battle-casualties in Italy.

Taurini Semigalli: This is Madvig's fine emendation (*E.L.* 219). The Taurini were Celts (Pol. III.60.8 ff., Appian, *Hann.* 5) intermixed with Ligurian elements (Pliny, *N.H.* III.123). They lived in Piedmont, and have given their name to Turin (Augusta Taurinorum).

6. eo magis miror: To the student inured to Livy's geographical failings, there are consoling evidences here of the Paduan's personal knowledge of the Alpine passes. The western Alps were of course the scene of extensive building operations in the Augustan period (see Chilver, *Cisalpine Gaul*, 38 ff.), so that the routes became more widely known.

ambigi . . . credere: For the characteristic Livian change from passive to active infinitive ("and that people commonly believe . . .") see V.20.8, V.30.3, V.39.11, etc.

Poenino: *i.e.* by the Great St Bernard. This route was used about 400 B.C. by the Boii.

atque inde nomen: As Livy indicates in § 9, this etymology is wrong. The correct form is Peninus, from Celtic *pen*, a peak.

7. Coelium: For Coelius Antipater, see Introduction, p. 41.

Book XXI

per Cremonis iugum: Presumably the Little St Bernard [see Hyde, *Roman Alpine Routes* (Philadelphia, 1935) 79 f.], since this is the other main pass debouching into the territory of the Salassi. Polybius too seems to indicate this as the pass chosen by Hannibal (III.56.3 with Walbank's n.). It had a carriage road over it during the Augustan period (Chilver, 40, quoting Strabo IV.6.7).

per Salassos montanos: They inhabited the upper valley of the Dora Baltea. Augusta Praetoria (Aosta) was established in their territory in the early Augustan period to control the area, so that the Salassi were in the public eye when Livy was writing this decade.

ad Libuos Gallos: Identical with the Libicii of Pliny, *N.H.* III.124; cf. Pol. II.17.4 with Walbank's note. They lived in the valley of the lower Sesia, and their capital was at Vercellae.

deduxerint: The use of the perfect subjunctive to express the potential is in early Latin hardly distinguishable from that of the present subjunctive. Later, however, it is employed to refer to the past "to express the writer's opinion as to what is likely to have been the case" (Woodcock, § 120, quoting Cic. *Off.* 1.75 and the present passage). The emendation to *deduxissent* (Madvig, *E.L.* 220, Weissenborn-Müller) is quite unjustified. The perfect has the generalising nuance, whereas the pluperfect would confine the truth of the observation to the single occasion in 218.

8. ea tum ... patuisse itinera: Again reflecting the Augustan standpoint. Livy is referring not so much to the difficulties of terrain, overcome by Gallic migrations earlier, as to the hostility of the inhabitants.
utique: "at any rate", or perhaps "in particular"; 29.7.n.

gentibus semigermanis: Livy refers here to the difficulties Hannibal would have encountered from the tribes north and west of the Pennine Alps. In particular he may have had in mind the Gaesatae, who dwelt in the area from the Rhône to the *vallis Poenina*. The Gaesatae have been claimed as German by some scholars partly on the basis of this passage, but Livy may be guilty of an anachronism. At any rate, the word *Germani* is not prominent in Latin till the first century; the historian may have been imaginatively transposing to Hannibal's day the difficulties encountered in the Roman pacification of the Alps (on which see Mommsen, *Provinces of the Roman Empire*, I.15 ff.). See Walbank on Pol. II.21.1.

9. ⟨nomen⟩: Some later manuscripts and editors supply this necessary insertion after *norint*.
Sedunoveragri: No extant citation of this form exists; Walters prints it here because the manuscripts have *sed uno velacri*. But this could easily have

been changed from *sed uni* through a scribe's construing *ab transitu . . . ullo sed uno*. *Seduni Veragri* is the safer reading. Cf. Caesar, *B.G.* III.1.1, *in Nantuates, Veragros Sedunosque . . . qui a finibus Allobrogum et lacu Lemanno et flumine Rhodano ad summas Alpis pertinent.*

norint: Subjunctive of "modest assertion", in origin potential. Cf. *fecerint* at 47.5.

inditum: 31.4 n.

sacratum: "hallowed". Cf. *Vesta sacrata*, Ovid, *Met.* XV.864; Livy VIII.6.5.

Poeninum: This suggestion of Livy reverses the logical order. The god is called Peninus (frequently on inscriptions *deus Peninus, Iuppiter Peninus*, etc.) because he is the *numen loci* in the Pennine Alps.

39.1-48.10. *Hannibal's first operations in Italy*

Chapter 39.

1. **peropportune ad:** So also I.42.2, *peropportune ad praesentis quietem status . . .*

Taurinis: For the dative, 34.9 n.; for the facts, see Pol. III.60.7.

Insubres: 16.4 n.

in reficiendo: "as they recovered"; the word is always transitive earlier. Livy frequently allows ellipse of *se*, especially in gerundival expressions; *e.g.* IX.37.3.

3. **P. Cornelio consuli:** 15.4 n.

Pisas: 32.5 n.

tirone: For the use of such substantives adjectivally, see Cic. *Phil.* XI.39, and Riemann, 74 f. (cf. 40.11 *ruptore*, 41.11 *victricem*, 30.8 *indigenas/advenas*). The sense of the ablative absolute ("though the army was newly recruited and . . . fearful") is concessive; Mikkola, 34 n. 1.

4. **venit . . . moverat:** Even in past time, when a *cum*-clause specifies the precise time of the action the indicative is used. "*cum venisset* here would make nonsense, for it would try to say '*after* the consul had come, Hannibal had *previously* moved'." (Woodcock, § 239, 5.)

stativis: 48.7 n.

Taurinorumque unam urbem . . . expugnarat: Polybius (III.60.9) states that Turin is "the most important" rather than the only city of the Taurini, and provides the extra detail that Hannibal took it in three days.

5. **non metu solum sed etiam voluntate:** The pattern of Livy's narrative is similar to Polybius', who however specifies the cause of fear (slaughter of the citizens of Turin who opposed Hannibal).

Book XXI

ni subito adventu ... oppressisset: Livy frequently employs such *nisi* clauses to express a sudden and unexpected reversal. See my *Livy*, 202 n. 3.

6. praesentem: i.e. *partem*, "those at hand".

7. sicuti ... ita: As often, the correlatives have a concessive (*quamquam ... nihilominus*) relationship.

9. et auxerant ... Scipio quod ... Hannibal: The same points are made at greater length in Pol. III.61.2-6.

10. tamen: Resumptive ("But to continue ...") rather than reflecting on Scipio's rashness, as Weissenborn-Müller suggests. See 46.9, and Ogilvie on I.12.1.

Padum traicere: *i.e.* at a point west of Placentia, where Scipio had marched from Pisa. This information provided by Livy is absent from Pol. III.61.1 and 64.1.

ad Ticinum amnem: on the eastern bank.

educeret: 47.3 n.

talem orationem: "A speech on these lines"; 12.8 n. The two orations which follow provide a good illustration of the exploitation of speeches by Roman historians to characterise speakers and occasion (Quint. X.1.101: *cum rebus tum personis accommodata*). The skirmish at the Ticinus has a symbolic importance as marking the onset of the struggle. The characterisation of the speakers is achieved by artistic editing of the traditional version of the speeches, which can be found at Pol. III.62-4. Polybius records two brief speeches, Scipio's being shorter than Hannibal's, which is placed first; both are partly in *oratio obliqua*. In Livy's version both orations are of identical length, and considerably longer than Polybius' versions; and they are in the more arresting *oratio recta* throughout. Scipio's is placed first, partly perhaps for patriotic reasons, partly because this provides a smoother transition from the preceding narrative, in which Livy describes how the Romans make the first challenge by crossing the Po. Livy deliberately introduces a balance of topics between the two speeches, almost as if Hannibal had been present at Scipio's speech and were answering it. Within this artistic structuring, the leaders are characterised especially by the arguments of the *tractatio*. Scipio is the god-fearing Roman, but underestimates the enormity of his task; Hannibal is the man who is the slave to Fortune, and his arguments stress the more materialistic motives. See Ullmann, 16 f.; Burck, *Einführung*, 71 f.

Scipio's speech is constructed as follows:—

40.1-4: Exordium Principium a re ipsa, ab audientibus, a nostra persona.

NOTES

5-6	κατάστασις, statement of the theme.
40.6-41.15	**tractatio**
40.7-10	*facile*
11	*religiosum*
41.1-7	*facile*
9	*pium*
10-12	*dignum*
13-15	*necessarium*
41.16-17	**conclusio** = amplificatio.

Chapter 40.

1. si educerem ... supersedissem: 13.1 n.

loqui: *supersedere* is found normally with the ablative, but Sisenna, fr. 108 has the infinitive; Kühner-Stegmann, 1. 669.

2. ad Rhodanum: cf. 29.1 ff.

vicissent ... habui: The variation in mood is attributable above all to the change from third to first person. The causal sense in *vicissent* could have been renewed by writing: *legiones quae ... hostem secutae ... habuissent,* but Livy prefers the variation of the factual indicative.

3. Hispaniae provinciae: This dative after *scribere* ("enrolled for the province of Spain") has no parallel in Livy, who normally writes *ad* or *in* to express this sense. See X.1.1, XLII.33.4, etc.; and Packard's *Concordance,* s.v. *scribere.*

meis auspiciis: In time of war, the right to take the auspices was the prerogative of the commander alone. Hence the phrases *meo auspicio, tuis auspiciis,* etc., symbolise the status of the commander. Scipio had been allotted Spain as his province (17.1), and his brother Gnaeus has the status only of *legatus.*

4. ego: This introduces the second and adversative part of the *quia* clause ("whereas I . . .").

5. Note the homoioteleuton (*vicistis/exegistis/habetis*) and anaphora (*a quibus . . . a quibus*).

stipendium: 1.5 n.

6. qui plures paene, etc. This strikingly alliterative phrase, characteristic of Livy (cf. XXX.42.17), appears in the manuscripts in § 7 between *amissis* and *plus,* where it is usually regarded as a gloss and excluded by editors. Walters' transposition is pleasingly ingenious. The subjunctive is causal.

8. at enim: Introducing the figure of *praesumptio,* the anticipated objection which lends an air of reasonableness to the speaker; 18.9 n.

Book XXI

robora ac vires: 1.2 n.

possit: Consecutive.

9. effigies immo, umbrae: Cicero employs the phrase *umbra et imago* (*Rab.* 41, etc.) in a similar sense. *effigies* with this meaning is not found before Livy, who uses a wider range of metaphors than Cicero. See Kühnast, 293 ff.

praeusti: "frost-bitten" as at Pliny, *N.H.* III.134, but not before Livy in this sense.

nive rigentes nervi/membra torrida gelu/ /quassata fractaque arma/claudi ac debiles equi. The careful balance of the phrases should be noted. In the first two, chiasmus reinforces the antithetical effect of the isocolon or syllabic balance. In the second two again there is an identical number of syllables in each.

11. ita forsitan decuit: *fors-sit-an* introduces an Indirect Question, and is accordingly in Cicero and Caesar followed by the subjunctive. So also in Livy on 13 occasions; but like the Augustan poets and later prose-writers, he sometimes employs it as a simple equivalent to *fortasse*, without affecting the mood of the verb, as at *Praef.* 12, X.24.13. See Kühner-Stegmann, I. 811; Riemann, § 117.

ruptore: 39.3 n.

deos ipsos: A rhetorical flight of fancy. The suggestion that the climatic sufferings are a divine visitation is not one that would appeal to Livy himself. He does not visualise the gods as personally vindictive; the divine element in the world moves on its ethically predetermined course through the actions of men. See 10.5 above, V.11.16, VI.18.9; and see my *Livy*, 60.

profligare bellum: "to polish off the war", perhaps a colloquialism in Cicero (*Fam.* II.30.2) but common in Livy (IX.29.1, XXVIII.2.11).

secundum deos: almost "on the level below ...."; cf. I.4.1.

Chapter 41.

2. licuit ... ire ... ubi ... haberem: "I could have gone ... and would have there". For the indicative of the modal verb, see Woodcock, § 200.

4. hostem fudi: Cf. 29.3.

fugientium: As at 40.2, rhetorical argument apposite for a battle-speech, but hardly relevant to the facts; see 31.3 for the Hannibalic strategy. Similar arguments appear in the Polybian version, III.64.6.

[neque] ... [erat]: This is the easiest solution to the textual difficulty, and the least likely. Wölfflin's *nequieram*, which excises *non poteram* as a gloss and *erat* as a later insertion, is an ingenious suggestion.

timendo: Ironical.

5. cum declinarem: The clause must be taken closely with *videor incidisse*—"do I appear to have run into the enemy through carelessness, when seeking to avoid a contest . . . ?"

in vestigiis eius: Not to be taken directly with *occurrere*. The sense is: ". . . or to be dogging his steps and advancing towards him".

6. terra ediderit: A poetic image to enhance the incongruity of the suggestion; cf. Ovid, *Met.* I.436.

ad Aegates . . . ab Eryce: The appropriate *exempla* demonstrate the traditional role of the Carthaginians. For Livy's use of *exempla* in speeches, see my *Livy*, 238 f.; for the historical events, 10.7 n.

duodevicenis denariis: The ransom of 18 denarii per capita is not mentioned in Polybius or any other source, though Dio remarks (cf. Zon. 8.17) that Hamilcar requested Catulus to dispense with the yoke. The detail was presumably in Livy's own lost account of the terms in Book 19.

7. aemulus itinerum Herculis: (*aemulus* here has substantival force; cf. Cic. *Marc.* 2, *illo aemulo atque imitatore studiorum ac laborum meorum*). Hercules was said to have returned from Spain via Gaul after his tenth labour, the capture of the oxen of Geryones, and to have crossed into Italy by the Graian Alps. Cf. Pliny, *N.H.* III.123: *Graiis Herculem transisse memorant*, and Livy V.34.6 and I.7.3 with Ogilvie's notes.

vectigalis stipendiariusque et servus: A rhetorical fantasy, as Livy well knows. The label of tributary and slave is in Polybius' version (III.64.4) attached to the Carthaginians as a whole. They had in fact paid the indemnity of 3,200 talents imposed by the treaty of Catulus by 231. Though initially there was a distinction between *vectigal*, payment in produce, and *stipendium*, the more humiliating money-tribute, the two words later become interchangeable (cf. Livy XXXIII.47.1 f.) and both are used here merely for rhetorical emphasis (*congeries verborum*) to accentuate Hannibal's subservience.

8. agitaret: "derange"; cf. Cic. *Rosc.* 67: *suum quemque scelus agitat amentiaque afficit*.

si non . . . certe: Cf. XXXI.7.3; Mikkola, 94 n. 1.

foedera Hamilcaris scripta manu: The Carthaginians entrusted to Hamilcar full discretion for negotiation, and Polybius praises him highly for his realistic assessment of the situation (Pol. I.62).

9. consule: Lutatius Catulus.

Book XXI

fremens maerensque: An imaginative touch in the tradition of dramatic historiography. So Hannibal is said to leave Italy for home, *frendens gemensque ac vix lacrimis temperans* (XXX.20.1).

10 quadam: "with a sense of outrage".

velut si: Note how in the speeches Livy uses the full Ciceronian expression (cf. §.15 below) whereas in the narrative *velut* and *tamquam* are frequently used without *si* (II.36.1, XXIX.22.1, etc.).

11. Licuit ... licuit: "We could have ...."; see § 2 above.

humanorum: sc. *suppliciorum*; at IV.9.3 Livy writes *ultima publicorum malorum*.

12. tutelae deinde: "Under our protection". The genitive with a verb (cf. VII.18.3, *fidei suae ... ducebant esse*) is sometimes labelled possessive (*e.g.* by Dimsdale), but it is better regarded as a genitive of quality or definition.

During the Mercenary War in which Carthage lost Sardinia to the rebels, Utica defected, and Carthage was under siege, the Carthaginians appealed for help to both Hiero and Rome. The Romans restored all prisoners, allowed their merchants to sail into Carthage with merchandise, and refused the *deditio* of both Utica and mercenaries in Sardinia (Pol. I.83). Naturally Scipio omits to mention Rome's almost immediate volte-face on Sardinia (Pol. I.88.8 with Walbank's n.).

13. furiosum: A regular strand in the traditional characterisation of Hannibal; cf. § 8 above, and 10.11.

atque utinam: With this *exclamatio*, yet another rhetorical figure evidenced in this speech, Scipio passes from the themes of easy victory and righteous war to the necessity of self-defence.

14. de quibus quondam agebatur: The First Punic War was fought for Sicily but hardly for Sardinia, which was seized in opportunist fashion after the close of hostilities; see § 12 above.

15. nisi: It is tempting to read here *nos si non vincimus*. For the distinction between *nisi* and *si non*, the first making negative the whole clause, the second a particular word, see Kühner-Stegmann, 2.411.

qui obsistat, quas dum superant ... possint: The relatives have a consecutive sense; *quas dum* is the compendious equivalent of *ut dum eas ...* or *quibus, dum eas ...*

velut si: See § 10 above.

16. The conventional appeal in the *conclusio* is to the emotions of the hearers, stressing their allegiance to kin and country.

NOTES

Chapter 42.

1. Hannibal: His precise position has not been given (cf. 39.6) but Polybius is equally vague. The following incident is recorded with more picturesque detail in Pol. III.62.2 ff.; parallels in syntactical structure and order of topics suggest that he may be Livy's source here.

armisque Gallicis: In Polybius, πανοπλίας Γαλατικάς, "such as usually adorn their kings when they intend to fight a single combat" (III.62.5).

interpretem: Not in Polybius, and presumably a careful addition by Livy in the interests of probability.

ecquis (= *ecce quis*), expressing more dramatic enquiry.

decertare: "to engage to the death".

2. cum ad unum: This section in particular reproduces closely the order of topics in Pol. III.62.7 f.

deiecta: The regular expression for dropping lots in an urn or helmet; cf. Caes. *B.C.* I.6.5, Virg. *Aen.* V.490.

fortuna: In Polybius, "the Gauls raised their hands and prayed to the gods" (III.62.8); Livy appears to have introduced the *fortuna* motif here.

3. sui moris tripudiis: An imaginative touch not in Polybius. Livy is fond of retailing such tribal behaviour. Compare his account of the priests of Gallograecia, *vaticinantes fanatico carmine* (XXXVIII. 18.9) where the source Polybius has φάσκοντες (XXI.37.5); also 28.1 above.

4. dimicarent: Frequentative; 4.4 n.

is habitus animorum: *is* points forward to the *ut* clause; "their mental attitude was such that . . ."

inter spectantes volgo: "amongst the spectators at large". Packard's *Concordance* lists eleven examples of this usage of *volgo*, all from the fourth and fifth decades; this passage is not cited.

Chapter 43.

1. spectatis: Participial here, picking up *spectantes*, rather than adjectival; *spectatus* as adjective conveys the notion of *moral* excellence inappropriate here.

ita locutus fertur: The formula again indicating Livy's free version, which is totally different from that in Polybius. The structure in Livy is as follows.

43.2: **Exordium:** principium ab auditoribus.

43.3-44.7: **Tractatio**

    43.3-5 *necessarium*

Book XXI

2. si, etc. A stylistic commencement parallel to that of Scipio's speech. In Polybius this topic is treated in *oratio obliqua*.

fortuna: here = *condicio*, as frequently.

veluti imago: "a type of your own situation"; 40.8 n.

3. fortuna: The *fortuna*-theme is likewise in the Polybian speech (III.63.3) at this point, but note how Livy reintroduces it (§ 5 *et eadem fortuna:* § 10, *terminum laborum fortuna dedit:* 44.8) to characterise Hannibal as a man who relies on fortune, and who later in his speech before Zama acknowledges this as an error (XXX.30.10 ... *ut rationem sequi quam fortunam malim*; cf. 30.5, 11, 12, 16, 18).

4. circa Padus: Not *a fronte*, presumably because the Po and its tributaries (the Sesia and the Dora Baltea) surrounded Hannibal on three sides.

maior ac violentior Rhodano: The Po falls 6,000 ft in 40 miles to Turin, and its displacement of 63,000 cubic feet per second is many times greater than that of the Rhône. The Rhône is of course considerably longer, but Livy is not concerned with overall length here. He can draw both on personal knowledge of the Po and on literary testimonies such as that of Pol. II.16.6 ff. and Virgil, *G.* I.482, *fluviorum rex*.

5. ne ab dis: In development of the theme of Hannibal's enslavement to *fortuna*, Livy here depicts her as the blind Tyche which has no connection with the gods.

7. agite dum: The use of *-dum* as an enclitic following an imperative or interjection is very common in early Latin; it is probably in origin an accusative of extent of time. *agedum* becomes so common later in the sense of "come now" that it is used indiscriminately with singulars and plurals (cf. Livy XXXVIII.47.11, *mittite agedum legatos,* and earlier Plaut. *Mil.* 928, *age.*). *agitedum* appears frequently in the first decade.

8. in vastis Lusitaniae Celtiberiaeque montibus: Not mentioned in the Polybian version, and much more relevant to second- and first-century Roman campaigns than to those of Hannibal. Celtiberia was earlier regarded by historians as in the north-east of Spain (so Walbank on Pol. III.17.2 f.), but in Livy's day it denoted the general area of the hinterland south of the Ebro. Lusitania lay further west in the modern Portugal, and gave its name to the western imperial province; it was not an area in which Hannibal had campaigned.

consectando: For the use of the gerund with participial force, see 2.1 n.

9. opulenta ... ac ditia stipendia: For *opulentus* in this military sense, see I.30.4, *exercitus opulentus praeda*; for *dis*, cf. IX.40.6, *ditem hostem ... victoris praemium*.

10. emeritis stipendiis: The stock military expression; so Cic. *Sen.* 49, Sall. *Jug.* 84.2, Livy IV.60.4, etc.

11. nec existimaritis: *nec = et ne* with a perfect subjunctive in a prohibition is common at all times following an affirmative imperative (Kühner-Stegmann, I.192 f.) ;Livy is fond of using it parenthetically, as here and V.53.3, etc.

quam ... tam: "Do not think that the difficulty of winning will be commensurate with the fame of the war". The *quam* in the correlative construction has a concessive force ("though the war be famed"); see Mikkola, 81, comparing Sall. *Hist.* I.55.24. There is no adjective in Latin which could be used with the precise sense of *magni nominis* (Wölfflin).

certamen edidit: cf. § 17 below, *ediderim facinus*, and 29.2, *proelium ... editur*.

perlevi momento: "through the slightest turning of the scales". For the thought, see XXV.18.3, XLII.50.5, etc.

12. nam: "This will certainly be the case, for ...".

fulgore nominis: The metaphorical use of *fulgor* does not occur in Latin till the Augustan period (cf. Ovid, *Trist.* V.12.39), and this represents a further example of the bolder use of metaphor in Livy than in Cicero.

13. ut ... taceam: The rhetorical device of *praeteritio* (παράλειψις). For the transitive use of *tacere*, see Cic. *De Or.* 1.119, etc.

viginti annorum: Hamilcar had crossed to Spain in 237 (2.1 n.), and many Carthaginians had served in Spain continuously since then.

ab Herculis columnis, ab Oceano: Rhetorical exaggeration; the troops had started from New Carthage (21.1, 22.5), though Hannibal himself had visited Gades, on the Atlantic close to Gibraltar (21.9).

14. tirone: 39.3 n.

caeso, etc. Near Mutina; cf. 25.9 ff.

15. An: In § 12, Hannibal had asked rhetorically if the Romans were comparable to the Carthaginians. He has first compared armies; *an* introduces a second point of comparison, the leaders.

Galliaeque: Specifically the Volcae, whose defeat is described at 28.1 ff.

Book XXI

semenstri ... duce: An effective rhetorical point, since Cornelius Scipio had been in office only since March, and it was now about the end of September. He would have had considerable military experience previously, but his actual career cannot be traced.

desertore exercitus sui: Again a rhetorical rather than substantial argument. Scipio had sent his army on to Spain (32.3 ff.). For the reflexive *sui* referring to the subject contained in the substantive (*desertore* = *qui deseruit*) see II.40.9, etc.: Riemann, 120.

17. cui non: "to whom I am unable to recount his own glorious deeds, designated by time and place". For *cui ... sua*, see Riemann, 124 f.

18. laudatis ... donatisque: For the stock military phrase ("given citations and decorations") cf. Sall. *Jug.* 8.2: *donatus atque laudatus.* For the use of *miliens* in such hyperbole, cf. V.51.1.

Chapter 44.

1. animorum ac roboris: "alacrity and vigour".

generosissimarum gentium equites: Referring to the Spanish contingents as well as the Masaesylii, the African neighbour on whom Carthage relied for provision of cavalry; see *JRS* (1965), 150 f.

frenatos infrenatosque: Spaniards and Numidians respectively (cf. 46.5). The Numidian cavalry was renowned for using no bridles; cf. Virg. *Aen.* IV.41 and the amusing description at Livy XXXV.11.8 ff. *infrenatus* normally means "bridled"; this is the sole passage in classical Latin where it bears the sense of *infrenis.*

4. dolor, iniuria, indignitas: "resentment at injustice and humiliation". *Indignitas* possibly has the subjective sense of indignation, as at V.45.6, but more probably it balances *iniuria* as a second objective statement of the causes of *dolor* (cf. I.34.5).

vos omnes: 30.3 n.

deditos adfecturi fuerunt: "Once we had surrendered, they intended to inflict ...". The use of the future participle to express purpose (Caesar would have written *in animo habuerunt adficere*) is one of the important syntactical shifts in Livy's Latinity. See 1.4 n.

5. crudelissima ac superbissima gens: This kind of indictment of Roman imperialism, ascribed by the historian to a hostile spokesman, is a frequent feature of Roman historiography, revealing the familiarity with such charges in the first century B.C. See 19.9 n.

suique arbitrii: 41.12 n.

cum quibus bellum habeamus, etc. Though the treaty of Catulus had stipulated that the allies of both sides were to be immune from attack

(Pol. III.27.3), this suggestion that Rome claimed the right to decide with whom the Carthaginians could go to war is justified only after 201 (Pol. XV.18.4, Livy XXX.37.4). The subjunctive *habeamus* is stipulative; Handford, § 51.

circumscribit: Again anachronistic, closer to the situation after 201 (Pol. XV.18.1 ff.).

quos non excedamus: The subjunctive is again stipulative. The accusative after this verb does not appear before Livy, in whom it is common (II.37.8, III.57.10, etc.: Kühnast, 145).

6. Ne transieris Hiberum: 2.7 n. This is the figure known as *fictio personarum,* by which the speaker momentarily assumes the identity of an opponent; cf. Quint. IX.2.29 ff.

ne quid rei: "You are to have no dealings with . . .".

nusquam . . . moveris: For the perfect subjunctive after *nullus, nunquam,* etc., cf. Sall. *Jug.* 110.4, Livy II.12.11, and above, 43.11. *Vestigio* may be an ablative of separation, "from your present place", or of measure of difference, "as much as a step".

7. ⟨ademisti?⟩: But it would be easier to explain the ellipse of *adimis,* as Heerwagen proposes.

⟨Transcendes⟩ autem?: This is Madvig's fine emendation. For *autem* rejecting a previous statement ("Do I say you *will* cross?"), cf. Cic. *Rab.* 10: *Att.* VI.2, etc.

in Africam . . . in Hispaniam: This had been the senate's intention (cf. 17.1); Sempronius had gone to Sicily to prepare an invasion of Africa (17.6), whilst Scipio had set out for Spain, so that Hannibal's allegation is strictly true.

8. respectum: "place of refuge", as at Cic. *Phil.* 10.9, 11.26.

pacata: "friendly"; 20.7, 26.6.

vobis . . . fortibus viris: With *esse* after *licet* a predicated noun or adjective is usually attracted into the dative, as at the beginning of this sentence. By Livy's time this convention has extended to other expressions like *necesse est;* cf. Woodcock, § 124 n. 1.

omnibus . . . abruptis: "renouncing any intermediate outcome between victory and death as an impossible prospect". *abrumpere* connotes the deliberate severance by the soldiers themselves from any other outcome (cf. *abrumpere vitam*); *certa desperatione* is best taken as causal.

9. [bene fixum]: Rightly excised as a gloss on *destinatum* by Hertz; the phrase is found nowhere else in Livy.

destinatum in animo: Though the simple dative might be expected, the presence of *omnibus* before the verb led Livy to use this variation, found also at VI.6.7.

nullum contemptu m⟨ortis incitamentum⟩: Frigell's speculative insertion would fill out a line of 18 uncials which might have dropped out of the archetype; see the *O.C.T.* Vol. 2, xvi. But Livy nowhere uses *incitamentum* (see Packard's *Concordance*); *hortamentum* would be a better solution.

Chapter 45.

1ff. Notice how, once these speeches detailing the attitudes of each side are completed, Livy develops the narrative with his technique of alternation of standpoint, beginning with the Romans (§ 1), continuing with the Carthaginians (§ 2), switching back to the Romans (§ 3), and finally to the Carthaginians (§ 4) whose detailed activities are then recounted (§ 4-9). In ch. 46 a similarly extended account of the Romans begins the chapter (§ 1-3), followed by further alternation of viewpoint.

1. ad certamen accensi: Livy omits to say, doubtless in the interests of a more dramatic narrative, that a night elapsed before the battle was joined (Pol. III.65.2).

ponte Ticinum iungunt: *i.e.* from the east to the west bank, and crossing close to the junction with the Po; cf. Pol. III.65.1. Here Livy provides extra detail, not in Polybius, of the operations.

castellum insuper imponunt: Livy clearly means that a defensive structure (presumably of timber like Agricola's *castella*) was erected on the western end of the bridge; *insuper imponunt* can hardly mean "they built as well". It is tempting to believe that Livy has misunderstood the account in his source, which may have described a bridgehead or perhaps merely a *praesidium militum*.

2. Poenus: For the variation between plural and singular, see 8.3 n.

opere: "on construction-work"; cf. 7.3.

Maharbalem ... mittit: A further detail not found in Polybius. On Maharbal at Saguntum, 12.1 n.

sociorum populi Romani: Though the Romans had recently settled Latin colonies at Placentia and Cremona, there is no evidence that she had made formal *foedera* with any peoples in this area north of the Po, so that the expression is anachronistic. Livy probably has in mind non-Gallic communities amongst the Taurini and the Laevi (cf. V.35.2, Pol. II.17.4 with Walbank's n.).

3. in agrum Insubrium: The Insubres, whose capital was at Mediolanum (Milan), must have regarded the area east of the Ticinus as likewise within their sphere of influence, so that this phrase seems otiose. But perhaps Livy wishes to stress that the crossing was not so far south as Ticinum, the capital of the Laevi, who though under Insubrian dominance were a Ligurian people.

Victumulis: There is dispute about the site of Victumulae. Strabo V.218 puts it near Placentia in the territory of Vercellae; cf. also Pliny, *N.H.* XXXIII.78. But it was more probably on the modern site of Biella, 20 miles north-west of Vercellae, and too far north for this operation. See the evidence of the Ravenna geographer cited by Nissen, *Ital. Landesk.* 2.174 f. The actual site of the skirmish of the Ticinus was in the vicinity of Laumellum (Lomello), midway between the Ticinus and the Sesia, and about 8 miles north of the Po (De Sanctis, III.2.25; Walbank on Pol. III.65).

4. vocatis ad contionem: Polybius has no record of this second harangue.

in quorum spem: The accusative expresses the aim or end to which they are to address their efforts. Cf. *mercedem*, 43.7.

4-5. pugnarent ... velit ... accepisset: After an introductory historic present, the tendency of Cicero and Caesar is to use primary subjunctives in *oratio obliqua*, but on occasion secondary subjunctives follow (Cic. *Verr.* II.1.66, Caes. *B.G.* V.47.5; Kühner-Stegmann, 2. 176 f.). Livy likewise varies his usage. Here *pronuntiat* is employed as a historic or secondary tense; for "Conway's Law" after such a tense, see 10.3 n.; but not infrequently as here we find a combination of primary and secondary subjunctives without such a logical pattern (cf. 30.2 ff.).

6. cives Carthaginienses: If the speech has any historical basis, which is improbable, this could be addressed to the Numidians who lived on the borders of Carthaginian territory, and who would benefit economically from such a change of status.

suorum popularium ... secum: "to obtain the lot of any of their fellow-countrymen in place of their own". For the reflexives referring to the subject of the subordinated clause, see Riemann, 137. For *secum* as a compendious comparison for *cum sua fortuna*, cf. 4.8 n.

8. silicem: Not "knife" (Dimsdale), as the verb *elisit* shows; it is a flint-stone. Cf. I.24.9 with Ogilvie's n. It will be noted that here as often the detailed portrait of Hannibal is at odds with the sketch in 4.9, *nullum iusiurandum, nulla religio*; see my *Livy*, 104.

9. quisque: Juxtaposed with *suam*, but illogically in the nominative, as if Livy had written *velut deos . . . quisque accepisset*.

morae: Predicative dative; Woodcock, § 68.

Book XXI

Chapter 46.

1. super cetera: 31.12 n.

prodigiis: Livy regularly sets down the prodigies which were reported each year to the *pontifex maximus* and listed in the *annales maximi*. By so doing he was going counter to the contemporary convention among historians (see his comments at XLIII.12.1), and this is an indication of his religious standpoint. Though he is aware that many of these reported prodigies are bogus (see 62.1 below; XXIV.10.6, XXVII.23.2, etc.) he accepts in principle that such manifestations can be a sign of divine displeasure, or (to express the matter in a Stoic way) a mark of cosmic disharmony. See my *Livy*, 61 ff. On prodigies in general, see R. Bloch, *Les prodiges dans l'antiquité classique* (Paris, 1963); F. B. Krauss, *An Interpretation of the Omens, Portents, and Prodigies reported by Livy, Tacitus and Suetonius* (Philadelphia 1930). On Livy's attitude, see J. Delgado, *Helmantica* (1961), 441 ff.: (1963), 383 ff. The lists placed here and at ch. 62 are of course juxtaposed with Roman defeats, and their importance as contributing to dramatic narrative and the creation of an atmosphere of gloom should not be overlooked.

2. lupus: An animal sacred to Mars (Hor. *Odes*, I.17.9) and doubtless interpreted by the credulous as symbolising Hannibal himself. Wolves are frequently cited amongst prodigies; cf. 62.5, XXVII.37.3, Hor. *Odes*, III.27.3, etc.

⟨**et**⟩: The copulative *et* is characteristic in prodigy-lists; cf. 62.3 ff.

examen apum: Another common prodigy. Cf. Pliny, *N.H.* XI.55: Cic. *Har. Resp.* 25: Livy XXIV.10.11, XXVII.23.2, etc. Such a swarm could presage prosperity (Cic. *Div.* 1.73); but in the Livian passages they regularly symbolise the hostile forces which are to defeat the Roman command. Likewise in the famous prodigy in the *Aeneid* (VII.64 ff.), bees settle on the ancient laurel which lent its name to Laurentum, symbolising the future dominion of the Trojans.

3. quibus procuratis: The signs of divine displeasure had to be expiated by appropriate sacrifices or other religious gestures. See the discussion by Cicero at *Div.* 1.95 ff.

Scipio, etc. So also Pol. III.65.3 ff., whose account of the skirmish is basically similar.

5. Romanos sociorumque quod roboris: These are the rest of the cavalry (see § 3). For *quod roboris* ("the flower" of the allied contingent) as a military cliché, see Caesar, *B.C.* III.87.4, Livy XXX.2.1, etc.

in subsidiis: "as reserve-ranks". In the formal disposition of a Roman army, the *subsidia* are the *triarii* or third line (Varro, *L.L.* 5.89), but in less formal engagements such as this they are reserves drawn up behind the front line.   Walbank, 399, believes there is a misunderstanding here by Livy or his source, for the corresponding phrase in Polybius ἐν μετώπῳ means "in line facing the front".   But this does not invalidate Livy's description, for they are certainly not in the front rank.

frenatos equites: *i.e.* the Spaniards (44.1 n.), the Numidian cavalry having no bridles.

   6. inter subsidia ac secundam aciem: "amongst the reserves in the second line".   Though the manuscripts, except perhaps M, read *ad*, not *ac*, this would give a false picture of a retreat *between* the subsidia *to* the second line; in fact the *subsidia are* the second line, with nothing behind them.   For the expression, cf. IV.28.2, *subsidia et secundam aciem adortus . . .*

aliquamdiu . . . dein: 7.8 n.

quia: The sentence is slightly illogical in construction.   The sense is: because the horses were disturbed by the intermingling of infantry (*i.e.* the *iaculatores*), many riders fell off; or they dismounted to lend aid to comrades, and so the battle became an infantry engagement.

vidissent: Frequentative; 4.4 n.

   7. ad pedes pugna abierat: There is no parallel in Livy to support Luterbacher's *abierat*.   Livy normally writes *ad pedes descendere, degredi, deduci* to describe this operation.   None of these verbs is close to the readings of the manuscripts, and Gron.'s *venerat* should be adopted on the analogy of II.46.3, *pugna iam in manus, iam ad gladios venerat.*   There is also a case for retaining *anceps* which appears in MDA, for Polybius has ἰσόρροπον (65.8). I would read: *ad pedes anceps pugna venerat.*

circumvecti paulum: "wheeled slightly".   But one wonders if *paulatim* ("gradually worked their way round") may not be the true reading here.

tum primum pubescentis: He was born in either 236 (Pol. X.6.10; *Vir. Ill.* 49) or 235 (Pol. X.3.4, Livy XXVI.18.7) and was thus 17 or 18 at this time.

   8. Hic erit iuvenis: (for the reading *erit*, cf. III.1.1, VII.1.1, Florus II.6.11, *hic erit Scipio . . .*).   This is the first mention of the great Scipio Africanus, Livy's hero and model of conduct, who dominates the second half of this decade.   For a detailed picture, see my *Livy*, 93 ff.

   9. tamen: Resumptive after the parenthesis; 39.10 n.

quos . . . invaserunt: For the direct object, already used by Sallust (Cicero almost invariably has *in* with the accusative) and regularly found in Livy, see Kühner-Stegmann, 1.334.

Book XXI

alius confertus equitatus: The previous sentence indicated by the use of *maxime* (*iaculatorum maxime*) that a few cavalry had fled; *alius* here bears the sense of "the rest" (11.3 n.).

cedendo: For the participial force of the gerund, see 2.1 n.

10. Coelius ad servum ... delegat: On Coelius, see Introduction, p. 41. The attribution of this deed of bravery to the young Scipio goes back to his intimate Laelius (Pol. X.3.2 ff.) though Laelius may not have known him at the time. The alternative explanations are that Scipio was the hero, and that the Ligurian slave has been introduced for derogation of his image; or that the slave was the saviour, and the attribution of the rescue to the son is an early attempt to build up the legend of Scipio as the rescuer as well as the avenger of his father. This seems to me more probable, but cf. Walbank on Pol. X.3.3 ff.

malim ... plures tradidere auctores: An engaging admission of Livy's partiality towards his hero. Presumably Antias as well as Polybius recorded this version.

obtinuit: Normally intransitive ("and this is the version that prevails"). so that *quod* has to be regarded as a loose internal accusative ("in this matter").

Chapter 47.

1. equitatu meliorem Poenum ... et ... campos patentes ... aptos non esse: Likewise joined in Pol. III.66.2, who adds the further reason for retiring that Scipio was severely wounded.

2. vasa colligere: "to pack up", the regular military expression; Cic. *Verr.* II.4.40, Livy XXVII.47.8, etc.

ad Padum: It is clear from Pol. III.66.3-4 (see Walbank's n.) that Livy is wrong here. "The first river" in Polybius must be the Ticinus, where a bridge had been built and guarded (45.1), and the river at which the Roman protecting force was captured (§ 3) must be the Ticinus.

ratibus: In Polybius the bridge over the Ticinus is of planks (III.66.4), as Livy earlier implies (45.1 and 3), so that Livy here describes the Ticinus action as if it were taking place at the Po, where the only practicable bridge was of boats.

3. Prius ... pervenere quam ... sciret: In the classical authors, the subjunctive after priusquam is normally regarded as expressing an idea of design or anticipation ("before Hannibal *could* realise ..."). But when the main verb is positive and past as here, the indicative is frequent only in early and colloquial Latin, and is never found for example in Caesar, where

NOTES

many of the subjunctives have only the merest hint of anticipation or purpose (*e.g. B.G.* III.26.3). In Livy on several occasions (cf. XXV.31.12) the subjunctive is found expressing a purely temporal idea. See Woodcock, § 228.

ad sescentos: So also Pol. III.66.4.

in citeriore ripa: from Hannibal's viewpoint—the north bank of the Po in Livy's version, but actually the west bank of the Ticinus.

tota rate: As at 28.7, the rafts lashed together are visualised as a single *rates* (cf. § 6 below); once the moorings at each end are unfastened, the whole structure is taken downstream by the current. For *secundam aquam*, cf. 27.3n.

4. Magonem: The younger brother of Hannibal (Pol. III.71.5 f.; cf. 54.2 below).

Hispanis: Compare their crossing of the Rhône, 27.5.

5. peritis: Including, of course, the Paduan himself.

fecerint: Perfect subjunctive of modest assertion; 38.7 n.

ut iam: "Even assuming that ..."; cf. XXXIV.32.13, *ut iam ita sint haec, quid ad vos, Romani?*

6. auctores: *i.e.* Polybius III.66.6: καταλύσας δὲ δευτεραῖος καὶ γεφυρώσας τοῖς ποταμίοις πλοίοις and perhaps Antias, for Polybius has no mention of Mago's going over first.

locum iungendo flumini: There are two such datives of the end aimed at attached to nouns in Caesar (*B.G.* III.4.1., V.27.5); the construction is much commoner in Livy (cf. 52.8).

7. Livy's independence of Polybius is especially notable here.

8. sex milia: So Pol. III.66.11, "about 50 stades". Livy like Polybius implies that the Roman camp was adjacent to the city, whereas the logic of the subsequent battle demands that this first camp was west of the Trebia. See Pol. III.67.9 ff. with Walbank's notes.

Chapter 48.

1. tumultu ... quam re maior: Livy makes less of the incident than does Polybius. The number of deserters is identical, but in Polybius it is not merely the guards who are slaughtered but a considerable number of troops encamped next to the Gauls.

2. Ad: adverbial = *circiter*; 8.3 n.

3. signum defectionis: "a signal *for* the rebellion ...".

4. quarta vigilia: "Shortly before daybreak"; cf. Pol. III.67.9.

impeditiores equiti: The enemy being superior in this arm; cf. 47.1.

castra movet: According to Livy's improbable version, the Romans now move westwards from Placentia towards the east bank of the Trebia.

5. utique: "at any rate", a usage common especially in Cicero's letters and perhaps a colloquialism earlier; 29.7n.

6. transgressos: From the east to the west bank. In Polybius, though the Romans are said to camp initially περὶ τὴν Πλακεντίαν (66.9), Scipio's movements are eastward to the Trebia, and the crossing of the river is from west to east.

7. collegam ... ratus expectandum: Since Sempronius was proceeding from Rimini, this is a further reason for assuming that Livy is incorrect, and that Scipio encamped east of the Trebia, with Hannibal to the west.

stativis: sc. *castris*. Livy uses the word to indicate Scipio's intention to dig in. But the *castra stativa* proper, the permanent camp constructed for long periods between campaigns, was much more complex than Scipio's on this occasion. On the permanent camp, see Pol. VI.27 ff. with Walbank's notes.

8. nec procul inde: 5 miles according to Pol. III.68.7.

quantum ... tantum: For the correlatives used concessively, ("though delighted ... none the less concerned"), see Mikkola, 81.n.4.

9. Clastidium: Its site has been established by inscriptions as Casteggio, 27 miles west of the Trebia (*CIL*, V. 827 f.). It had been important as a Roman base in their operations against the Gauls in 222 (Pol. II.34.5). Its position further reinforces the view that Hannibal was west of the Trebia, and Scipio east.

nummis aureis quadringentis: Gold coins were not minted at Rome till the following year (cf. Pliny, *N.H.* XXXIII.47; for a useful summary of the earlier development of Roman coinage, see Scullard, *Roman World*, ch. 16 § 4). It is possible that Livy is here indicating the amount paid anachronistically (the *nummus aureus* being equivalent to 100 sesterces). But more probably he is describing Carthaginian gold coins here; the Carthaginians had struck issues in gold as early as 400 in Sicily, and at Carthage itself from earlier in the third century. The obverse was a head of Tanit in the guise of Persephone, the reverse usually a horse and/or a palm-tree. For a popular account see Harden, *The Phoenicians*, 166 ff.

Dasio: Polybius does not provide the name (III.69.1); the form appears also in Livy XXIV.45.1, XXVI.38.6.

10. ut fama clementiae colligeretur: "To win a reputation for clemency". The use of *colligere* is fully Ciceronian.

NOTES

49.1-51.7. Sicilian operations. Sempronius joins Scipio at the Trebia

Livy's neat organisation of the historical material is notable here. Sempronius is now introduced into the narrative of the Italian campaigning. As a preliminary, Livy marshals events in Sicily during the earlier months of 218, and then translates the reader with Sempronius from Sicily to Ariminum and the Trebia. For other examples of this technique, by which operations in different theatres are skilfully united, see my *Livy*, 180 f.

The information given in these chapters is all the more precious since Polybius provides no detail (cf. III.41.2, III.61.9 f.). The sequence of events must have been: (*a*) The praetor Aemilius Lepidus is despatched to Sicily after the outbreak of war to prepare the way for the invasion of Africa (see § 6 below). (*b*) Sempronius sails for Sicily after Aemilius has repelled a surprise attack on Lilybaeum. (*c*) Sempronius takes over at Lilybaeum, leads a flotilla to Malta, returns to Lilybaeum, and takes a second force to Volcanum. (*d*) On his return to Sicily he is informed of Hannibal's invading march, and plans the return of his army to Italy.

Chapter 49.

1. constitisset: "had come to a halt"; cf. Cic. *Mur.* 33, Livy XXXV. 4.1.

insulasque: The Liparaean islands had been earlier under Carthage, but were ceded to Rome by the treaty of 241 (Pol. III.27.2 ff. with Walbank's n.) so that the Carthaginians were closely familiar with them.

2. viginti quinqueremes, etc. This detail of Carthaginian offensive operations, not in Polybius, is an example of the positive gains derived from consultation of the Roman annalists.

Liparas ... Volcani: The Carthaginians sailed round the east of Sicily with the intention of attacking the west coast of Bruttium. These islands are the most southerly of the Lipari islands.

tenuerunt: "held course", an abbreviated form of *cursum tenuerunt* (cf. XXII.31.5).

in fretum: *i.e.* the *fretum Siculum* between Rhegium and Messana.

aestus: "swell" or "current" caused by the storm mentioned in § 5. For *aestus* in this sense, cf. XXIV.1.11.

3. eas: *i.e.* the three just mentioned, in the straits.

Hierone: Hiero II of Syracuse is one of Livy's model faithful allies; cf. 50.7 ff., XXII.37, XXIV.4. His *fides* is enhanced by the implicit comparison made with his young successor Hieronymus. Hiero had been king of

Book XXI

Syracuse since 270 (Pol. I.8.3 with Walbank's n.). Though he had allied himself with Carthage after the incident of the Mamertines in 264, he had concluded peace with Rome in 263, and thereafter preserved the alliance till his death in 216. He was about 90 at this time; cf. Pol. VII.8.7.

4. veteres socios: Livy thinks especially of the areas around Lilybaeum, Panormus, Soluntum, Agrigentum, and Phintias, the main centres of Carthage's former influence.

5. Lilybaeum: The modern Marsala on the west coast, it had been virtually the capital of Carthaginian Sicily after the destruction of Motya in 408 by Dionysius of Syracuse, and the focus of Carthaginian resistance from 250 onwards. See Pol. I.42 ff.; Warmington, *Carthage*, 158 ff.

disiecti ... deiectam: The first verb refers to the *scattering* of the 20 quinqueremes (for *disicere* of vessels on the sea, cf. Virg. *Aen.* I.43, Livy XXX.24.7, etc.), the second to the 35 quinqueremes being *driven off course* (*deicere* as at Caes. *B.G.* IV.28.2, Livy XXIII.34.16, etc.).

6. M. Aemilio praetori: This is the first mention of M. Aemilius Lepidus as praetor, and of Sicily as his province. It has already been stated that Africa and Sicily were the province of the consul Sempronius (17.1), but this is an inexactitude (Sumner, *PACA*, 1966, 19; Broughton, I.238).

7. Extemplo, etc. For an understanding of this textually controverted passage it should be remembered that Aemilius is at Lilybaeum with some Roman forces at his disposal. The legates, who have a status higher than military tribunes (see Walbank on Pol. VI.35.4), carry the praetor's instructions to the coastal cities; the military tribunes supervise the guard-posts as part of their regular duty (Pol. VI.34.8 ff.). Hence insert a colon after *legati*, and take *intendere* and *tueri* as historic infinitives. There is in fact no reason why the *teneri* of the manuscripts should not be retained against Sauppe's *tueri*; "the tribunes directed their men to guard-duties, and Lilybaeum pre-eminently was protected by engines of war." For *teneri*, cf. Caes. *B.G.* III.2.1, VII.69.6, etc.

8. socii navales: After Rome achieved dominance in southern Italy, she entered into alliances with Greek cities which retained their autonomy (Tarentum excepted) but which provided transport-ships and later crews for Roman warships in the First Punic War. Later the phrase *socii navales* means "ships' crews" *simpliciter*, irrespective of provenance. At XXXVI. 2.15, *libertini* at Rome are enrolled as *socii navales*; cf. also XL.18.7. At 50.3 below the Carthaginian sailors are given this title. It is clear in the present case that Sicilian towns are being asked to provide some crews for Roman warships.

cocta cibaria: "The meal-ration, already baked"; ten days' rations are likewise taken aboard at XXVI.7.10.

9. pernox: Not found before the Augustan period; Ovid, *Met.* VII.268 uses it of the moon, as does Livy elsewhere (V.28.10, XXXII.11.9).

sublatis armamentis: "under full sail", so that the sails were visible in the moonlight. The *armamenta*, ship's tackle, sometimes includes sails, sometimes excludes them.

10. Extemplo, etc. The alternation of description from the viewpoints of Romans (§§ 10, 13, 50.4) and Carthaginians (§§ 11, 50.2, 5) is especially common in Livy's accounts of naval engagements; see my *Livy*, 251 ff.

11. demendis armamentis . . . aptandaque . . . classe: This use of the gerundive in the instrumental ablative is almost equivalent in force to a present participle; "they spent the time clearing the decks . . ."; cf. III.65.4, *insectandis patribus tribunatum gessit;* Woodcock, § 207.4.

13. memoria gestarum rerum: The culminating battle of the First Punic War had taken place off the Aegates Islands in March 241, when the Romans under Lutatius Catulus defeated the Carthaginian fleet as it tried to relieve Hamilcar on Mt Eryx.

Chapter 50.

1. Ubi in altum, etc. This sentence well summarises the traditionally differing approaches of the two nations towards fighting at sea. The Roman technique of the *corvus*, first devised at Mylae in 260 and apparently abandoned after Ecnomus in 256, was introduced for this purpose of making the struggle a *certamen virorum aut armorum*. See Polybius I.22 f.

velle: Historic infinitive to be taken with *conserere* as well as *conferre*.

2. eludere: (sc. *velle*), "dodge", used also of ships' manoeuvres at XXXVI.45.3; Caes. *B.C.* I.58.1.

3. sociis navalibus: 49.8 n. As often Livy applies the Roman technical term to Carthaginian conditions, rather incongruously in this instance.

sicubi (= **si ubi**) **esset:** *sicubi* is not uncommon in Terence and Cicero, but has the indicative. The subjunctive here is of course frequentative; 4.4 n.

4. Romanis multitudo sua: *suus* is used much more freely than is *se* in reference to the logical rather than the grammatical subject. Cf. Woodcock, § 36 n. 1.

Book XXI

6. reduce: The word does not imply that the ship was towed back. "Only one ship was holed, and even that was brought to harbour". *Reduce* is here the equivalent of a participle in the ablative absolute, such a predicative use of adjectives being common at all periods. See Kühner-Stegmann, 1.779 f.

7. gnaris: See the previous note. For the use of the participle (here adjective) alone without substantive, cf. 23.1 above, and Woodcock, § 93.1.
Messanam venit: Estimates of the time of year range between May and August 218. Polybius III.41.2 need not be interpreted as saying that the two consuls set out simultaneously, so the fact of Scipio's departure in August is irrelevant. This chapter shows that Aemilius Lepidus had been in the province for some time before Sempronius' arrival; assuming that the praetor arrived shortly after entering office—in April, say—Sempronius can hardly have arrived before May. He has undertaken and carried through expeditions to Malta and the Liparaean islands by mid-September (51.5 n.), so that he may have arrived at Messana by May or June.

8. praetoriam navem: The flagship was so called by extension of the title *praetorium* for the general's tent. Cf. Paulus ap. Fest. p. 249 Lindsay: ... *initio praetores erant qui nunc consules, et hi bellum administrabant, quorum tabernaculum quoque dicebatur praetorium.*
precatusque transitum: Referring, of course, to future operations; "after praying that the crossing would prove successful ..."

9. senem: See 49.3 above.

10. et quibusdam volentibus novas res fore: "and a revolution would be welcome to some of them"; this Greek construction (τοῦτο βουλ<ο>μέν<ῳ> μοι ἔστιν) is earlier imitated by Sallust at *Jug.* 84.3, *neque plebi militia volenti putabatur;* also 100.4. See Riemann, 267.

11. nihil cunctandum quin ...: *nihil* when used as a substantive and direct object of a transitive verb is frequently followed by *quin/quominus;* so Cic. *Phil.* 2.23, *nihil praetermisi ... quin ...;* Livy III.54.4, *nihil moror quominus ...* In the present passage *nihil* has adverbial force, but it is strictly an internal accusative after the gerund, so that the construction is analogous.
navigantes inde: *i.e.* in the course of their journey from Messana.

Chapter 51.

1. a Lilybaeo: 5.7 n.
Melitam: There is surprisingly little evidence in classical writers about Malta. The descriptions in Diodorus (V.12) and the elder Pliny are jejune.

But it is clear from the evidence of tombs and inscriptions that Carthaginians had settled on the island as early as, if not earlier than, the eighth century. There is, however, no trace of the Phoenician town mentioned by Livy here (§ 2); presumably it lies beneath the modern Valetta. See Harden, *The Phoenicians*, 40. At the end of the 2nd Punic War, Carthage was deprived of all her overseas territories, but Rome did not immediately take over the island; see the anecdote about a visit of Massinissa's fleet there at Cic. *Verr.* 4.103. It subsequently fell under the jurisdiction of the governor of Sicily, but there was little supervision, and in Cicero's time it was a refuge for pirates in the winter (*Verr.* II 4.104). See in general J.Weiss, *RE* 15.1, 543 ff. **traiecit:** 19.6 n.

2. Hamilcar, Gisgonis filius: Otherwise unknown; perhaps his father was the Gisgo who negotiated for peace in 241 (Diod. XXIV.13) and was foully executed by the insurgents in the Mercenary War (Pol. I.80). **traditur:** Zeugma; "Hamilcar surrendered himself . . . and the town and island were handed over . . ."

reditum Lilybaeum: Perhaps it was at this time that Sempronius sent a ship from Lilybaeum to reconnoitre the African coast. Charisius has preserved a fragment of Coelius Antipater (*HRR* 12): *Sempronius Lilybaeo celocem in Africam mittit visere locum ubi exercitum exponat.*

a consulibus . . . venierunt: As *veneo* is employed as the passive of *vendo*, from Livy's time it is frequently found with *a* and the ablative. Cf. Quint. XII.1.43, etc.

sub corona: War-captives were originally crowned with chaplets when sold; cf. Coelius Sabinus *ap.* Gell. VI.4.3: *sicuti antiquitus mancipia iure belli capta coronis induti venibant, et idcirco dicebantur sub corona venire.* See the quotation from Cato in the same passage of Gellius.

3. ab ea parte: *i.e.* the west and south.

insulas Volcani: Though the one island (Vulcano) was known as *insula Volcani*, the Liparaean islands as a whole were formerly known as *insulae Volcaniae*; see Cic. *N.D.* 3.55.

4. depopulato: Though the active present *depopulo* is not used by the best writers of the first century B.C., the perfect participle in the passive sense survives in Caesar (*B.G.* I.11.4, VII.77.14) as well as frequently in Livy. **iam forte:** Madvig. *E.L.* 224, emends to *nam forte* (cf. XXXIII.9.2) but *iam forte* is found at X.40.6. **Vibonensi agro:** The territory of the Roman colony Vibo (called Vibo Valentia at Mea. II.4.9, the name it now bears), built on the site of the Greek city of Hipponium, of which 5th/4th-century remains still survive.

BOOK XXI

5. escensio: A word favoured in this sense by Livy (XXII.20.4, XLIV.10.11) and not found in earlier prose.

litteraeque de transitu in Italiam: The date is approximately mid-Sept. (Walbank on Pol. III.61.10). Scipio would have reported urgently to the Roman senate on returning to Pisa in early September.

6. Ariminum: Rome had founded a Latin colony there as early as 268 (Livy *Per.* 15; Vell. Pat. 1.14).

mari supero misit: Polybius and Livy are here wholly at odds. According to Polybius, the army was sailed across the straits and proceeded on foot via Rome, led by Sempronius (III.61.10, 68.12). Appian too (*Hann.* 6) implies the short sea-journey. The circumstantial detail in Polybius (oath exacted from the soldiers, march through Rome, period of 40 days' marching) and the dangers of a sea-journey late in the season make the land-route more likely. But Livy may well be right in sending the consul by sea, otherwise what point would there have been in exacting an oath from the soldiers to appear at Ariminum, if Sempronius personally led them on the march? See Walbank, I. 396.

Sex. Pomponio: Not otherwise known.

52-56. *The Battle of the Trebia*

Chapter 52.

2. equestri proelio uno et volnere suo comminutus: There is a strong case for reading, with Sigonius and Conway, *una* for *uno*, since *uno* would strike an inappropriately derogatory note ("dismayed by a single cavalry engagement"). Moreover, *una et* would help to bring together the disparate ideas in the two ablatives. *Comminutus* is Drakenborch's emendation of the manuscript readings *minutus/et minutus*; since *comminutus* is not used elsewhere by Livy, a more probable solution is *et⟨iam⟩minutus*.

recentis animi: In battle-contexts, *recens* is the antonym of *defatigatus*, precisely the note of contrast with Scipio required here.

ferocior: For Livy, *ferocitas* is an irrational emotion which puts a commander at the mercy of an opponent who is *callidus*; it is the mental state which encourages *temeritas*, the antonym of the *prudentia* which is the mark of the good general. See my *Livy*, 71 ff.

3. Inter Trebiam Padumque: The vague topography reflects the words of Polybius III.69.5.

4. modo ne: "As long as they refrained from hostilities". *modo*, though similar in meaning to *dummodo*, "provided that", is not a true subordinating conjunction. Like *tantum* similarly used it remains an adverb, and the construction is an independent jussive. *Modo ne* is found in Cicero (*Off.* I.89) as well as elsewhere in Livy (X.43.4, etc.). See Handford, § 63; Woodcock, § 220.

5. praeda . . . aleret: So *B.G.* VIII.47.3, *latrociniis se suosque alebat.*

deinceps: The sense is "district by district". Though the *TLL* states that this local as against the temporal sense of "successively" is rare, it is found several times in Livy; see I.44.3, II.39.4, XXIX.3.3.

6. ad id: sc. *temporis.* Cf. III.22.8, IX.15.1, etc.

declinant: The verb indicates a movement away from the path of opportunist neutrality.

terrae . . . laboranti: "suffering damage". At Caes. *B.C.* II.6.5 the verb is used of damage to colliding triremes.

7. Cornelio, etc. It would be interesting to know how much of this psychological and moralising detail is attributable to Livy himself. In Polybius the Gauls merely ask for help, without claiming *nimia fides*; likewise there is no mention of Scipio's suspicious unwillingness to help them, though he is opposed to engaging with Hannibal later (III.70.4). These additional hesitations in Livy's account accentuate the *temeritas* of Sempronius, which is to be delineated as the cause of the Trebia disaster.

ut . . . obsolevissent: "Even assuming that time had blotted out the rest . . ."; Kühner-Stegmann, 2. 251 n.3.

recentem Boiorum perfidiam: Cf. 25.2 ff., esp. 25.7.

8. continendis . . . sociis: 47.6 n.

10. sparsos et incompositos . . . ingentem terrorem caedemque ac fugam: Pol. III.69.9 indicates a more orderly retreat; Livy incorporates the characteristic clichés of annalistic historiography.

11. varia inde pugna: The contrast with Polybius is notable here. In his account we read that Hannibal drew up his forces in front of the camp, refusing to allow them to engage in an unplanned operation (III.69.12).

⟨**inter recedentes in**⟩**sequentesque:** This is Conway's intelligent improvement on earlier speculative solutions for filling this lacuna in the text.

cumque ad extremum aequassent certamen: "Though ultimately the exchanges had been even". *aequare* is here used in extension of the sense "to make level or even". Cf. I.25.11 (Horatii v Curiatii), *iamque aequato Marte singuli supererant.*

⟨**cum caedes esset, penes**⟩: This again is Conway's speculative solution, accommodated to the length of a line assumed to have fallen out of the codex Puteanus. It is consonant with the facts described at Pol. III.69.14.

Book XXI

Chapter 53.

1. nemini omnium: "to no-one in the world"; cf. XXXVII.53.20, etc. **iustior:** "more complete"; likewise *iusta victoria* at Cic. *Fam.* II.10.3.

2. restitutos ac refectos, etc. This psychological analysis of Sempronius' attitude, depicted by Livy's regular technique of *oratio obliqua* (cf. 16.3 ff.), is important for its characterisation of the *superbia* and *temeritas* of the consul. Contrast Pol. III.70.2: "It was open to him to follow his own judgment in the present situation since Scipio was ill, but he wished to consult his colleague's opinion." Scipio's advice follows in Polybius, but no comments are attributed to Sempronius, and it seems likely that Livy's own imagination is at work here.

3. differri ... expectari: *differri* is impersonal here. For the regular use of accusative and infinitive in rhetorical questions in *oratio obliqua*, see Woodcock, §267.

4. cis Hiberum: *i.e.* north of the river.

5. circa moenia Carthaginis: The sort of exaggeration apposite for a leader unhinged by *ferocitas*; the fiasco of Regulus' invasion in 256-5 would hardly have been recalled by a more sensitive spokesman.
Appenninum: Regularly singular in classical Latin; cf. below 58.3, 59.1, etc.
suae dicionis: 41.12 n.

6. prope contionabundus: 36.1 n. Livy is, as it were, accounting for the highly rhetorical nature of the speech he has attributed to Sempronius, which is hardly appropriate to sick-bed conversation.
tempus propinquum comitiorum: It was now the end of November (54.7 n.); the new consuls would be elected early in the new year to take office on March 15th.
occasio ... vertendae gloriae: The accusation of *prava ambitio* echoes Pol. III.70.7.

7. Hannibal, etc. The psychological assessment is similarly placed in Polybius' account, but Livy intensifies the motifs of Sempronius' *ferocitas* and *temeritas*. So *temere atque improvide* here, *temeritas* being the antonym of *prudentia*; then *percitum ac ferox* (§ 8), *percitus* implying irrational emotion as at Cic. *Mil.* 63, *animo irato ac percito*.

8. gerendae rei fortunam: "opportunity"; for *fortuna* with the genitive in this sense, cf. VII.35.5, *delendi omnis exercitus fortuna*.

9. tiro: 39.3 n.
dum ... esset ... faceret ... vigerent: The suggestion that *dum* meaning "while" with the present indicative resists transference into the

NOTES

subjunctive in *oratio obliqua* has no foundation so far as Golden Latin is concerned. See *e.g.* Sall. *Cat.* 7.6, Livy XXV.20.6, where as here the subjunctive is imperfect after a historic introductory verb. In Tacitus, and occasionally in Livy, the indicative is retained. See Riemann, 290 n.2; Woodcock, § 221 n.iv.

11. speraret ... certamen et facere ... cuperet: "hoped for a battle, and was eager to precipitate it".

cessaretur: Subjunctive in *oratio obliqua*.

paratos pugnae: The dative, not found in Cicero or Caesar (*B.C.* I.30.5, *omnia ad bellum apta ac parata*), is frequent in Livy (I.1.8, VII.16.4, etc.).

Chapter 54.

1. in medio: "between the two camps". The topography as described here is very close to Pol. III.71.1.

quem ubi, etc. It is instructive to compare the Polybian passage to see how Livy injects an imaginative note. Polybius tells us that Hannibal had long marked out the spot for an ambush, and the plan is worked out in camp. Livy pictures the brothers surveying the spot, and the *oratio recta* reports their imaginary conversation.

equites ... tegendo ... locum: For the dative, 47.6 n. The gerund of a transitive verb in the dative governing an accusative other than a neuter pronoun or adjective is rare in late Republican prose, though commoner earlier. Cicero and Caesar would have written *tegendis locis*, as Livy elsewhere (52.8 above) writes *contlnendis sociis*.

2. Magoni fratri: 47.4 n.

ait: Though *ait* is normally employed for indirect speech, Livy uses it for variation in *oratio recta* when *inquit* is also pressed into service as here (§ 3). See *e.g.* I.24.4, XXXII.32.13 ff.

centenos: *i.e.* 100 infantry and 100 cavalry.

3. praetorium missum: For *praetorium = concilium imperatoris*, (which consisted of *legati, tribuni, praefecti*), cf. XXVI.15.6, XXX.5.2; Caesar uses *concilium*. For *mittere* in the sense of *dimittere*, cf. Caesar, *B.C.* I.3.1, *misso ... senatu*, Livy XXVI.14.4.

novenos ex turmis manipulisque: In Polybius III.71.8 the 200 selected men are told to choose ten each to make the number up to 2,000; notice how Livy is a stickler for accuracy in such minor matters.

insideatis: "where you are to lie in ambush". For the accusative (not in Cicero/Caesar after *insidere*), cf. IX.34.3, XXVI.44.2 and frequently in later authors.

Book XXI

hostem caecum: Further Livian characterisation without parallel in Polybius.

4. obequitare: Not found before Livy.

iniecto ... certamine: For this phrase, "prompting an engagement", cf. X.6.3.

5. ut prandere omnes iuberent ... armatos ... instratisque equis: All emphasising the meticulous preparation of the prudent commander, and thereby characterising by contrast the foolhardiness of Sempronius.

6. ferox: "aggressively confident"; 52.2 n.

ad destinatum iam ante consilio: i.e. *ad id quod iam ante consilio destinaverat* (Weissenborn-Müller).

7. brumae tempus: Sempronius had received the instruction to leave Sicily about mid-September (51.5 n.), and the army had forty days' marching through Italy, not counting the period necessary for preparation and the march from Lilybaeum to Messana. They could hardly have been assembled and fit for operations at Rimini before mid-November. The march to the Trebia and the preliminary operations there would entail the lapse of two or three weeks more, so that it was now December, near "the time of the solstice".

praegelidis: Not found before Livy. The historian here is close to Polybius, but with extra detail about the climate and terrain of which he has personal knowledge.

8. non ope ulla: For the significance of this, cf. 55.1, *ignibus ... oleo*.

quidquid aurae ... appropinquabant: "Whenever the breath of the river-breezes was felt". *quidquid* in such indefinite relative clauses is an internal accusative; cf. *si quid* in such sentences as *si quid in te peccavi, ignosce* (Cic. *Att.* III.15.4). So Livy VII.32.6: *quidquid ... longius proferrent arma* (in *oratio obliqua*), VIII.39.5; *quidquid progrediebantur*, etc.

9. utique egressis: "Particularly after they emerged".

Chapter 55.

2. Baliares ⟨ac⟩ levem armaturam: Though Pol. III.72.7 distinguishes two kinds of light infantry, the insertion of ⟨ac⟩ by editors seems unjustified. In his account of the battle, Livy equates the Baliares and the *levis armatura* (55.5 f.) and does not mention the pikemen at all.

quod virium, quod roboris: "The strength and sinew of his army"; 1.2 n. Note that no figure is given; Polybius gives the strength as 20,000, made up of Celts, Spaniards, and Africans, so that the total engaged on the

NOTES

Carthaginian side is 38,000, with 2,000 more in ambush. Of the 40,000, 11,000 are cavalry; he had arrived at the Po with 6,000 (Pol. III.56.4), but they have been reinforced by Gallic contingents. For suspicions about the round figure, see § 4 below.

ab cornibus . . . elephantos: Livy visualises the elephants outside the cavalry (§ 7 *ab extremis cornibus*); much more probably they were in front of the wings of the phalanx, with the cavalry outside them. See Walbank on Pol. III.72.9.

diversos: "in two sections". This sense of *diversus* ("separated") is common in Latin, and there is no need (*pace* Walbank) to amend the manuscript reading.

3. revocatos circumdedit peditibus: "he flanked the infantry with the cavalry, which were brought back". Note that here the common construction after *circumdare*, with the persons surrounded in the dative and those put round them in the accusative, describes *protective* dispositions; occasionally *circumdare* has the accusative of the body surrounded and the ablative of a circumvallating force, where the dispositions are *aggressive* (Caesar, *B.C.* III.9.4).

4. duodeviginti milia: Polybius' figure is 16,000, the difference being attributable to a different reckoning of the legionary complement. Livy has already indicated this as 4,000 (17.2 f.), so that he must be in error here.

socium . . . viginti, auxilia praeterea: Polybius' figure for the allied forces is likewise 20,000, but he does not mention the contingent of the Cenomani (on whom, see 25.14 n.) who are to be one of the scapegoats in Livy for the defeat. Both Polybius and Livy reckon the Roman cavalry at 4,000. Thus the total figure on each side is reckoned at 40,000, suspiciously like a later estimate. The Carthaginians certainly had a strong numerical advantage in cavalry.

5. diducta . . . levis armatura: Livy means the Baliares (§ 6) who divide and move to the flanks; in Polybius the pikemen later operate there (III.73.7).

6. decem milibus . . . quattuor milia: Livy has refrained from giving the cavalry figures earlier so that the disadvantages under which the Roman cavalry laboured can be assembled in one sentence.

per se: "unaided".

plerisque: Some Numidians had of course provoked the battle and forded the Trebia twice.

insuper: "in addition", not "from above"; cf. 1.5.

BOOK XXI

iaculorum: Livy seems confused. The Balearic slingers are earlier distinguished from *iaculatores* (21.11), but here he seems to regard them as like the Roman *velites*.

7. odore insolito territis: Cf. XXX.18.7, XXVII.14.6. Horses had to be specially trained to face elephants, and Roman forces had not experienced them since the Sicilian and African fighting in the Ist Punic War (Pol. I.19, 34 ff., 40).

fugam faciebant: Here, as at 5.16, to cause flight; elsewhere (Sall. *Jug.* 53.3, 58.4) to flee.

8. animis: Ablative; "by mental determination".

9. Livy's schematic picture—Baliares attacking the flanks, the elephants the front centre, the Numidians the rear—is too neat; the elephants operated throughout on the flanks of the infantry (Pol. III.74.2). Notice Livy's skilful variation of tenses here—imperfect for the continual hail of the light-armed, pluperfect for the recent change of direction by the elephants, and perfect for the sudden emergence of the ambuscade.

simul for *simul ac* is frequent at all periods; see *e.g.* Cic. *Tusc.* 4.12, Caes. *B.G.* IV.26.5.

improvida: continuing the emphasis on Roman *temeritas*.

ingentem tumultum ac terrorem: Cf. XXV.25.9; 52.10 n.

10. maxime: with *adversus elephantos*.

11. velites: For their equipment at this time, cf. XXVI.4.4: *parmae breviores quam equestres et septena iasula*. Since they were not officially formed till 211 (XXVI.4.10) and since there is no trace of this mode of attack in Polybius, the historicity of this detail is dubious. (On the deficiencies of Livy's account of the elephants at the Trebia, see Walbank on Pol. III.72.9 with bibliography).

avertere: Perfect indicative rather than infinitive.

sub caudis ... fodiebant: Later the standard technique was *"vitare impetum beluae et ex transverso aut pilis lacessere aut ... gladio nervos incidere"* (XXXVII.42.5).

Chapter 56.

1. in suos consternatos: "maddened against their own troops"; 11.13 n.

Gallos: The Cenomani (55.4), conveniently in the rôle of scapegoats for the defeat.

2. in orbem: The circle is more appropriate to a defensive stance, familiar to us from Western films and Caesar's Gallic Wars (IV.37.2,

NOTES

V.33.3). If an army wishes to move in close order, it adopts a square formation permitting retention of ranks (*quadrato agmine*, 5.16, 57.7). Livy uses *in orbem* again in this sense at XXII.29.5.

decem milia ferme: So Pol. III.74.6; if all were legionaries, representing the salvage of well over a half the total force.

alia ... media Afrorum acie: The construction after *perrumpere* elsewhere in Livy is *in, per,* or simple accusative. The ablative *media acie* here shows that the preceding *alia* (*Aldus*; alii, *Mss:* alibi, *Weiss.*: aliter, *dett. aliq.*) is likewise ablative with *via* understood. "Since they had been unable to escape by any other route, they broke through by way of the African centre." Cf. XLIV.43.2: *alii alia in civitates suas dilapsi sunt;* otherwise the use of *alia* is poorly attested.

3. neque prae imbri, etc. This was not the only reason; Polybius adds that they feared the enemy cavalry.

Placentiam recto itinere: Since Polybius and Livy both say that the Romans could not return to the camp because of the obstacle of the river (Pol. III.74.5), they must have marched north and crossed the Trebia nearer to the confluence with the Po. Some assume a bridge there (cf. Walbank on Pol. III.74.6), perhaps defended by troops from Placentia (Dimsdale), for the Carthaginians in pursuit were unable to cross because of the wintry weather which had presumably raised the river beyond fording-level. T. Frank, *JRS* (1919), 202, argues that Placentia before 190 B.C. was west of the Trebia at Stradella, but cf. Walbank, I. 401.

4. Plures ... eruptiones: Livy now returns to the battlefield, where the example of the 10,000 prompts other attempts to break out of the Carthaginian encirclement.

6. Imber nive mixtus, etc. This sentence should be transposed with the following one. *Finis insequendi hostis ...* (§ 7) should follow *pervenerunt*; then the Carthaginians return to the camp numb after the pursuit, and the deaths of men and beasts follow. Cf. Pol. III.74.9-11.

elephantos prope omnes: Pol. III.74.11 says that all except one died; at 58. 11 Livy records the death of seven more (but the whole operation there is dubious) with one surviving (XXII.2.10, a description inspiring Juvenal's splendid line, *cum Gaetula ducem portaret belua luscum*).

7. ut vix laetitiam ... sentirent: An improbable picture, in the strongest contrast to Pol. III.74.10, καὶ πάντες ... περιχαρεῖς ἦσαν, a chief cause of joy being the small number of African and Spanish dead.

8. ⟨ex fuga semermium⟩: There is certainly a lacuna in the text here; this insertion of Luchs' presupposes the loss of a line by haplography (*ex ... ex*), but *semermium* is less likely than *sauciorum*.

ratibus Trebiam traicerent: (For *traicere*, 19.6 n.). Since Livy has staged the battle on the eastern bank, with the Roman camp on the west side, these Roman forces in his version have to cross the river to reach Placentia, and a reason has to be fabricated for the Carthaginian inaction as they cross.

9. Pado traiectus Cremonam: "put across the Po to Cremona". For the ablative, cf. XXXV.48.3, *traici Hellesponto in Europam*. For Cremona, 25.2 n. This information on the division of the consular forces is not in Polybius; cf. App. *Hann*. 7.

57-59. Roman reactions; further Italian operations

Chapter 57.

1. Tantus terror: No such panic is recorded by Pol. III.75.4, who on the contrary stresses that the Romans immediately took emergency action. Livy does not record the allegations, discreditable to Sempronius, that the consul tried to conceal the defeat. He prefers the more dramatic version which will allow him to depict, by his favourite technique of *oratio oblicua*, the anxieties in the capital; cf. 16.1 n.

2. quos alios duces . . . esse? 53.3 n.
arcessantur: 10.3 n.

3. ingenti periculo . . . transgressus: This is probably exaggerated, since Sempronius would have set out as early as possible to reach Rome by the end of the year. With the Carthaginians still west of the Trebia, he could return to Rome via Ariminum unimpeded. Later in the winter such travelling would have been more difficult (cf. 57.5).
falleret: Subjunctive in *oratio obliqua*, as part of the *consilium* or *spes* which he rejects.

4. quod unum maxime: Referring to the election in the ablative absolute, not the return to camp, and therefore illogically expressed.
Cn. Servilius: The Servilii were a patrician gens, with a record of offices going back to the early days of the republic. At this period they were part of a highly influential group in the senate with the Aemilii and the Cornelii Scipiones (Scullard, *Roman Politics*, 39 ff.). The new consul was probably the son of the consul of 252, but nothing is known of his earlier career. He is overshadowed by Flaminius in 217, and perished at Cannae in the following year (XXII.49.16).
C. Flaminius: A plebeian and a "novus homo," with an earlier record of anti-senatorial activity, so that his election reflects the Romans' disquiet at

the senatorial conduct of the war so far. In 232 as tribune he had carried through an agrarian law apportioning Gallic territory near Ariminum; this had been done in the plebeian assembly without consultation of the senate. In 223, during his first consulship, having ignored a senatorial instruction to return to Rome on the grounds of invalid election, he gained a triumph in operations against the Insubres. In 220 he held the censorship, and had begun the great north road to Ariminum that bore his name. He was therefore a man of proved experience, unjustly denigrated in the accounts of Polybius (II.21.8, III.80.3 ff.) and Livy, who both reflect the senatorial standpoint. See Scullard, *Roman Politics*, 44; Walbank, I. 192 ff.

5. ceterum, etc. Polybius does not record the winter operations that follow. Livy has probably turned here from Coelius to Antias, though Klotz believes that Coelius is the source for the rest of this chapter. Indications of the use of Antias are: (1) vague Roman successes (§ 8); (2) inflated figures (§ 12); (3) emphasis on the vices of Hannibal (§ 14).

⟨**ut**⟩ **quaeque his impeditiora erant:** (sc. *loca*. On the uses of *quisque* in the plural, see Riemann, 183 ff.). The Numidian cavalry was less accustomed to mountain fighting than were the Spaniards; see 43.8 n.

clausi = *interclusi*. So XXVII.18.20, *fuga clausa*.

subveherent: The subjunctive is not frequentative (as Weissenborn-Müller, Dimsdale), but generic; Woodcock, § 155 ff.

6. Emporium: The Romans had constructed a number of these supply-centres during their Gallic operations in the 220's. There was one at Clastidium (48.9) and another at Victumulae (57.10). It has been suggested that the port of Placentia on the Po (cf. Appian, *Hann.* 7) is referred to here, but Livy seems to visualise a stronghold some miles west of the city (§ 7).

plurimum . . . ad effectum spei: *spei* here does double service with both *plurimum* and *effectum*; "though he had rested his highest hopes on concealing his plan to achieve his aspiration . . ."

7. repente: 9.2 n.

consul: Since Scipio was at Cremona (56.9), either he has taken up residence at Placentia in Sempronius' absence, or more probably Sempronius has now returned and is referred to here.

8. saucius . . . pugna excessit: So also 7.10.

9. percurato: The verb is not found earlier; Kühnast, 387.

Victumulas: 45.3 n.

10. emporium: See § 6 above.

Book XXI

12. ad triginta quinque milia: The inflated assessment suggests the hand of Valerius Antias.

13. signum repente: All this is so much out of character with Hannibal's previous treatment of the Gauls that the whole account must be suspect— an attempt to brand Hannibal as treacherous, lustful, cruel, and tyrannical. But cf. Diod. 25.17.

14. libidinis, crudelitatis ... superbiae: Continuing the traditional portrait; 4.9 n.

exemplum: "type" or "manner"; cf. XXV.31.9, XLII.8.5, etc.

Chapter 58.

1. This chapter excellently exemplifies the thrills and chills of rhetorical historiography. There is no trace of these operations in Polybius, and this unsuccessful attempt to cross the Apennines anticipates the trials experienced in the crossing described in Book XXII.2 f.

frigora: Livy is fond of such abstract plurals; for *frigora*, cf. XXII.1.1; the sense may be "the cold weather of successive days" (Riemann, 59).

2. adiuncturus: For the expression of purpose, 1.4 n.

3. Transeuntem Appenninum: It is unprofitable to speculate on the route, in view of the doubts surrounding this operation, and the absence of sign-posting.

foeditatem: "foul conditions".

aut ... aut: "because they would have had to abandon their weapons, or in struggling on in the face of the storm they were sent spinning and crashing down by the hurricane". *aut ... aut* do not express alternatives, but express two possible reasons for halting. *aut quia* would have been a more logical formulation.

vertice intorti: A bold poetic image. *intorquere* is the favourite Virgilian word for hurling weapons (*Aen.* II.231, X.323 and 382, etc.).

4. spiritum includeret nec reciprocare animam sineret: "restricted their breathing, and did not allow them to get their breath". Livy elsewhere (XXII.51.8, XL.24.7) prefers *spiritum intercludere*, which may be the correct reading here (though cf. *vocem includere*, II.2.8, *spiritum includere* Val. Max. IX.12.7). *reciprocare* with *animam* (to breathe in and out) is not found before Livy.

5. strepere ... micare ... torpere: The staccato effect of the historic infinitives accentuates the vividness of the rolls of thunder and shafts of lightning. The abstract plural *fragores* (cf. 58.1) and the chiasmic order (*caelum strepere, micare ignes*) should also be noted.

capti auribus et oculis: "deafened and blinded"; so Cic. *Tusc.* 5.117, *Div.* 2.9; Livy XXII.2.11, etc. The use is found only in the passive.

7. explicare ... statuere: For *explicare* of unfolding canvas, Plaut. *Mil.* 1317; for *statuere* of erecting tent-poles, and hence the tents themselves, cf. Caes. *B.C.* I.81.2, Livy XXXIX.46.3, etc.

perscindente ... rapiente: The first preventing the opening of the canvas, the second the implanting of the poles.

8. aqua levata vento: Not mist (as Dimsdale), a hardly likely feature of a hurricane, but the moisture from the rain in the air and on the ground. For such action by the wind, cf. Lucr. VI.495 ff. with Bailey's notes.

tegminibus: The word occurs only once in Cicero, in translation from Greek (*Tusc.* 5.90), but becomes common in Augustan prose and poetry.

9. strage: The sense of "carnage", common in Cicero, is the secondary meaning, the first being "litter" or "wreckage" left by storm or human agency. The word is very common in this sense in Livy.

10. movere ac recipere animos: sc. *coeperunt.*

ad alienam opem quisque inops: "Those whose resource was spent turned to the resource of others."

11. elephanti ... septem absumpti: 56.6 n.

Chapter 59.

1. ad Placentiam: "towards Placentia". For *ad*, cf. Caesar, *B.G.* VII.79.1; Woodcock, § 8.

ad decem milia: sc. *ab urbe.* For *ad = circiter,* B.3 n.

postero die: Such prompt aggression is hardly consonant with the deprivations described in the previous chapter. In view of this and of the candid admission of Roman losses in this chapter, Livy may well have turned back to Coelius at this point.

2. ab Roma: 5.7 n.

4. The balanced alliteration—*paucis propugnatoribus ... portisque positis/ ceteros confertos ... castra recepit*—is noteworthy here.

7. raro magis ulla saeva: (Madvig, *E.L.* 229 prefers *raro ulla magis saeva*). In his attempts to enliven a battle with no idiosyncrasies, Livy regularly introduces phrases like *raro alias*; cf. IX.32.9, 37.2, 39.5: XXVII. 49.5, etc. The numbers in this operation are comparatively small, hardly justifying such hyperbole.

8. accensum ... proelium: "set alight"; the metaphor is used again with *certamen* at XXXV.10.5.

9. maior quam pro numero: 29.2 n.

equestris ordinis aliquot: The term *equester ordo* is here used anachronistically to refer to the cavalry section of the Servian military classification, the 18 centuries of *equites equo publico*. The traditionalism by which the state cavalry had been restricted to a small number of wealthy citizens was the main reason for Roman inefficiency in this military arm. In fact the *equites equo publico* consisted of senators, their relatives, and others with the requisite property; the non-senatorial element amongst them gradually developed into a middle class, which by the first century B.C. is called *equester ordo*. See H. Hill, *The Roman Middle Class*, chs. 2-3.

tribuni militum quinque: The legionary complement was six (Pol. VI.19) and this loss would therefore be considerable in a consular army already depleted by the Trebia disaster.

praefecti sociorum tres: There were three of these supervising the allied contingent attached to each legion. Those commissioned were Roman citizens, and their supervisory duties over the allies were similar to those of the tribunes over the legionaries. See Walbank on Pol. VI.27.5.

10. Hannibal in Ligures, Sempronius Lucam: Though Hannibal's alleged movements further west towards the maritime Alps involve no improbabilities, this statement that Sempronius crossed the Apennines to Lucca, presumably to counter a possible thrust down the coast road, is rejected by most modern scholars. Apart from the difficulty of the journey, it directly contradicts 63.1, unless a return march is presumed from Lucca to Rimini. See Walbank, I. 410 f.

quaestores . . . C. Fulvius et L. Lucretius: Two of the eight quaestors were assigned to the consuls to administer the finances; it is likely that these men were dispatched from the winter-quarters on the Po, perhaps to negotiate for ships and supplies at Genoa or Pisa for P. Scipio's forthcoming journey to Spain (XXII.22).

senatorum ferme liberis: "chiefly senators' sons". They were a regular source of recruitment into the eighteen centuries; see § 9 above, and Hill, ch. 2.

cum iis: One might have expected *secum* here, laying greater stress on the Ligurians' intention to make Hannibal believe in the stability of their allegiance; *iis* expresses more objectively the thought Hannibal was to entertain. See Riemann, 141.

60-61.11.   Roman operations in Spain

The close resemblance to the Polybian account, but with some differences and additions, suggests that Coelius is the source here (so Klotz, 136).

NOTES

Chapter 60.

1. Dum haec: Notice how, when Livy wishes to summarise economically such preliminary operations, he uses the period-sentence with its complex of subordinate clauses and participial phrases; the parallel passage in Polybius III.76.1-2 has two sentences with more co-ordinate structure.

in Hispaniam ... missus: See 32.3.

2. Emporias (The accusative of the town is regular in Livy after this verb; cf. IX.38.2, XXIII.38.3, XLV.5.1.) Emporiae was a Phocaean foundation, and one of the two Spanish outposts retained by Massilia after the Ebro treaty. There is an interesting account of the divided city at XXXIV.9.1 ff.

3. a Laeetanis: A detail additional to Polybius. PMA² have Lacetanis here, and Livy is vague about the location of the Lacetani. At 23.2 Lacetania is juxtaposed with the Ausetani, "*subiecta Pyrenaeis montibus*"; at 61.8 the Ausetani and Lacetani are "*prope Hiberum*". Hence emendation to *Laeetanis* here may be more accurate geographically (Strabo III.4.8, Ptol. 2.6) but Livy may well have written Lacetanis.

usque ad Hiberum: A little less than 200 miles.

partim renovandis ... partim novis: In Livy's schematic presentation, Scipio tries peaceful techniques before resorting to war. Polybius makes it clear (III.76.2) that he laid siege to towns which opposed him in his expedition down to the Ebro.

Romanae dicionis: For the genitive with a verb, 41.12 n.

4. in mediterraneis ... ac montanis: sc. *locis*. For *mediterranea*, cf. 31.2; for *loca montana*, XXXIX.1.5.

ad populos ... ac gentes ... valuit: For the frequent use of *ad* with the sense of *apud*, cf. Cic. *Brut.* 57 (*ad populum valuisse dicendo*) with Douglas' note.

5. Hannonis: 23.2 n.

priusquam alienarentur omnia: The subjunctive clearly expresses design or anticipation; 47.3 n.

6. Hasdrubale: left by his brother Hannibal in command of Carthaginian Spain; 22.2 n.

7. magni certaminis ... dimicatio: The descriptive genitive in the Latin can be rendered as complement in English; "the engagement was no stern contest".

sex milia, duo: Polybius offers no such figures; Livy's seem unduly high.

cum aliquot principibus: Polybius names only one such chief, Andobales (Indibilis) king of the Ilergetes, who must have been released as a good-will gesture by Scipio, for he is fighting the Romans again in 217 (XXII.21.2).

capiuntur: the reading of the Puteanus is justified by similar *constructiones ad sensum* at I.59.11, XXII.21.4, etc.

Cissis: The Κίσσα of Polybius, in the vicinity of Tarraco (61.2) and the town of the regio Cessetania (Pliny, *NH* III.21), it is possibly the Iberian name (Cese) of Tarraco, as Vallejo suggests.

8. praeda oppidi ... rerum: See § 7 above; "the town-booty comprised things..."

supellex barbarica: "primitive utensils"; *barbaricus* does not appear in prose before Livy. For *supellex* in apposition to *praeda* rather than *rerum*, cf. XXII.15.2.

ac vilium mancipiorum: Editors seem happy to take this as a "rather broken" construction, with *supellex* in apposition to *praeda* and *mancipiorum* to *rerum*, but a parallel would be difficult to find, and one wonders if a word has dropped out, e.g. *vilium ⟨vulgus⟩ mancipiorum*.

9. ditavere: So 43.9, *ditia stipendia facere*. The verb appears earlier in the *ad Herennium*, IV.66.

Chapter 61.

1. accideret: *accidere* is found in this sense at VIII.24.11, X.41.7, and there is a case for emending *accedere* at 10.12 to *accidere*, as Weissenborn-Müller. The subjunctive here contains no hint of purpose or anticipation, as the following *postquam*-clause shows ("before definite information ... reached him; but when he heard ..."). The purely temporal sense of the subjunctive becomes increasingly common from Livy onward; 47.3 n.

octo milibus ... mille: The figures are also in Pol. III.76.10.

2. classicos milites: The marines of the warships as distinct from the crews; Tacitus (*Hist.* I.36, II.11, etc.) uses *classici* alone in this sense.

navalesque socios: 49.8 n.

vagos palantesque: Perhaps intensifying the notion of the diaspora with the two adjectives; 10.1 n.

quod ferme fit ut ... creent: *quod* is best taken as introducing a causal clause in parenthesis rather than as a loose relative; the *ut* introduces a consecutive noun-clause (Woodcock, § 168). Translate: "for it usually happens that success breeds carelessness". Cicero uses *creare* in this sense, e.g. *Div.* 2.55.

3. circa ea loca: "in the vicinity"; for *loca* ("region") as distinct from *loci*, see Krebs, *Antibarbarus*, 666 ff.

4. in paucos praefectos ... animadvertisset: Polybius says that

NOTES

"he ordered the customary punishment to those responsible for what had occurred". On such military punishments, see Pol. VI.37 f.

4-5. Emporias rediit. vixdum digresso ...: It is generally held that 61.5-11 is a doublet of previous operations; but those now described are inland, not coastal, and they do not duplicate what goes before but are additional, taking place in the winter not the autumn. Antias may well be the source as Klotz suggests, but this need not wholly invalidate the picture. Scipio could have first subdued the coastal cities, then advanced inland to repress the Ilergetes whose revolt was prompted by Hasdrubal, sailed north to Emporiae to quell the Ausetani and Lacetani, and spent the rest of the winter at Tarraco.

5. Ilergetum: 22.3 n. Their chief had already been captured at Cissa (60.7 n.), which is good evidence that they had taken up arms against the Romans.

6. excito ... hibernis: Livy's geographical vagueness may have confused the order of events. Emporiae could have been his base against the Ausetani (see § 8) but not against the Ilergetes.

Atanagrum urbem: Take with both *compulsis* and *circumsedit*. The town is not otherwise known, but presumed to be in the vicinity of Ilerda (Lerida), the capital of the Ilergetes; 22.3 n.

8. Inde in Ausetanos prope Hiberum: In fact they are 200 miles further north (23.2 n.), so that he must have returned to Emporiae *after* subduing the Ilergetes and before conducting this expedition.

urbe eorum: Vich (23.2 n.).

haud procul iam urbe: Cicero and Caesar write *procul ab*, but the simple ablative becomes frequent from the Augustan age onward; cf. II.13.6, IV.10.5, etc.

9. ad duodecim milia: The confident, inflated figures make Antias the probable source.

diffugere: Probably perfect indicative. Livy favours *-ēre*, the archaic and poetical form, against *-erunt* especially in the first decade (over 70 per cent.). In this book the figure is 40 per cent., and it gradually diminishes as the poetic content recedes. See Palmer, *The Latin Language*, 138 f.

10. nix iacuit: Conditions much more appropriate to a site in the foot-hills of the Pyrenees than to one on the Ebro, but if accurately described they could scarcely be characteristic of Vich.

minus quattuor pedes: The ellipse of *quam* is common after *minus* at all periods; see Cic. *Quinct.* 41, *plus onnum*; Livy XXIX.34.17, etc.

pluteos ac vineas: The *pluteus* was a simple semi-circular curtain of wicker-work faced with leather and on three wheels (*ternis rotulis ... more* *carpenti*, Veg. IV.15). The *vinea* was a more ambitious shed-structure with a roof and sides, attacks on the wall being made through the open ends.

sola ... etiam ... fuerit: "The snow was the sole protection remaining"; *etiam* is here used in its temporal sense.

tutamentum: Only here in the classical period; Virgil, *Aen.* V.262 has *tutamen*.

11. Amusicus: Not otherwise known, but yet another distinctive detail authenticating the operation at Vich.

viginti argenti talentis pacti: (For the ablative of price after *pacisci*, cf. XXV.33.3). The Carthaginians had begun to mint silver in Spain under Hamilcar earlier in the third century, and tribes with whom they were allied would possess such coins. See E.S.G. Robinson, "Punic coins of Spain", *Essays in Roman Coinage presented to H. Mattingly* (Oxford 1956), 34 ff. At XXII.31.2, XXIII.13.7, XXIII.32.5 the phrase *argenti talenta* is used to denote Carthaginian coinage, and the same may be the case here. On the Carthaginian coinage, see Harden, *The Phoenicians*, 166 ff. The Spaniards began minting their own Oscan silver by the end of the century; see *e.g.* XXXIV.10.4.

Tarraconem: So also Pol. III.76.12.

62.1-63.15. *Prodigies expiated. Flaminius' inauspicious departure*

Chapter 62.

1. prodigia: 46.1 n. This list inserted here, between the disasters of the Trebia and Lake Trasimene, provides the appropriate framework of cosmic gloom and disorder.

quod evenire solet: Livy is well aware of the likelihood of religious psychosis in such times of strain, and passages like this (for others, see my *Livy*, 63) should not be forgotten in assessing Livy's attitude to such phenomena. He accepts in principle the possibility of a connection between such cosmic disturbances and historical events, but he is frequently scathing about particular occurrences reported as supernatural events.

2. in quis: The archaic flavour of this form helps to evoke the antique registers. Note that Livy's list tidily starts with Rome, proceeds south (Lanuvium), west (Amiternum/Picenum), and north (Caere/Cisalpine Gaul).

ingenuum infantem: The fact that the child was free-born presumably caused the cry to be interpreted as an omen affecting the body politic.

in foro holitorio: There is a tradition that children in need of sustenance were taken to the vegetable market where they received milk at the *columna lactaria* (Paul. ap. Fest. p. 105 Lindsay). Perhaps one of these uttered the cry thus interpreted.

triumphum clamasse: On the occasion of triumphal processions, the bystanders cried *"Io triumphe "*(cf. Hor. *Od.* IV.2.49 f., Suet. *Caes.* 49, etc.), so that the child's cry, like that of the unborn infant at XXIV.10.10, would be interpreted as foretelling a notable victory.

3. ⟨in⟩ foro boario: The cattle market lay opposite the Aemilian bridge and north-west of the Circus Maximus.

in tertiam contignationem: This provides interesting evidence of the existence of three-storey *insulae* already in third-century Rome. See Carcopino, *Daily Life in Ancient Rome*, ch. 2.

habitatorum: "tenants"; cf. Cic. *Q.Fratr*, II.3.7.

4. aedem Spei quae est in foro holitorio: So distinguished from other temples of Hope on the Esquiline and elsewhere in the city (II.51.2, XXV.7.6, etc.). The remains of three temples in the *forum holitorium* are still visible. The temple of Hope, built in 258, was the oldest, vowed by Atilius Caiatinus. The second, the temple of Janus, dates from the the same era, and the third to Juno Sospita from 194 B.C. See E. Strong, *Art in Ancient Rome*, I 41; Anderson-Spiers-Ashby, *The Architecture of Ancient Rome*, 17 ff.

Lanuvi: 20 miles from Rome along the via Appia, this town had been prominent in the Latin Federation, and was later famous for the cult of Juno Sospita, traces of whose temple, mentioned in this passage, still remain.

hastam: The Mss have *hostiam*, retained by Weissenborn-Müller, but cf. XXIV.10.10, *hastam Martis Praeneste sua sponte promotam*, and XL.19.2, *hastas motas*. The spear would be the sacred spear of Juno in the temple; hence the special ceremonial enjoined in § 8.

5. in agro Amiternino: Amiternum (Aquila) in Sabine territory was the birthplace of Sallust; for an amusing commentary on the local manners, see Syme, *Sallust*, 8 ff.

lapidibus pluvisse: A particularly frequent theme in the prodigy-lists (XXIII.31.15, XXV.7.7, etc.), probably falling meteors.

Caere: (Cerveteri), locative; the noun does not usually decline.

sortes extenuatas: So also at Falerii, XXII.1.11. The tablets were of wood (see *e.g.* Plaut. *Cas.* 384) and tended to shrink or swell, changes regarded as evil and good omens respectively (Pliny, *N.H.* XXXIV.137).

6. libros: sc. *Sibyllinos*. These books, which purported to come from the Cumaean Sibyl in the reign of Tarquinius Superbus, were kept in the temple of Capitoline Jupiter. They comprised a collection of oracles written in Greek hexameters (Tibullus II.5.16) and were consulted for methods of placating deities. See III.10.7, IV.25.3, V.13.5 (with Ogilvie's notes).

decemviri: sc. *sacris faciundis*, the college of priests of Apollo who had charge of the books. See X.8.2.

novendiale sacrum: A nine-day festival regularly instituted for this particular prodigy; see I.31.4.

aliis = *ceteris*; 11.3 n.

operata fuit: (For the use of *fuit* with the participle as adjective denoting a state, "was busy on", cf. Woodcock, § 100). *operari* is the technical expression for conducting a sacrifice; cf. I.31.8, IV.60.2, X.39.2.

7. iam: Wrongly emended by Madvig to *nam*; cf. I.1.1.

lustrata est: In the lustration, the victims (pig, sheep, and bull) were led in procession round the city to purify it, and then sacrificed. See I.44.2 with Ogilvie's n.

hostiae maiores: Full-grown victims as against sucklings were sacrificed at more urgent crises; cf. XXII.1.15.

quibus ... dis: Cf. Cic. *Leg.* 2.29; the priests of Apollo, in interpreting the Sibylline books, specified not only the size of victims to be sacrificed but also the god to whom they were to be offered. (Supply *ut caederentur* after *editum est*.)

8. donum ex auri pondo quadraginta: "A gift made from 40 lbs of gold", presumably of the type mentioned at V.25.10, a golden bowl sent to Delphi. Though *pondo* is orginally used with *librae* as the ablative of *pondus*, in the classical period it is regarded as an indeclinable noun = *librae*. Cf. Cic. *Clu.* 179, Caes. *B.C.* II.18.4, etc.

matronae Iunoni: The temple to Juno on the Aventine had been vowed and dedicated by Camillus (V.22.7, 396 B.C.), outside the pomerium because it housed the statue of Juno from the enemy town of Veii (V.22.5 ff., 31.3 with Ogilvie's n.). The exact site of the temple is unknown.

lectisternium: The ceremony of inviting the gods to participate in the sacrificial feast by placing their images on the couches was in origin Greek, introduced to Rome about 400 B.C. probably from southern Italy. At V.13.6 six deities with Greek connections are so honoured.

supplicatio Fortunae in Algido: Fors Fortuna, a deity of Etruscan origin, had as her province "the incalculable element in life" (Warde Fowler, *Roman Festivals*, 67 ff.). Hor. *Odes* I.35 is addressed to Fortuna in this role. At Praeneste, she was especially worshipped as protectress of matrons and promoter of fertility. The prayers addressed to her here, juxtaposed with the special cult of Juno, suggest that Fortuna and Juno are linked as the goddesses to whom matrons address this expiation. Mt Algidus (near Tusculum, south-east of Rome) had a town, Algidum, on it, where the shrine to Fortuna must have stood.

9. Iuventati ... Herculis: This association of Iuventas (= Hebe) and Hercules again reflects Greek influence; see Homer, *Od.* 11.603, Paus. 1.19.3. Hercules was chosen since the ox had leapt into the *forum Boarium*, centre of the oldest cult of Hercules at the Ara Maxima.

10. Genio: Was this special sacrifice to the *Genius populi Romani* stimulated by the report of ghostly figures at Amiternum and ghostly ships at Rome? The Romans envisaged every person and province of life as having its own genius or protective spirit. This seems to be the first occasion attested of sacrifice to the *Genius populi Romani*.

C. Atilius Serranus: He had relieved Manlius Vulso at Tannetum (26.2), handed over his forces to Scipio at Pisa (39.3), and returned to Rome.

vota suscipere iussus ...: "was ordered to vow offerings, should the state remain unharmed ten years hence". The whole relationship of the Roman state with its gods is visualised as contractual. The characteristic formula of prayer is: "I will do this if you do that." So, *e.g.* the formula of evocation of deities from Carthage in 146 B.C. at Macr. *Sat.* III.9.7: *si ita feceritis, voveo vobis templa ludosque facturum.* Also Livy I.24 (prayer before a solemn treaty), etc.

Chapter 63.

1. Flaminius: 57.4 n.

quae Placentiae hibernabant: 59.10 n.

sorte: It was commoner at this period for the senate to assign the legions to individual magistrates proceeding to separate provinces (XXV.3.3, XXVII.7.9); but where the consuls operated in the same province, they decided between them which forces each should have (cf. XXII.27.10).

edictum et litteras: *edictum* is the technical expression for a Roman magistrate's ordinance, whether aedile, tribune, praetor (especially his legal ordinances), or consul (often, as here, a command to troops to assemble, cf. XXIV.8.19).

consulem: *i.e.* Sempronius; cf. § 15 below.

2. Hic in provincia: *i.e.* at Ariminum. The whole of this highly coloured, moralising account is suspect (cf. Scullard, *Roman Politics*, 44 n. 3). Would Flaminius have commanded the troops wintering at Placentia to meet him at Ariminum, only to march them back westward, like the Grand Old Duke of York, to Arretium (63.15, XXII.2.1; Pol. III.77.1)? The Roman strategy was that Servilius should bar the east coast route to Hannibal, and Flaminius the way through Etruria. One wonders if Livy or his source has confused Ariminum with Arretium.

inire consilium erat: Though the gerundial genitive is also found with *consilium est* (Cic. *Fam.* V.20.4, Livy XXXIII.6.8, etc.). the infinitive is commoner, *consilium est* being analogous to *decernit*. So Cic. *Att.* V.5.1, Sall. *Cat.* 4.1, Caes. *B.G.* VII.26.1, *consilium ceperunt . . . profugere.*

tribunus plebis: 57.4 n. On the land-bill of 232 B.C., apportioning lands in Picenum to Roman citizens, which was carried in the plebeian assembly in the face of senatorial hostility, see Pol. II.21.8: Cic. *Sen.* 11 and *Inv.* 2.52; Val. Max. V.4.5: Frank, *CAH* 7.806 f.

consul . . . de consulatu: As consul fighting against the Insubres in 223, he had received a communication from the senate demanding his recall for an allegedly invalid election (§ 7 and § 12: XXII.3.4 and 13: Oros. IV.13.12 ff.). Like Nelson he ignored the signal till after the battle. Pol. II.32 f. has no trace of the story.

abrogabatur: A conative imperfect, "which the senate sought to annul".

de triumpho: The senate tried to refuse this, but was overruled by the assembly; Zon. VIII.20.

3. ob novam legem: The *lex Claudia* is dated to 218 by Broughton, *Magistrates*, ad loc., and Frank, *Economic Survey*, I. 74, on the basis of this passage, where it is suggested that Flaminius' advocacy gained him public support and the consulship.

Q. Claudius: The praenomen Quintus is not found in any patrician branch of the gens.

uno patrum adiuvante C. Flaminio: The statement is so surprising, senators being traditionally aloof from commercial undertakings, that one must suspect an exaggerated picture here of Flaminius' isolation on this issue.

plus quam trecentarum amphorarum: Ancient ships were normally measured by cargo capacity in talents or amphorae. The 300 jars here mentioned, corresponding to 225 bushels, would each weigh ½ cwt, so that the limit imposed here was a cargo of 8 tons. The largest merchant-vessels carried about 250 tons; see C. Torr, *Ancient Ships*, 25 ff.

4. quaestus omnis patribus indecorus: In this main argument advanced for the bill, gain is characteristically visualised as commercial profit; there was notoriously no objection to senators increasing their wealth by land-tenure or usury.

NOTES

5. auspiciis ementiendis: "by false interpretation of the auspices". Political manipulation of such religious phenomena by the *nobiles* was a notorious feature of Roman life. Auspices were twofold—those unsought (*oblativa*), such as a roll of thunder during an election, and those sought out (*impetrativa*) on the day and at the place of the election. If the augurs pronounced the omens unfavourable, the auspices had to be consulted again the following day; if a magistrate commenced his duties in defiance of the auspices, he was required to resign. Bibulus' attempt to block Caesar's policies in 59 by observing the sky, and Mark Antony's adjournment of an election when Dolabella was almost voted in, are well-known first-century examples of such manipulation of the auspices. Livy at VIII.23.15-17 (327 B.C.) records an earlier case, but the detail may well be anachronistic. See Scullard, *Roman Politics*, 27 f.

Latinarum feriarum mora: Once the consuls were elected, they were required to arrange and to attend this sacred festival on the Alban Mount in honour of Jupiter Latiaris. The festival was of great antiquity, attended by the dignitaries of local Latin towns and perhaps as old as the Etruscan occupation. See Ogilvie on I.31.3, V.17.2.

consularibus aliis impedimentis: "Other delays imposed by consular duties", such as presiding at senatorial debates, consulting the pontiffs, etc.

in provinciam: across the Rubicon to Cisalpine Gaul.

6. non cum senatu modo, etc. This evocation of the senatorial reaction, achieved by Livy's favourite technique of *oratio obliqua*, should be noted as an effective illustration of his psychological approach.

7. consulem non paruisse: *i.e.* in 223; see § 2 above.

inauspicato: The word is used also by Cic. *Div.* 1.33; see § 9 below (*auspicato*).

conscientia spretorum . . .: i.e. *deorum atque hominum*, "through guilty awareness of having spurned them . . ."

et Capitolium . . . votorum nuncupationem: On the day of the election (at this period the Ides of March) the consuls, attended by the Senate, proceeded to the Capitol to offer sacrifice to Jupiter (Ovid, *Fasti* I.79 with Frazer's n.) and make public vows for the safety of the state (Tac. *Ann.* XVI.22.1 with Furneaux's n.).

8. ne senatum, etc. The consul next presided over a meeting of the Senate in the Capitoline temple, at which there was a religious agenda, notably the arrangements for the *feriae Latinae*.

Latinas: sc. *ferias* as at V.17.2, Cic. *Att.* I.3.1, etc.

9. auspicato: Ablative absolute, "after taking the auspices", frequent in Cicero as in Livy; hence the analogous *inauspicato* in § 7 above.

sine insignibus: The consul formally departed to his province in a red or white cloak, any other colour being inauspicious. See Val. Max. I.6.11, the account of Crassus' departure against the Parthians wearing not red or white but gray. The lictors bearing the fasces were likewise *de rigeur*.

solum vertisset: "had emigrated", an archaic legal phrase which Cicero explains, as being obscure; *Caecin.* 100: *solum vertunt, hoc est sedem ac locum mutant.* Also *Dom.* 78, with Nisbet's n. Cf. III.13.9.

10. videlicet: Announcing the ironical tone of the suggestion, it is well placed between *maiestate* and *imperii*.

praetextam sumpturum: The formal donning of the magistrate's toga took place before proceeding to the Capitol (§ 7 above).

12. Q. Terentius et M. Antistius: Not otherwise known, a fact which must accentuate suspicions about the historicity of the whole episode. See § 2 above; *CAH* 8.43.

13. immolantique: Such an inauspicious omen at Rome would have caused postponement of the induction-ceremony.

14. fuga ... et concursatio: "The withdrawal and the jostling was even more marked on the outskirts of the crowd, where they did not know the cause of the panic."

in omen magni terroris: Though Livy writes at X.11.2 *quo velut omine belli accepto*, the reading of the manuscripts, *in omen*, need not be changed; see Tac. *Ann.* I.14.3 with Furneaux's note.

15. duabus ... duabus: Suggesting that Flaminius commanded four legions. This would have left Servilius without any, whereas his forces are taken over at XXII.11.3 by Fabius Cunctator. Moreover, the terrain at Trasimene could hardly have accommodated four legions. Hence it is best to assume, with Walbank, *Commentary*, 410 f., that Flaminius led only two legions.

Vocabulary

A

abduco, ere, *withdraw.*
abeo, ire, *leave.*
abhorreo, ēre, *differ from.*
abiegnus, *fir-.*
ablego, are, *remove.*
abnuo, ere, *deny, refute.*
abrogo, are, *annul.*
abrumpo, ere, *break off.*
abscedo, ere, *retire.*
absisto, ere, *desist from.*
abstineo, ēre, *keep away from.*
abstuli, see aufero.
absum, esse, *be away from.*
absumo, ere, *destroy, consume.*
abundo, are, *have plenty of.*
accedo, ere, *reach, approach.*
accendo, ere, *ignite, fire.*
accerso/arcesso, ere, *summon, seek.*
accido, ere, *happen, befall.*
accio, ire, *summon.*
accipio, ere, *submit to, receive, accept; hear.*
accola, ae, m., *neighbour.*
acer, *keen.*
acerbitas, atis, f., *harshness.*
acerbus, *harsh.*
acetum, i, n., *vinegar.*
acies, iei, f., *battleline.*
actuarius, *swift, light.*
addo, ere, *append; inflict.*
adduco, ere, *bring to.*
adeo, *to such a degree.*
adeo, ire, *approach.*
adfatim, *adequately.*
adfero, ferre, *bring to; report.*
adfirmo, are, *maintain.*
adfligo, ere, *oppress.*
adflo, are, *blow upon.*
adfluo, ere, *flock to.*
adfulgeo, ēre, *shine on.*
adhibeo, ēre, *employ.*
adhortatio, onis, f., *exhortation.*

adhortor, ari, *encourage.*
adicio, ere, *add.*
adigo, ere, *bind.*
adimo, ere, *take away.*
adiungo, ere, *attach.*
adiuuo, are, *aid.*
adminiculum, i, n., *support.*
admiratio, onis, f., *surprise, admiration.*
admisceo, ēre, *mingle.*
admitto, ere, *receive.*
admodum, *quite.*
admoveo, ēre, *propel, bring up.*
adnecto, ere, *attach.*
adnitor, i, *exert oneself.*
adorior, iri, ortus, *attack; arise.*
adoro, are, *adore.*
adpello, ere, *bring to.*
adplico, are, *attach.*
adscensus, us, m., *ascent.*
adscisco, ere, *adopt.*
adsensus, ūs, m., *approval.*
adsentior, iri, adsensus, *agree with.*
adsequor, i, *overtake.*
assideo, ēre, *sit by, blockade.*
adsigno, are, *allocate.*
adsuefacio, ere, *accustom.*
adsuesco, ere, *grow accustomed.*
adsum, esse, *be present.*
adsumo, ere, *adopt.*
adsurgo, ere, *rise.*
aduena, ae, m., *foreigner.*
aduenio, ire, *arrive.*
aduento, are, *arrive.*
aduentus, ūs, m., *arrival.*
aduersus, adj., *frontal;* adv., prep., *against;* ex aduerso, *opposite;* aduerso flumine/aduersā ripā, *upstream.*
aduoco, are, *summon.*
aedes, is, f., *temple.*
aedifico, are, *build.*

243

aegre, *with difficulty;* **aegre patior,** *be indignant at.*

aeneus, *brazen.*

aequalis, *fellow-.*

aequo, are, *equal, make even.*

aequus, *equal, level; just;* **aequo animo,** *with equanimity.*

aestas, atis, f., *summer.*

aestus, ūs, m., *swell.*

aetas, atis, f., *age.*

affectus, *weakened.*

ager, agri, m., *field.*

aggredior, i, *attack.*

agito, are, *ponder.*

agmen, inis, n., *column.*

ago, ere, egi, actum, *drive; do; plead; treat.*

agrestis, *country-.*

ala, ae, f., *wing.*

alacer, *alert.*

alieno, are, *estrange.*

alienus, *another's.*

aliquamdiu, *for some time.*

aliquando, *finally.*

aliquantum, *some;* **aliquanto,** *somewhat.*

aliquis, quid, *someone, something.*

aliquot, *several.*

alo, ere, ui, *nourish.*

altaria, ium, n., *altar.*

altitudo, inis, f., *height, depth.*

altus, *high, deep;* **altum,** *deep water.*

alueus, i, m., *channel; tub.*

ambigo, ere, *contend.*

ambiguus, *ambivalent.*

ambitus, ūs, m., *detour.*

ambo, *both.*

amicitia, ae, f., *friendship.*

amitto, ere, *lose.*

amnis, is, m., *river.*

amphora, ae, f., *large jar.*

amplector, i, xus, *embrace.*

an, *or.*

anceps, cipitis, *double; doubtful, dangerous.*

anfractus, ūs, m., *bend.*

ango, ere, anxi, anctum, *nettle.*

angulus, i, m., *corner.*

angustiae, arum, f., *narrows.*

angustus, *narrow.*

animaduersio, onis, f., *inquiry.*

animaduerto, ere, *realise; punish.*

animalis, *living.*

animans, antis, *living, creative.*

animus, i, m., *mind, spirit.*

annales, ium, m., *annalistic history.*

annus, i, m., *year.*

antiquus, *ancient.*

anxius, *troubled.*

apertus, *open.*

apparatus, ūs, m., *provision.*

appareo, ēre, *become clear; appear.*

appello, are, *hail.*

appendix, icis, f., *complement.*

appropinquo, are, *approach.*

appuli, see **adpello.**

apricus, *sunny.*

apto, are, *fit.*

aptus, *fitted.*

aqua, ae, f., *water.*

arbiter, tri, m., *witness; umpire.*

arbitrium, i, n., *authority.*

arbor, oris, f., *tree.*

arceo, ēre, *exclude.*

arcesso, see **accerso.**

ardeo, ēre, arsi, arsum, *blaze.*

arduus, *difficult.*

argentum, i, n., *silver.*

arguo, ere, *assert.*

aries, iei, m., *ram.*

arma, orum, n., *arms.*

armamentum, i, n., *tackle.*

armatura, ae, f., *armament.*

armo, are, *arm.*

arrectus, *precipitous.*

arripio, ere, *seize.*

ars, artis, f., *skill, technique.*

artus, *narrow.*

artus, ūs, m., *limb.*

arx, arcis, f., *citadel.*

asper, *harsh.*

aspernor, ari, *spurn.*

at, *but;* **at enim,** *but, you may say . . .*

atrox, ocis, *fierce.*

attollo, ere, *raise up.*
attribuo, ere, *allot.*
auarus, *greedy.*
auctor, oris, m., *author.*
auctoritas, atis, f., *authority.*
audacia, ae, f., *boldness.*
audax, *bold.*
audeo, ēre, ausus, *dare.*
audio, ire, *hear.*
auerto, ere, *divert.*
aufero, -ferre, abstuli, ablatum, *bear away.*
augeo, ēre, auxi auctum, *increase, extend, swell.*
auidus, *eager.*
aura, ae, f., *breeze.*
auris, is, f., *ear.*
aurum, i, n., *gold.*
auspicato, *after taking the auspices.*
auspicia, orum, n., *auspices.*
auxiliaris, is, m., *auxiliary.*
auxilium, i, n., *help.*

B

ballista, ae, f., *catapult.*
barbaricus, *primitive.*
barbarus, *barbarian.*
bellicosus, *warlike.*
belligero, are, *wage war.*
bello, are, *make war.*
bellum, i, n., *war.*
benignus, *kind.*
biduum, i, n., *period of two days.*
bini, *two each;* **bina castra,** *two camps.*
blandior, iri, *coax.*
boarius, *cattle-.*
bonus, *good;* **bonum,** *blessing.*
bos, bouis, m., *ox.*
breuis, *short;* **breui,** *soon.*
bruma, ae, f., *winter-solstice.*

C

cacumen, inis, n., *peak.*
cado, cadere, cecidi, casum, *fall.*
caecus, *blind.*
caedes, is, f., *slaughter.*

caedo caedere, cecīdi, caesum, *cut, cut down.*
caelum, i, n., *sky, weather.*
caementum, i, n., *rubble.*
caetra, ae, f., *Spanish shield.*
caetratus, *Spanish targeteer.*
calor, oris, m., *heat.*
calx, calcis, f., *mortar.*
campester, *flat.*
campus, i, m., *plain.*
candidus, *white, bright.*
cantus, ūs, m., *singing.*
capesso, ere, *lay hold of.*
capio, ere, cepi, captum, *capture; entice.*
captiuus, i, m., *captive.*
caput, itis, n., *head; capital.*
carus, *dear, precious.*
castellum, i, n., *fortified settlement.*
castigo, are, *rebuke.*
castra, orum, n., *camp; day's march.*
casus, ūs, m., *chance, accident; fall.*
catapulta, ae, f., *catapult.*
cauda, ae, f., *tail.*
caueo, ēre, caui, cautum, *safeguard.*
cauo, are, *hollow out.*
causa, ae, f., *cause;* after noun, *for the sake of;* **vestrā causā,** *for your sakes.*
cedo, ere, cessi, cessum, *yield, retire.*
celeber, *famed.*
celer, *swift.*
celeritas, atis, f., *speed.*
celo, are, *conceal.*
celox, ocis, f., *cutter.*
censeo, ēre, ui, *propose; suppose.*
centeni, *a hundred each.*
centum, *hundred.*
cerno, ere, crevi, cretum, *see.*
certamen, inis, n., *contest, conflict.*
certo, are, *struggle, dispute.*
certus, *certain.*
cesso, are, *abandon, decline.*

ceteri, orum, m., *the rest.*
ceterum, *but.*
cibaria, orum, n., *rations.*
cibus, i, m., *food.*
circa, *around.*
circumdo, dare, *surround.*
circumduco, ere, *lead round.*
circumeo, ire, *go round.*
circumfundo, ere, *pour round.*
circumiectus, *surrounding.*
circumligo, are, *bind round.*
circumpadanus, *around the Po.*
circumsedeo, ēre, *invest.*
circumspecto, are, *look round.*
circumspicio, ere, *look round.*
circumsto, stare, *stand round, encompass.*
circumueho, ere, *bear round;* pass., *ride round.*
circumuenio, ire, *encompass.*
citerior, *nearer.*
citra, *on this side.*
citus, *swift.*
ciuis, is, m., *citizen.*
ciuitas, atis, f., *state.*
clades, is, f., *disaster.*
clam, *secretly.*
clamo, are, *shout.*
clamor, oris, m., *shouting.*
classicus, *belonging to the fleet.*
classis, is, f., *fleet.*
claudo, ere, si, sum, *close.*
clementia, ae, f., *clemency.*
cliuus, i, m., *hill.*
coepi, ptum, *began.*
coeptum, i, n., *undertaking.*
coerceo, ēre, ui, itum, *confine.*
coetus, ūs, m., *crowd.*
cognosco, ere, novi, nitum, *recognise.*
cogo, ere, coegi, coactum, *gather; compel.*
cohors, hortis, f., *detachment.*
collega, ae, m., *colleague.*
colligo, ere, egi, ectum, *gather.*
collis, is, m., *hill.*
colo, ere, ui, cultum, *cultivate; dwell.*
colonia, ae, f., *colony.*

comitia, orum, n., *elections.*
commeatus, ūs, m., *furlough; supplies.*
comminuo, ere, *impair.*
comminus, *at close quarters.*
committo, ere, *join.*
commoveo, ēre, *move.*
communio, ire, *fortify.*
comparo, are, *prepare; compare.*
compello, ere, *drive.*
comperio, ire, *find.*
compono, ere, *arrange.*
comprendo, ere, *seize.*
comprobo, are, *approve.*
conatum, i, n., *attempt.*
conatus, ūs, m., *attempt.*
concedo, ere, *yield, retire.*
conceptus, *afire.*
concilio, are, *win over.*
concilium, i, n., *council.*
concio, ire, *rouse in unison.*
concito, are, *arouse.*
conclamo, are, *call in unison.*
concremo, are, *burn out.*
concretus, *hardened.*
concurro, ere, *join battle.*
concursatio, onis, f., *jostling.*
concurso, are, *charge repeatedly.*
concursus, ūs, m., *gathering; onset.*
condicio, onis, f., *condition, terms.*
confero, ferre, *join; collect.*
confertim, *closely.*
confertus, *in close order.*
confessio, onis, f., *admission.*
conficio, ere, *complete.*
confido, ere, fisus, *trust.*
confiteor, ēri, fessus, *confess.*
confluo, ere, *merge.*
confragosus, *rough.*
confugio, ere, *flee together.*
confundo, ere, *confuse.*
congredior, i, *join, grapple.*
congrego, are, *assemble.*
congressus, us, m., *meeting.*
conicio, ere, *hurl together.*
coniecto, are, *guess.*
conitor, i, *struggle.*

coniunx, iugis, c., *spouse.*
conloquium, i, n., *parley.*
conloquor, i, *discuss.*
conor, ari, *try.*
conquiesco, ere, *rest.*
conquisitor, oris, m., *recruiting-officer.*
conscendo, ere, *embark.*
conscientia, ae, f., *guilty aware-ness.*
conscribo, ere, *enrol.*
consero, ere, ui, tum, *join.*
consido, ere, sedi, sessum, *settle.*
consilium, i, n., *plan, consultation, planning.*
consisto, ere, stiti, *halt.*
conspectus, ūs, m., *sight.*
conspicio, ere, spexi, spectum, *observe.*
constans, *firm.*
consterno, are, *infuriate, alarm.*
consterno, ere, straui, stratum, *cover, pave.*
consto, are, *halt;* **satis constat,** *it is certain/agreed.*
consul, is, m., *consul.*
consularis, *consular.*
consulatus, ūs, m., *consulship.*
consulo, ere, *consult, deliberate.*
consulto, are, *deliberate.*
consumo, ere, *spend.*
contendo, ere, *march.*
contentio, onis, f., *dispute.*
contignatio, onis, f., *storey.*
continens, *unbroken.*
contineo, ēre, *restrain, retain.*
contingo, ere, tigi, tactum, *touch.*
contio, onis, f., *gathering, parade.*
contionabundus, *haranguing.*
contraho, ere, *assemble; incur.*
conuenio, ire, *assemble.*
conuerto, ere, *direct; attract.*
coorior, iri, ortus, *arise together.*
copia, ae, f., *abundance.*
copulo, are, *join.*
coquo, ere, coxi, coctum, *cook.*
cornu, us, n., *wing of army.*

corona, ae, f., *wreath;* 51.2 n.
corpus, oris, n., *body.*
corrumpo, ere, *damage; bribe.*
corruo, ere, *fall headlong.*
coruus, i, m., *crow.*
credo, ere, didi, ditum, *believe.*
creo, are, *appoint; breed.*
cresco, ere, crevi, cretum, *grow.*
crimen, inis, n., *charge.*
crudelis, *cruel.*
crudelitas, atis, f., *cruelty.*
cruor, oris, m., *gore.*
culpa, ae, f., *blame.*
cultor, oris, m., *inhabitant.*
cultus, ūs, m., *cultivation.*
cunctanter, *with hesitation.*
cunctor, ari, *delay, hesitate.*
cunctus, *all.*
cupido, inis, f., *longing.*
cupio, ere, *desire.*
cura, ae, f., *care, diligence, anxiety, eagerness, curiosity.*
curo, are, *tend, care.*
cursus, ūs, m., *course.*
custodia, ae, f., *guardpost; protection.*
custos, odis, m., *guard.*
cutis, is, f., *skin.*

D

damnum, i, n., *loss.*
decemuir, i, m., *decemvir;* 62.6 n.
decerno, ere, *decide, decree; assign.*
decet, ēre, *it is fitting.*
declaro, are, *declare.*
declino, are, *veer.*
decurro, ere, *run down.*
dedico, are, *dedicate.*
deditio, onis, f., *surrender.*
dedo, ere, didi, ditum, *surrender.*
deduco, ere, *bring down; escort; withdraw; launch; found.*
defectio, onis, f., *secession.*
defendo, ere, di, sum, *defend.*
defensor, oris, m., *defender.*

defero, ferre, carry down/over, transfer; proffer; report.

deficio, ere, revolt; fail.

defigo, ere, xi, xum, render motionless.

deflecto, ere, turn aside.

degredior, i, go down.

deicio, ere, cast off/down, fell.

deinceps, successively.

delectus, chosen.

deleo, ēre, destroy.

deligo, ere, egi, ectum, choose.

deminuo, ere, reduce.

demitto, ere, send/let down.

demo, demere, take down, stow away.

denuntiatio, onis, f., declaration.

denuntio, are, intimate.

depopulor, ari, pillage.

deposco, ere, demand.

deprendo, ere, catch.

derectus, forthright.

deruptus, precipitous.

descendo, ere, di, sum, descend.

descisco, ere, secede.

desero, ere, abandon.

deses, idis, idle.

desiderium, i, n., longing.

desidero, are, long for.

designo, are, designate.

desperatio, onis, f., despair.

despero, are, give up hope.

destino, are, allocate, decide.

destituo, ere, forsake.

desum, esse, be lacking, fail.

detestor, ari, abominate.

detracto, are, decline.

detrunco, are, lop.

deueho, ere, bear away.

deuersorium, i, n., inn.

deuius, untrodden.

deuolo, are, fly down.

deuoluo, ere, roll down.

deus, i, m., god.

dextra, ae, f., right hand, right side.

dicio, onis, f., control, sway.

dictum, i, n., command.

diduco, ere, divide.

dies, iei, m., day; **in dies,** daily.

differo, ferre, postpone.

difficilis, difficult.

diffido, ere, fisus, distrust.

diffugio, ere, scatter in flight.

dignitas, atis, f., dignity.

dignus, worthy.

digredior, i, separate, deviate; depart.

dilabor, i, melt away.

dilatio, onis, f., delay.

dilectus, ūs, m., levy.

dimicatio, onis, f., battle.

dimico, are, fight.

dimitto, ere, disband, release.

dirimo, ere, break off.

diripio, ere, plunder.

diruo, ere, destroy.

disceptatio, onis, f., dispute.

discepto, are, dispute.

discerno, ere, distinguish.

disciplina, ae, f., discipline.

disco, ere, didici, learn.

discors, ordis, disunited.

discrimen, inis, n., distinction.

discrimino, are, delineate.

discutio, ere, break down.

diserte, explicitly.

disicio, ere, scatter.

dispono, ere, deploy.

dissentio, ire, disagree.

dissimulo, are, pretend not to.

distineo, ēre, distract.

distribuo, ere, divide out

dito, are, enrich.

diu, for a long time.

diuendo, ere, sell piecemeal.

diuersus, different, apart.

diuido, ere, divide.

diuinus, godlike.

do, dare, dedi, datum, give.

doceo, ēre, ui, ctum, teach.

documentum, i, n., proof.

dolabra, ae, f., pickaxe.

dolor, oris, m., pain.

dominus, i, m., lord, master.

domo, are, ui, itum, subdue.

domus, ūs, f., house, home.

donum, i, n., gift.

dubius, doubtful.

ducenti, *two hundred.*
duco, ere, duxi, ductum, *lead; construct.*
ductus, ūs, m., *leadership.*
dummodo, *provided that.*
duo, *two.*
duodecim, *twelve.*
duodeuiginti, *eighteen.*
duro, are, *harden.*
dux, ducis, m., *leader.*

E

edico, ere, *proclaim.*
edictum, i, n., *proclamation.*
editus, *raised.*
edo, edere, edidi, editum, *produce; ordain.*
edoceo, ēre, *inform.*
educo, ere, *lead out.*
effectus, ūs, m., *completion.*
efferatus, *savage.*
effero, ferre, *raise, transport.*
efficio, ere, *ensure.*
effrenatus, *uncontrolled.*
effundo, ere, *pour out, scatter; loosen.*
effuse, *spread out.*
egeo, ēre, ui (+ abl.), *be without.*
egero, ere, *dig out.*
egredior, i, *go out from.*
egregius, *outstanding.*
elephantus, i, m., *elephant.*
elicio, ere, *entice.*
eligo, ere, elegi, electum, *choose.*
emensus, *traversed.*
ementior, iri, *fabricate.*
emergo, ere, *come out.*
emetior, iri, mensus, *traverse.*
emineo, ēre, *stick out, be conspicuous.*
eminus, *at a distance.*
emitto, ere, *send out.*
emporium, i, n., *market.*
emunio, ire, *build up.*
enitor, i, nisus/nixus, *struggle on/up.*
eo, *thither.*
eodem, *to the same place.*

eques, itis, m., *horseman.*
equester, *equestrian.*
equitatus, ūs, m., *cavalry.*
equus, i, m., *horse.*
erigo, ere, rexi, rectum, *lead up; arouse.*
error, oris, m., *detour, wrong turning.*
erumpo, ere, *burst out.*
eruptio, onis, f., *sally.*
escendo, ere, *climb.*
escensio, onis, f., *disembarkation.*
euado, ere, *escape, emerge from.*
eueho, ere, *bear out.*
euenio, ire, *result.*
euentus, us, m., *outcome.*
euoco, are, *summon forth.*
excedo, ere, *quit; extend (into).*
excellens, *outstanding.*
excidium, i, n., *destruction.*
excĭdo, ere, *fall off.*
excīdo, ere, *destroy.*
excio, ire, *rouse.*
excipio, ere, *except; receive; cut off.*
exemplum, i, n., *type, example.*
exeo, ire, *leave.*
exerceo, ēre, *engage.*
exercitus, ūs, m., *army.*
exhaurio, ire, *endure.*
exiguus, *slight.*
exitus, ūs, m., *departure; end, death.*
exordior, iri, orsus, *begin.*
exorior, iri, ortus, *sally forth.*
exortus, ūs, m., *rising.*
expeditio, onis, f., *campaign.*
expeditus, *unencumbered.*
experior, iri, *try out.*
expertus, *proved.*
expleo, ēre, *fill up.*
explico, are, *unfold.*
exploro, are, *reconnoitre.*
expono, ere, *disembark; relate.*
expostulo, are, *complain.*
exprimo, ere, *wring.*
expugno, are, *take by storm.*
exsequor, i, *execute.*
exsilium, i, n., *exile.*

exsolvo, ere, *pay out; discharge.*
exspectatio, onis, f., *prospect.*
exspecto, are, *await.*
exsto, are, *project.*
exsuscito, are, *kindle.*
extemplo, *immediately.*
extendo, ere, *extend.*
extentus, *broad.*
extenuo, are, *diminish.*
externus, *outer.*
extollo, ere, *praise.*
extremum, i, n., *tip.*
exturbo, are, *dislodge.*
exul, ulis, m., *exile.*
exuo, exuere, ui, utum, *strip.*

F

fabrico, are, *fashion.*
facilis, *easy.*
facilitas, atis, f., *ease.*
factio, onis, f., *party.*
fallo, ere, fefelli, falsum, *deceive.*
falsus, *untrue.*
fama, ae, f., *report; reputation.*
fames, is, f., *hunger.*
fateor, ēri, fassus, *admit.*
fatigo, are, *tire.*
fatum, i, n., *fate.*
fauces, ium, f., *defile.*
fauor, oris, m., *good will.*
fax, facis, f., *torch.*
feliciter, *successfully.*
felix, *fortunate.*
femina, ae, f., *female.*
femur, oris, n., *thigh.*
feriae, arum, f., *holidays.*
ferio, ire, *strike.*
ferme, *approximately, almost, mostly;* haud ferme, *scarcely.*
ferox, *fierce.*
ferro, ferre, tuli, latum, *carry; lead; obtain; say, propose.*
ferrum, i, n., *iron.*
fessus, *weary.*
festino, are, *hasten.*
fides, ei, f., *good faith, trust, guarantee;* in fidem recipere, *guarantee protection.*

fido, ere, fisus, *trust.*
filius, i, m., *son.*
finio, ire, *limit, end.*
finis, is, m., *limit, boundary;* fines, *territory.*
fingo, ere, finxi, fictum, *picture.*
finitimus, *neighbouring.*
firmo, are, *strengthen.*
firmus, *strong.*
flagro, are, *be ablaze.*
flecto, ere, flexi, flexum, *bend, diverge.*
flos, oris, m., *flower.*
flumen, inis, n., *river.*
fluo, ere, fluxi, xum, *flow.*
fodio, ere, *hack out, pierce.*
foeditas, atis, f., *foulness.*
foedus, *foul.*
foedus, eris, n., *treaty.*
forte, *by chance.*
fortis, *brave.*
fortuna, ae, f., *fortune, condition.*
forum, i, n., *market-place.*
fragor, oris, m., *din.*
frater, tris, m., *brother.*
fraus, fraudis, f., *duplicity.*
fremitus, ūs, m., *din.*
freno, are, *bridle.*
frequens, *crowded.*
frequento, are, *crowd into.*
fretum, i, n., *strait.*
frigus, oris, n., *cold.*
fructus, ūs, m., *harvest.*
frumentum, i, n., *corn.*
fruor, i, fructus, *enjoy.*
fuga, ae, f., *flight.*
fugio, ere, i, *flee.*
fugo, are, *put to flight.*
fulmen, inis, n., *thunderbolt.*
fumus, i, m., *smoke.*
funditor, oris, m., *slinger.*
fundo, ere, fudi, fusum, *rout.*
fungor, i, functus (+ abl.) *perform.*
furia, ae, f., *fury.*
furtum, i, n., *theft.*

VOCABULARY

G

gaudium, i, n., *joy.*
gelidus, *cold.*
gelus, ūs, m., *frost, cold.*
gener, eri, m., *son-in-law.*
gens, gentis, f., *race, nation.*
genu, ūs, n., *knee.*
genus, eris, n., *kind; class, race;*
genere, *after the fashion of.*
gero, ere, gessi, gestum, *wage, perform.*
gigno, ere, genui, genitum, *beget.*
glacies, iei, f., *ice.*
gladius, i, m., *sword.*
glareosus, *gravelly.*
gloria, ae, f., *glory.*
gnarus, *aware.*
grando, inis, f., *hail.*
gratificor, ari, *show favour to.*
gratis, *free.*
gratulor, ari, *congratulate.*
gratus, *welcome.*
grauate, *reluctantly.*
grauis, *heavy, burdened.*
grauiter, *seriously.*
grauo, are, *oppress.*
grex, gregis, m., *herd.*
gurges, itis, m., *deep water.*

H

habeo, ēre, *have, hold; regard.*
habilis, *apt.*
habitator, oris, m., *tenant.*
habito, are, *dwell.*
habitus, ūs, m., *appearance.*
haereo, ēre, haesi, *stick.*
hasta, ae, f., *spear.*
hastile, is, n., *shaft.*
haud, *not at all.*
haudquaquam, *by no means.*
hercule, *indeed.*
hereditarius, *inherited.*
hiberna, orum, n., *winter-quarters.*
hiberno, are, *winter.*
hibernus, *of winter.*
hiemps, hiemis, f., *winter.*

hinc . . . hinc, *on one side . . . on the other.*
holitorius, *vegetable-.*
horrendus, *fearful.*
horreo, ēre, *tremble at.*
horreum, i, n., *granary.*
hortator, oris, m., *one lending encouragement.*
hortor, ari, *encourage.*
hospes, itis, m., *guest-friend.*
hospitalis, *hospitable; taking guests.*
hospitium, i, n., *hospitality, entertainment, guest-friendship.*
hostia, ae, f., *victim.*
hostilis, *hostile.*
hostis, is, m., *enemy.*
humus, i, f., *ground, earth;*
humi, *on the ground.*

I

iaceo, ēre, ui, *lie.*
iactatio, onis, f., *tossing.*
iacto, are, *throw, strike.*
iactura, ae, f., *loss.*
iaculator, oris, m., *darter.*
iaculor, ari, *throw darts.*
iaculum, i, n., *dart, javelin.*
icio, ere, ici, ictum, *wound, strike.*
ictus, ūs, m., *blow.*
idūs, iduum, f., *Ides.*
ieiunus, *fasting.*
ignarus, *unaware.*
ignis, is, m., *fire.*
ignominia, ae, f., *shame.*
ignoro, are, *be unaware of.*
ignotus, *unknown.*
imbellis, *unwarlike.*
imber, bris, m., *rainstorm.*
imbuo, ere, ui, utum, *tinge.*
immanis, *huge.*
immensus, *boundless.*
immineo, ēre, *overhang.*
immisceo, ēre, *mingle.*
immitto, ere, *send/let in.*
immobilis, *motionless.*
immodicus, *boundless.*

immolo, are, *sacrifice.*
immortalis, *immortal.*
immotus, *unmoved.*
imparatus, *unprepared.*
impauidus, *fearless.*
impedimentum, i, n., *obstacle; baggage.*
impedio, ire, *hinder.*
impeditus, *difficult.*
impello, ere, *drive.*
imperator, oris, m., *general.*
imperito, are, *govern.*
imperium, i, n., *command, jurisdiction; empire.*
impero, are, *command.*
impetus, ūs, m., *charge, force.*
impiger, *energetic.*
impono, ere, *put into/on; impose.*
improuidus, *thoughtless.*
improuisus, *unexpected.*
impudens, *shameless.*
imus, *lowest;* **ab imo,** *from elow.*
inanimus, *lifeless.*
inauspicato, *without taking the auspices.*
incautus, *careless.*
incedo, ere, *advance.*
incendium, i, n., *blaze.*
inceptum, i, n., *attempt.*
incertus, *uncertain.*
incessus, ūs, m., *advance.*
incido, ere, *fall on.*
incipio, ere, *begin.*
incito, are, *rouse.*
includo, ere, si, sum, *enclose; restrict.*
incoho, are, *begin.*
incola, ae, m., *inhabitant.*
incolo, ere, ui, *dwell (in).*
incolumis, *safe, unharmed.*
incompositus, *disordered.*
inconditus, *untrained.*
incrementum, i, n., *growth.*
incruentus, *bloodless.*
incubo, are, ui, *lie in.*
incultus, *uncultivated.*
indecorus, *inappropriate.*
indico, ere, *declare.*

indigena, ae, m., *native.*
indignor, ari, *be angry.*
indignus, *undeserving.*
indo, ere, didi, ditum, *attach.*
indoles, is, f., *character, attributes.*
indomitus, *unsubdued.*
induco, ere, *lead into/against, prompt.*
industria, ae, f., *diligence;* **de industriā,** *on purpose.*
ineo, ire, *begin; enter.*
inermis, *unarmed.*
inexpertus, *inexperienced.*
inexplorato, *without reconnaissance.*
inexsuperatus, *impassable.*
infamis, *notorious.*
infans, fantis, c., *child.*
infero, ferre, *bear into;* **arma/ bellum inferre,** *attack.*
infestus, *hostile, hazardous.*
infidus, *faithless.*
infimus, *bottom.*
informis, *rough, unsightly.*
infrenatus, *without bridle.*
infundo, ere, *pour on.*
ingemisco, ere, gemui, *groan.*
ingenium, i, n., *nature, talent.*
ingens, gentis, *mighty, loud.*
ingenuus, *freeborn.*
ingredior, i, *enter, walk on to.*
inicio, ere, *throw on, cast into; prompt.*
inimicitia, ae, f., *enmity.*
iniquitas, atis, f., *unevenness.*
iniquus, *unfavourable.*
iniuria, *injustice;* **iniuriā,** *wrongly.*
iniustus, *unjust.*
inlucesco, ere, luxi, *grow light.*
inluuies, iei, f., *filth.*
inno, are, *float on.*
inopia, ae, f., *shortage.*
inopinato, *unexpectedly.*
inops, opis, *insufficient.*
inquam, inquit, *say.*
inquiro, ere, *investigate.*
inrito, are, *stir up, goad.*
inritus, *vain.*

insequens, *ensuing; attacking.*
insequor, i, *follow, attack.*
insideo, ēre, *occupy.*
insidiae, arum, f., *ambush.*
insignis, *signal, notable;* **insignia,** *badges of office.*
insimulo, are, *indict.*
insisto, ere, *stand on.*
insolitus, *unusual.*
inspicio, ere, *examine.*
instabilis, *unsteady.*
insterno, ere, stravi, stratum, *saddle.*
instituo, ere, *begin; resolve.*
instrumentum, i, n., *equipment.*
instruo, ere, *equip.*
insuetus, *unaccustomed.*
insula, ae, f., *island.*
insuper, *additionally.*
insuperabilis, *impenetrable.*
integer, *whole, virgin, fresh;* de **integro,** *afresh.*
intendo, ere, *consign, direct.*
intentus, *attentive.*
intercipio, ere, *snatch.*
intercludo, ere, clusi, clusum, *cut off.*
intercurso, are, *rush between.*
interdiu, *during the day.*
interdum, *occasionally.*
interficio, ere, *kill.*
interiaceo, ēre, *lie between.*
interiacio, ere, ieci, iectum, *set between.*
interim, *meanwhile.*
interior, *inner.*
interlino, ere, levi, litum, *smear between.*
interpres, etis, m., *negotiator.*
interrumpo, ere, *break apart.*
intersum, esse, *lie between.*
interuallum, i, n., *distance.*
intolerabilis, *unbearable.*
intonsus, *shaggy.*
intorqueo, ēre, torsi, tortum, *send spinning.*
intro, are, *enter.*
introduco, ere, *usher in.*
intueor, ēri, itus, *observe.*

inuado, ere, *attack.*
inualidus, *weak.*
inuictus, *unconquerable.*
inuidia, ae, f., *odium.*
inuiolatus, *unharmed.*
inuiso, ere, *visit.*
inuisus, *hated.*
inuius, *pathless.*
ira, ae, f., *anger.*
irascor, i, iratus, *be angry.*
ita, *so; only.*
iter, itineris, n., *journey.*
iubeo, ere, iussi, iussum, *order.*
iudex, icis, m., *judge.*
iugum, i, n., *ridge.*
iumentum, i, n., *pack-animal.*
iungo, ere, iunxi, iunctum, *join.*
ius, iuris, n., *right; law; authority;* **iure,** *rightly;* **iusiurandum,** *oath.*
iussus, ūs, m., *command.*
iustus, *just; regular; full-scale.*
iuuenis, is, m., *young man.*
iuuentus, tutis, f., *youth.*
iuuo, are, iuui, iutum, *help.*
iuxta, *alike.*

L

labor, oris, m., *toil.*
laboro, are, *be in difficulties, suffer harm.*
lacero, are, *mangle.*
lacrima, ae, f., *tear.*
lacesso, ere, *assail, challenge.*
laetitia, ae, f., *joy.*
laetor, ari, *rejoice.*
laetus, *joyful.*
laeva, ae, f., *left hand, left side.*
lapis, idis, m., *stone.*
lapsus, sūs, m., *fall.*
largus, *generous.*
lassitudo, inis, f., *weariness.*
latebrae, arum, f., *hiding-place.*
latebrosus, *concealed.*
latrocinium, i, n., *brigandage.*
latus, *wide.*
latus, eris, n., *flank, side.*
laxo, are, *abandon.*

lectisternium, i, n., *gods' banquet.*

legatio, onis, f., *embassy.*

legatus, i, m., *ambassador.*

lego, ere, legi, lectum, *choose; skirt.*

lenis, *gentle.*

lēvis, *smooth.*

lĕvis, *light.*

levo, are, *lighten; lift up.*

lex, legis, f., *law, condition.*

liber, bri, m. *book.*

līber, *free.*

liberi, *children.*

libero, are, *free.*

libertas, tatis, f., *freedom.*

libido, inis, f., *lust.*

libo, are, *pour out; impair.*

licet, ēre, *it is possible.*

lictor, oris, m., *lictor, attendant.*

lignum, i, n., *log.*

lineamentum, i, n., *line.*

lino, ere, levi, litum, *smear.*

liquesco, ere, *liquefy.*

lis, litis, f., *dispute.*

litterae, arum, f., *letter.*

lixa, ae, m., *camp-trader.*

loco, are, *place, pitch.*

locus, i, m., *place;* **loca,** *district.*

longinquitas, atis, f., *distance.*

longinquus, *distant.*

longus, *long;* **longe,** *far, by far.*

lorum, i, n., *reins.*

lubricus, *slippery.*

luctatio, onis, f., *struggle.*

lugubris, *mournful.*

luna, ae, f., *moon.*

lupus, i, m., *wolf.*

lustro, are, *purify.*

lux, lucis, f., *light;* **prima luce,** *at dawn.*

M

maeror, oris, m., *grief.*

magistratus, ūs, m., *magistrate, magistracy.*

magnitudo, inis, f., *size.*

maiestas, atis, f., *majesty.*

maior natu, *older.*

malo, malle, malui, *prefer.*

mancipium, i, n., *slave.*

mando, are, *order, allot.*

maneo, ēre, si, sum, *remain.*

manes, manium, m., *shades, spirit.*

manipulus, i, m., *maniple, infantry detachment.*

mano, are, *seep through.*

manus, ūs, f., *hand; band;* **manūs conserere,** *join battle.*

mare, is, n., *sea.*

maritimus, *sea-.*

materia, ae, f., *timber.*

matrona, ae, f., *matron.*

maturus, *early.*

maxime, *especially.*

mediterraneus, *inland.*

medius, *middle, intermediate.*

memor, *mindful.*

memorabilis, *remarkable.*

memoria, ae, f., *recollection.*

memoro, are, *relate.*

mensis, is, m., *month.*

mentio, onis, f., *mention.*

mereo, ēre, ui, itum, *serve;* **meritum,** *deserving deed.*

metor, ari, *mark out.*

metus, ūs, m., *fear.*

mico, are, *flash out.*

migro, are, *migrate.*

miles, itis, m., *soldier.*

militaris, *military.*

militia, ae, f., *war-service.*

milito, are, *be on service.*

mille/milia, *thousand/thousands.*

minime, *by no means.*

minor, *smaller.*

minuo, ere, ui, utum, *diminish.*

miror, ari, *wonder.*

mirus, *remarkable.*

misceo, ēre, ui, xtum, *mingle, confuse.*

misericordia, ae, f., *pity.*

missilis, *thrown;* **missile, missile.*

mitis, *gentle.*

mitto, ere, misi, missum, *send.*

mobilis, *mobile.*

modicus, *modest, small.*

VOCABULARY

modo, *only.*
modus, i, m., *way, limit, level;*
modo/in modum, *after the fashion of.*
moenia, ium, n., *walls.*
moles, is, f., *mass; trouble.*
mollio, ire, *soften.*
mollis, *soft, gentle.*
momentum, i, n., *instant; importance.*
moneo, ēre, *warn.*
mons, montis, m., *mountain.*
monstro, are, *show.*
montanus, i, m., *mountain-dweller.*
mora, ae, f., *delay.*
morior, i, mortuus, *die.*
moror, ari, *delay; hinder.*
mors, mortis, f., *death.*
mos, moris, m., *custom.*
motus, ūs, m., *movement; insurrection, tumult; emotion.*
moveo, ēre, vi, tum, *move; arouse, affect, unleash; achieve;* **mota arma,** *insurrection.*
multifariam, *in many places.*
multitudo, inis, f., *crowd, population, manpower.*
multo, are, *fine.*
munimentum, i, n., *fortification.*
munio, ire, *build, fortify;* 37.2 n.
munitio, onis, f., *construction.*
munus, eris, n., *gift.*
murus, i, m., *wall.*
mutuus, *reciprocal.*

N
naturalis, *natural.*
naualis, *naval.*
nauigo, are, *sail.*
nauis, is, f., *ship;* **longa nauis,** *warship.*
nauta, ae, m., *sailor.*
necdum, *not yet.*
necessarius, *inevitable.*
neglegentia, ae, f., *carelessness.*
neglego, ere, *neglect.*
nego, are, *deny.*
nemus, oris, n., *woodland.*

nequaquam, *by no means.*
nequeo, ire, *be unable.*
nequiquam, *to no purpose.*
neruus, i, m., *sinew.*
nimbus, i, m., *storm-cloud.*
nimis, *too, too much.*
nimius, *excessive.*
nitor, niti, nisus/nixus, *struggle.*
niualis, *snowy.*
niuosus, *snowy.*
nix, niuis, f., *snow.*
no, nare, *swim.*
nobilis, *noble.*
nobilitas, itatis, f., *nobility.*
nocturnus, *night-.*
nomen, inis, n., *name.*
nominatim, *by name.*
nomino, are, *name.*
nonaginta, *ninety.*
nondum, *not yet.*
nonus, *ninth.*
notus, *known.*
nouendialis, *lasting nine days.*
noueni, *nine each.*
nouus, *new;* **nouae res,** *political upheaval.*
nox, noctis, f., *night;* **noctu,** *by night.*
noxa, ae, f., *guilt.*
nubes, is, f., *cloud.*
nudo, are, *expose, strip.*
nudus, *unprotected.*
numerus, i, m., *number.*
nuncupatio, onis, f., *proclamation.*
nuntio, are, *announce.*
nuntius, i, m., *messenger.*
nuper, *recently.*
nusquam, *nowhere.*

O
obeo, ire, *undertake.*
obequito, are, *ride up to.*
obicio, ere, *expose.*
obligo, are, *bind.*
obliquus, *sideways.*
oblittero, are, *expunge.*
oboedienter, *obediently.*
obruo, ere, *bury.*

obsaepio, ire, *bar.*
obsero, ere, sevi, situm, *cover over.*
obses, sidis, m., *hostage.*
obsideo, ēre, *blockade.*
obsidio, onis, f., *blockade.*
obsisto, ere, *resist.*
obsitus, see obsero.
obsolesco, ere, solevi, soletum, *fade away.*
obstrepo, ere, *create din.*
obtero, ere, triui, tritum, *tread down.*
obtesto, are, *attest.*
obtineo, ēre, *hold.*
obtrunco, are, *slay.*
obuius, *confronting;* obuiam ducere, *lead to meet;* obuiam mittere, *send to meet.*
occasio, onis, f., *opportunity.*
occasus, ūs, m., *setting.*
occīdo, ere, cidi, cisum, *kill.*
occido, ere, occidi, occasum, *fall, set.*
occultus, *secret, hidden.*
occupo, are, *be first to; seize.*
occurro, ere, *meet.*
occurso, are, *oppose, confront.*
octauus, *eighth.*
octingenti, *eight hundred.*
octoginta, *eighty.*
oculus, i, m., *eye.*
odi, isse, *hate.*
odium, i, n., *hatred.*
odor, oris, m., *smell.*
offero, ferre, *offer.*
officium, i, n., *duty.*
oleum, i, n., *oil.*
omen, inis, n., *omen.*
omitto, ere, *relinquish; cease.*
onus, eris, n., *burden.*
opera, ae, f., *work;* 9.3 *n.*
operio, ire, ui, tum, *cover.*
operor, ari, *be busy at.*
opinio, onis, f., *belief.*
opperior, iri, *await.*
oppidanus, i, m., *townsman.*
oppidum, i, n., *town.*
oppleo, ēre, *fill.*

oppono, ere, *expose.*
opportunitas, atis, f., *chance.*
opportunus, *convenient.*
opprimo, ere, pressi, pressum, *quash, put down.*
oppugnatio, onis, f., *attack.*
oppugno, are, *attack.*
ops, opis, f., *resource.*
opulentus, *wealthy.*
opus, eris, n., *work, siegework, fortification.*
ora, ae, f., *shore, boundary.*
oratio, onis, f., *speech.*
orator, oris, m., *orator, spokesman.*
orbis, is, m., *circle;* in orbem, *in circular formation;* orbis terrarum, *world.*
ordior, iri, orsus, *begin.*
ordo, dinis, m., *order.*
orior, iri, ortus, *originate.*
oriundus, *sprung from.*
orno, are, *decorate.*
oro, are, *beg.*
os, oris, n., *face.*
ostendo, ere, di, sum, *show, afford.*
ostento, are, *point out.*
ostium, i, n., *mouth.*
otium, i, n., *leisure.*

P

pabulum, i, n., *fodder.*
pacatus, *peaceable, friendly.*
paciscor, i, pactus, *make agreement.*
paco, are, *pacify.*
palam, *openly.*
palor, ari, *wander.*
paludatus, *wearing a general's cloak.*
palus, udis, f., *marsh.*
palustris, *marshy.*
pando, ere, i, *open.*
par, *equal.*
parco, ere, peperci, parsum (+ dat.), *spare.*
pareo, ēre, ui (+ dat.), *obey.*
pario, ere, peperi, partum, *bring forth; win.*

pariter, *alike.*
paro, are, *prepare.*
pars, partis, f., *part, party.*
partior, iri, itus, *apportion.*
parturio, ire, *bear in labour.*
parumper, *briefly.*
paruus, *small.*
passim, *here and there.*
passus, ūs, m., *step;* **mille passus/milia passuum,** *mile/miles.*
patefacio, ere, *lay open.*
patens, *open.*
pateo, ēre, *lie open.*
pater, tris, m., *father.*
paternus, *a father's.*
patiens, *enduring.*
patientia, ae, f., *endurance.*
patior, i, passus, *allow.*
patria, ae, f., *native land.*
pauci, *few.*
paucitas, atis, f., *small number.*
paueo, ēre paui, *be fearful.*
pauidus, *fearful.*
paulatim, *gradually.*
paulisper, *for a short time.*
paulum, *a little.*
pauor, oris, m., *fear.*
pax, pacis, f., *peace;* **cum bona pace,** *unmolested.*
pectus, toris, n., *heart, chest.*
pecunia, ae, f., *money.*
pecus, oris, n., *cattle.*
pedes, ditis, m., *footsoldier.*
pedester, *on foot.*
pedetemptim, *step by step.*
pedica, ae, f., *snare.*
pello ,ere, pepuli, pulsum, *drive out/back.*
pendo, ere, *pay.*
penes, *in the hands of.*
penetro, are, *pierce.*
penitus, *utterly.*
peragro, are, *traverse.*
percello, ere, culi, culsum, *shatter, discourage.*
percitus, *excitable.*
percontatio, onis, f., *inquiry.*
percontor, ari, *ask.*

percuro, are, *tend.*
perdo, ere, didi, ditum, *destroy.*
perduco, ere, *lead to.*
pereo, ire, *die.*
perfero, ferre, *report.*
perficio, ere, *complete.*
perfidia, ae, f., *treachery.*
perforo, are, *hole.*
perfringo, ere, *break through.*
pergo, ere, perrexi, perrectum, *proceed.*
periculum, i, n., *danger.*
perimo, ere, emi, emptum, *destroy.*
perinde ac, *as if.*
periniquus, *very aggrieved.*
perlicio, ere, pellexi, ectum, *entice.*
perlustro, are, *survey.*
permisceo, ēre, *mingle with.*
pernicies, iei, f., *destruction.*
pernox, *throughout the night.*
peropportunus, *convenient.*
peroro, are, *wind up a speech.*
perrumpo, ere, *force a way through.*
perscindo, ere, *tear in pieces.*
perscribo, ere, *send dispatch.*
persequor, i, *pursue.*
perseuerans, *tenacious.*
pertraho, ere, *tow/draw over.*
peruado, ere, *spread through.*
peruasto, are, *ravage thoroughly.*
peruenio, ire, *arrive.*
peruerto, ere, *bring low.*
peruius, *penetrated.*
pes, pedis, m., *foot.*
peto, ere, ii, itum, *seek; attack.*
phalarica, ae, f., *Spanish missile.*
piaculum, i, n., *expiation.*
piger, *lazy.*
pignus, noris, n., *pledge.*
pigritia, ae, f., *weariness.*
pinna, ae, f., *feather, wing.*
pix, picis, f., *pitch.*
placet, ēre, *it is decided.*
planus, *level.*
plebs, plebis, f., *common folk.*

plerique, *several;* **plerumque,** *often.*

pluo, ere, pluui, *rain.*

plurimus, *very much.*

pluteus, i, m., *siege-cover.*

pluuia, ae, f., *rain.*

poena, ae, f., *punishment.*

polliceor, ēri, itus, *promise.*

pondo, *pound;* 62.8 *n.*

pondus, eris, n., *weight.*

pono, ere, posui, positum, *put, pitch.*

pons, pontis, m., *bridge.*

populatio, onis, f., *plundering.*

populor, ari, *ravage.*

populus, i, m., *people.*

porrigo, ere, rexi, rectum, *extend.*

porta, ae, f., *gate.*

portendo, ere, *presage.*

porto, are, *carry.*

portus, ūs, m., *harbour.*

possum, posse, potui, *be able.*

post, *after;* adv., *later.*

posterus, *next.*

postquam, *after.*

postremus, *last.*

postulatio, onis, f., *demand.*

postulo, are, *demand.*

potentia, ae, f., *power, ability.*

potestas, atis, f., *power.*

potio, onis, f., *drink.*

potior, iri, itus (+ abl.), *gain.*

potissimum, *especially.*

potius, *rather.*

prae, *because of.*

praealtus, *very deep.*

praebeo, ēre, *render, present;* *induce.*

praeceps, cipitis, *steep;* *hasty, uncompromising.*

praecipio, ere, *anticipate; order.*

praecipito, are, *throw headlong;* *fall headlong.*

praecipuus, *especial.*

praeda, ae, f., *booty.*

praedator, oris, m., *plunderer.*

praedico, ere, *tell beforehand.*

praedor, ari, *plunder.*

praeduco, ere, *set in front.*

praefectus, i, m., *prefect, commander.*

praeficio, ere, *put in charge.*

praefor, fari, *state first.*

praegelidus, *bitterly cold.*

praegredior, i, *go ahead* (*of*).

praemitto, ere, *send ahead.*

praemium, i, n., *reward.*

praeoccupo, are, *win beforehand.*

praeparo, are, *predispose; prepare.*

praepono, ere, *prefer.*

praepotens, *outstandingly powerful.*

praerogativa, ae, f., *prior choice.*

praeruptus, *precipitous.*

praesens, *present;* **in praesentia** (sc. **tempora**), *for the immediate situation.*

praesentio, ire, *discover beforehand.*

praesidium, i, n., *defensive force; defence.*

praestans, *outstanding.*

praeter, *except; beyond.*

praeterea, *moreover.*

praetereo, ire, *leave undone.*

praeterfero, ferre, *carry past;* passive, *rush past.*

praetermitto, ere, *neglect, ignore.*

praeterquam, *except.*

praetexta, ae, f., *purple-bordered robe worn by consul.*

praetor, oris, m., *praetor, general.*

praetorium, i, n., *general's tent; general's council.*

praetorius, *general's, admiral's.*

prandeo, ēre, *take breakfast.*

precor, ari, *pray.*

premo, ere, pressi, pressum, *oppress.*

pretiosus, *valuable.*

pretium, i, n., *price.*

prex, cis, f., *prayer.*

primor, oris, m., *leader.*

primus, *first.*

princeps, ipis, *first;* noun, m., *chief, leading citizen.*

principium, i, n., *beginning.*
priuatus, *private.*
priusquam, *before.*
procedo, ere, *advance, travel out to.*
procido, ere, *collapse.*
procliuis, *downhill.*
procul, *far.*
procumbo, ere, *lie prostrate.*
procuro, are *expiate.*
procurro, ere, *rush forward.*
prodigium, i, n., *prodigy.*
prodo, ere, didi, ditum, *betray.*
proelium, i, n., *battle.*
profectio, onis, f., *departure.*
profecto, *certainly.*
proficiscor, i, fectus, *set out.*
profiteor, ēri, fessus, *claim.*
profugio, ere, *flee.*
profugus, i, m., *fugitive.*
progenies, iei, f., *offspring.*
progredior, i, *advance.*
prohibeo, ēre, *prevent, hinder.*
proinde, *accordingly.*
prolabor, i, psus, *fall forward.*
prolato, are, *delay.*
promissum, i, n., *promise.*
promoveo, ēre, *advance.*
promuntorium, i, n., *promontory.*
pronus, *inclined, sloping.*
prope, *near;* **propius,** *nearer.*
propinquitas, atis, f., *proximity.*
propinquus, *near.*
propono, ere, *place before; publish.*
propugnator, oris, m., *defender.*
proripio, ere, *move violently forward.*
prospectus, ūs, m., *view.*
prosperus, *successful.*
prospicio, ere, *keep watch.*
protinus, *at once.*
prouideo, ēre, *foresee.*
prouincia, ae, f., *province, sphere of duty.*
proximus, *nearest.*
pubes, eris, *adult.*
publicus, *state-.*
pudor, oris, m., *shame.*

puer, eri, m., *boy.*
puerilis, *boyish.*
pueritia, ae, f., *boyhood.*
pugno, are, *fight.*
puluinar, aris, n., *couch.*
puppis, is, f., *stern.*
purgo, are, *clear, level.*
putrefacio, ere, *make to crumble.*

Q

quadraginta, *forty.*
quadriduum, i, n., *period of four days.*
quadringenti, *four hundred.*
quadriremis, is, f., *quadrireme.*
quadro, are, *square.*
quaero, ere, quaesivi, situm, *seek.*
quaestio, onis, f., *investigation.*
quaestus, ūs, m., *gain.*
quamquam, *although.*
quamuis, *although.*
quandoque, *sometime.*
quasso, are, *shatter.*
quaterni, *four each.*
quatio, ere, quassum, *shake.*
quattuordecim, *fourteen.*
quemadmodum, *as.*
querimonia, ae, f., *complaint.*
quies, etis, f., *rest.*
quiesco, ere, quievi, etum, *remain undisturbed.*
quietus, *untroubled; without stirring.*
quinam, *who, pray?*
quingenti, *five hundred.*
quinquaginta, *fifty.*
quinqueremis, is, f., *quinquereme.*
quippe, *for;* **quippe qui** + subj., *inasmuch as.*
quisquam, *anyone.*
quoniam, *since.*
quoque, *also.*

R

radix, dicis, f., *root.*
rapio, ere, ui, tum, *snatch, ravish.*

raptim, *hastily.*
rarus, *occasional.*
ratis, is, f., *raft.*
ratus, *secure;* see also **reor.**
recedo, ere, *retire.*
recens, *recent, fresh.*
recenseo, ēre, *review.*
receptus, ūs, m., *retreat.*
recessus, ūs, m., *retreat.*
recipio, ere, *recover, receive, take back.*
reciproco, are, *draw back and forth.*
recreo, are, *revive.*
rector, oris, m., *rider.*
rectus, *direct, perpendicular.*
reddo, ere, didi, ditum, *restore;* **res reddere,** *make restitution.*
redeo, ire, ii, itum, *return.*
redigo, ere, *drive back, obtain.*
reditus, ūs, m., *return.*
redux, ducis, *returned.*
refero, ferre, *consult, refer;* **pedem referre,** *retreat.*
rēfert, *it matters.*
reficio, ere, *repair, restore.*
refugio, ere, *flee backward.*
regio, onis, f., *route, territory.*
regius, *royal.*
regnum, i, n., *kingship, kingdom.*
regredior, i, *return.*
regressus, ūs, m., *return.*
regulus, i, m., *petty king.*
religio, onis, f., *religious scruple.*
religo, are, *fasten.*
relinquo, ere, *leave.*
reliquiae, arum, f., *remains.*
remigium, i, n., *oarage, oars.*
remitto, ere, *send back; relax.*
renouo, are, *renew.*
reor, reri, ratus, *think.*
repens, pentis, *sudden.*
repente, *suddenly.*
repentinus, *sudden.*
repercussus, *reverberating.*
repeto, ere, *go back for; return to; seek back;* **res repetere,** *seek restitution.*
repudio, are, *reject.*

repugno, are, *resist.*
res, rei, f., *thing, affair, state;* **respublica,** *state.*
resisto, ere (+ dat.), *resist.*
resoluo, ere, *unfasten.*
respectus, ūs, m., *refuge.*
respergo, ere, spersi, spersum, *sprinkle.*
respicio, ere, *look back.*
respondeo, ēre, di, sum, *reply.*
responsum, i, n., *reply.*
restituo, ere, *restore.*
retinaculum, i, n., *cable.*
retineo, ēre, *detain; hold on.*
retraho, ere, *drag back.*
reuoco, are, *recall.*
reus, i, m., *guilty man, defendant.*
rex, regis, m., *king.*
rideo, ēre, risi, risum, *smile.*
rigeo, ēre, ui, *be stiff.*
ripa, ae, f., *bank; river-course.*
risus, ūs, m., *laughter.*
riuus, i, m., *stream.*
robur, oris, n., *vigour; flower.*
rudimentum, i, n., *initiation.*
rudis, *inexperienced.*
ruina, ae, f., *destruction, collapse; fallen masonry.*
rumor, oris, m., *tidings.*
rumpo, ere, rupi, ruptum, *break.*
ruo, ere, i, tum, *fall; rush.*
rupes, is, f., *rock.*

S

sacrifico, are, *sacrifice.*
sacro, are, *hallow.*
sacrum, i, n., *sacred object; sacred ritual.*
saeuio, ire, *savage, rampage.*
sagulum, i, n., *cloak.*
saltus, ūs, m., *pass; woodland.*
salus, utis, f., *safety.*
sanctitas, atis, f., *integrity.*
sanctus, *sacred; upright.*
sane, *certainly, absolutely;* **haud sane,** *by no means.*
sanguis, guinis, m., *blood.*
sarcina, ae, f., *baggage.*

satis, *sufficiently.*
satisfacio, ere, *make satisfaction.*
sator, oris, m., *sower.*
saucius, *wounded.*
scio, ire, *know.*
scribo, ere, psi, ptum, *write; enrol.*
scriptor, oris, m., *writer.*
scutum, i, n., *shield.*
secessio, onis, f., *withdrawal.*
seco, are, ui, *cut.*
secundus, *successful;* secundā aquā, *downstream.*
sedecim, *sixteen.*
sedes, is, f., *abode.*
seditio, onis, f., *insurrection.*
sedo, are, *quell.*
segnis, *sluggish.*
semenstris, *six months old.*
semermis, *half-armed.*
semigermanus, *half-German.*
senatus, ūs, m., *senate.*
senesco, ere, *grow old.*
senex, senis, m., *old man.*
sensim, *gradually.*
sententia, ae, f., *opinion, proposal.*
sentio, ire, sensi, sensum, *realise, feel.*
separatim, *separately.*
septingenti, *seven hundred.*
sequor, i, secutus, *follow.*
series, iei, f., *chain.*
sero, ere, sevi, satum, *sow.*
serpens, pentis, f., *snake.*
seruio, ire (+ dat.), *serve.*
seruitus, tutis, f., *slavery.*
seruo, are, *preserve.*
serus, *late;* sero, adv., *late.*
sescenti, *six hundred.*
sexaginta, *sixty.*
sidus, eris, n., *constellation.*
significo, are, *signal.*
signum, i, n., *signal; military standard.*
silentium, i, n., *silence.*
silua, ae, f., *forest.*
simul, *together.*
simulo, are, *feign.*

singuli, *one each.*
sinister, *left.*
sino, ere, siui, situm, *allow.*
sinus, ūs, m., *fold.*
situs, *situated.*
socialis, *allied.*
societas, atis, f., *alliance.*
socius, i, m., *ally.*
sollemnis, *annual.*
sollicito, are, *disturb, rouse.*
sollicitus, *anxious.*
sŏlum, i, n., *soil, solid ground;* solum uertere, *emigrate.*
soluo, ere, solui, solutum, *unfasten.*
somnus, i, m., *sleep.*
sonus, i, m., *sound.*
sors, sortis, f., *lot.*
sortior, iri, *draw lots; draw by lot.*
sospes, pitis, *safe.*
spargo, ere, sparsi, sparsum, *scatter.*
spatium, i, n., *space, extent.*
species, iei, f., *appearance;* in speciem, *as a pretence.*
specto, are, *look to.*
specula, ae, f., *watch-tower.*
speculator, oris, m., *scout.*
speculor, ari, *reconnoitre.*
sperno, ere, sprevi, spretum, *despise.*
spero, are, *hope, expect.*
spes, spei, f., *hope.*
spiritus, ūs, m., *spirit, breath.*
sponte, *willingly;* sua sponte, *of his/their own accord.*
squalidus, *foul.*
stabilis, *steady, sure-footed.*
statim, *at once.*
statio, onis, f., *watch-station.*
stativa, orum, n., *camp.*
statuo, ere, *decide; erect.*
status, ūs, m., *condition.*
sterno, ere, straui, stratum, *level.*
stimulo, are, *rouse.*
stipendium, i, n., *pay; tribute; army-service.*

stirps, pis, f., *stock, root.*
sto, stare, steti, statum, *stand.*
stolidus, *foolish.*
strages, is, f., *slaughter, destruction.*
stratum, i, n., *bed.*
strenuus, *zealous.*
strepo, ere, ui, *resound.*
stringo, ere, inxi, ictum, *draw.*
structura, ae, f., *construction.*
strues, is, f., *heap.*
stuppa, ae, f., *tow.*
suadeo, ēre, si, sum, *urge.*
suasor, oris, m., *sponsor.*
subiectus, *lying below.*
subigo, ere, egi, actum, *reduce.*
subinde, *forthwith; from time to time.*
subitus, *sudden.*
sublatus, see **tollo.**
sublimis, *aloft.*
subruo, ere, *undermine.*
subsidium, i, n., *help.*
subsisto, ere, *halt.*
subueho, ere, *bring up.*
succedo, ere, *succeed.*
succendo, ere, *kindle.*
succingo, ere, *gird up.*
succlamo, are, *shout in answer.*
sufficio, ere, *suffice.*
summa, ae, f., *whole.*
summoueo, ēre, *dislodge, disperse.*
sumo, ere, sumpsi, sumptum, *take.*
supellex, ectilis, f., *utensils.*
super, *over; on.*
superbia, ae, f., *arrogance.*
superbus, *arrogant.*
supero, are, *overcome.*
superpono, ere, *put on top.*
supersedeo, ēre, *refrain from.*
supersum, esse, *remain, survive.*
superuacaneus, *superfluous.*
superus, *upper;* **mare superum,** *Adriatic.*
supplementum, i, n., *reinforcements.*

supplicatio, onis, f., *public prayer.*
suscipio, ere, *undertake.*
suscito, are, *stir up.*
suspicio, ere, *suspect.*
sustuli, see **tollo.**

T

tabes, is, f., *slush; putrefaction.*
tabidus, *slushy.*
tabulatum, i, n., *storey.*
taedet, ēre, *tire of.*
taedium, i, n., *weariness.*
taeter, *grisly.*
talentum, i, n., *talent.*
tango, ere, tetigi, tactum, *touch.*
tantus, *so great;* **tantum,** *only;* **tantum ne,** *provided that . . . not.*
tectum, i, n., *dwelling.*
tegmen, minis, n., *covering.*
tego, ere, xi, ctum, *protect; hide.*
telum, i, n., *dart, javelin.*
temere, *blindly, rashly, haphazardly.*
tempero, are, *control.*
tempestas, atis, f., *storm; time.*
templum, i, n., *temple.*
temptabundus, *attempting.*
tempto, are, *try out; attack.*
tempus, oris, n., *time; opportunity;* **ad tempus,** *temporary.*
tendo, ere, tetendi, tensum, *strive; march.*
teneo, ēre, *keep, retain; bind.*
tentorium, i, n., *tent.*
tenus (+ abl.), *up to.*
teres, etis, *rounded.*
tergum, i, n., *rear.*
tero, ere, triui, tritum, *rub, tread;* **tempus terere,** *waste time.*
terreo, ēre, *frighten.*
terrestris, *land-.*
terribilis, *awe-inspiring.*
territo, are, *inspire terror.*
terror, oris, m., *alarm, terror.*
testis, is, m., *witness.*
timeo, ēre, *fear.*
timor, oris, m., *fear.*

tiro, onis, m., *recruit;* adj., *raw.*

titubo, are, *stagger.*

tollo, ere, sustuli, sublatum, *raise.*

tormentum, i, n., *torture.*

torpeo, ēre, *be numb.*

torpidus, *shrivelled.*

tot, *so many.*

totus, *entire.*

trado, ere, didi, ditum, *surrender; relate.*

traduco, ere, *put across.*

tragula, ae, f., *javelin.*

traho, ere, xi, ctum, *drag; attract.*

traicio, ere, ieci, iectum, *put across; go across.*

trames, itis, m., *path.*

trano, are, *swim over.*

tranquillitas, atis, f., *calm.*

transcendo, ere, *scale.*

transeo, ire, *cross.*

transfero, ferre, *transfer.*

transfigo, ere, *penetrate.*

transfuga, ae, m., *deserter.*

transgredior, i, *cross.*

transitus, ūs, m., *passage.*

transmitto, ere, *put across, let through; cross.*

transueho, ere, *carry across.*

treceni, *three hundred each.*

trecenti, *three hundred.*

tredecim, *thirteen.*

trepidatio, onis, f., *panic.*

trepido, are, *panic.*

tribunus, i, m., *tribune.*

triduum, i, n., *period of three days.*

triennium, i, n., *period of three years.*

triginta, *thirty.*

tripertito, *in three sections.*

triremis, is, f., *trireme.*

tristis, *grim.*

tritus, see **tero.**

triumphus, i, m., *triumph.*

triumuir, i, m., *triumvir.*

trucido, are, *slaughter.*

tueor, ēri, tuitus, *defend.*

tumultuarius, *skirmishing.*

tumultuor, ari, *skirmish.*

tumultus, ūs, *din, confusion; insurrection.*

tumulus, i, m., *hill-top.*

tunc, *then.*

turba, ae, f., *crowd.*

turbo, are, *throw into confusion.*

turma, ae, f., *squadron.*

turris, is, f., *tower.*

tutamentum, i, n., *protection.*

tutor, ari, *defend.*

tutus, *safe.*

U

uado, ere, *advance.*

uadum, i, n., *shallows.*

uagina, ae, f., *sheath, scabbard.*

uagor, ari, *wander.*

uagus, *roaming.*

ualeo, ēre, *be strong.*

ualidus, *strong.*

ualles, is, f., *valley, low ground.*

uallum, i, n., *rampart.*

uanus, *fruitless.*

uario, are, *diversify.*

uarius, *differing.*

uastitas, atis, f., *devastation.*

uasto, are, *ravage.*

uates, is, m., *prophet.*

uecto, are, *carry often.*

ueho, ere, uexi, uectum, *carry, convey.*

uel, *or, or at any rate, even.*

ueles, itis, m., *light-armed soldier.*

uelut, *as if.*

uendo, ere, didi, ditum, *sell.*

uentus, i, m., *wind.*

uepres, is, m., *bush.*

uer, ueris, n., *spring.*

uerecundia, ae, f., *shame, shamelessness.*

uereor, ēri, itus, *fear.*

uergens, *facing.*

uerso, are, *affect.*

uertex, ticis, m., *whirlpool; top.*

uerticosus, *eddying.*

uerto, ere, ti, sum, *turn;* **uersus,** *facing.*

uerum, i, n., *truth;* **ueri similis,** *probable.*

uerus, *true.*

uerutum, i, n., *dart.*

uestigium, i, n., *track.*

uestimentum, i, n., *garment.*

uestio, ire, *clothe.*

uestis, is, f., *clothes.*

uestitus, ūs, m., *clothing.*

ueteranus, *experienced.*

ueto, are, ui, itum, *forbid.*

uetus, eris, *old, veteran.*

uetustus, *ancient.*

uia, ae, f., *path, journey.*

uibro, are, *wave.*

uicinalis, *neighbouring, local.*

uictor, oris, m., *conqueror.*

uictoria, ae, f., *victory.*

uiculus, i, m., *hamlet.*

uicus, i, m., *village.*

uidelicet, *doubtless.*

uideo, ēre, uidi, uisum, *see;* **uideor,** *seem.*

uigeo, ēre, *thrive.*

uigil, ilis, m., *guard.*

uigilia, ae, f., *watch.*

uiginti, *twenty.*

uigor, oris, m., *liveliness.*

uilis, *cheap.*

uinco, ere, uici, uictum, *conquer, prevail.*

uinculum, i, n., *rope; bond.*

uindex, icis, m., *avenger.*

uinea, ae, f., *siege-shed.*

uiolo, are, *lay hands on, break.*

uir, uiri, m., *man.*

uirgultum, i, n., *shrub.*

uirtus, tutis, f., *virtue, courage.*

uis, uis, f., *force;* plur. **uires,** *strength.*

uiso, ere, *view, visit.*

uisus, ūs, m., *sight, apparition.*

uitium, i, n., *vice.*

uitulus, i, m., *calf.*

uiuo, ere, uixi, uictum, *live.*

uiuus, *alive.*

uix/uixdum, *scarcely.*

ulciscor, i, ultus, *avenge.*

ulterior, *further;* **ultimus,** *last.*

ultra, *beyond; further.*

ultro, *unprovoked.*

ululatus, ūs, m., *wailing.*

undique, *from all sides.*

unicus, *sole.*

uolgus, i, n., *crowd.*

uolnero, are, *wound.*

uolnus, eris, n., *wound.*

uolo, uelle, uolui, *wish, would have it.*

uoltus, ūs, m., *face, expression.*

uoluntarius, *unforced.*

uoluntas, atis, f., *wish.*

uoluptas, atis, f., *pleasure.*

uoluto, are, *roll;* passive, *reel.*

uotum, i, n., *vow.*

uox, uocis, f., *utterance.*

urbs, bis, f., *city.*

urgeo, ēre, ursi, *oppress, jostle.*

usquam, *at all.*

usus, usūs, m., *use.*

utcumque, *according as.*

uter, tris, m., *skin.*

uter, utra, utrum, *which of two?*

uterque, *each of two;* **utrimque,** *on both sides;* **utroque,** *in both directions.*

uti, alternative form of **ut.**

utique, *especially.*

utrum . . . an, *whether . . . or.*

PRINTED IN GREAT BRITAIN BY UNIVERSITY TUTORIAL PRESS LTD, FOXTON, NEAR CAMBRIDGE